Reference Manual for STENOGRAPHERS and TYPISTS

Fourth Edition

D0465544

RUTH E. GAVIN

WILLIAM A. SABIN

Gregg Division/McGraw-Hill Book Company
New York   St. Louis   Dallas   San Francisco
Düsseldorf   London   Mexico   Panama   Sydney   Toronto

Ruth E. Gavin, whose untimely death occurred a few months before the publication of this edition, had taught office education courses in public high schools in California. At the time of her retirement, she was a member of the faculty of the City College of San Francisco.

William A. Sabin is editor in chief of office education in the Gregg Division of McGraw-Hill Book Company. He is also a coauthor, with Mary Butera and Ruthetta Krause, of *College English: Grammar and Style.*

REFERENCE MANUAL FOR STENOGRAPHERS AND TYPISTS, Fourth Edition
Copyright © 1970, 1961, 1956 by McGraw-Hill, Inc. All Rights Reserved.
Copyright 1951 by McGraw-Hill, Inc. All Rights Reserved. Printed in the United States of America. No part of this publication may be reproduced, stored in a retrieval system, or transmitted, in any form or by any means, electronic, mechanical, photocopying, recording, or otherwise, without the prior written permission of the publisher. *Library of Congress Catalog Card Number 71-88882*

89 WCWC 98765

ISBN 07-023068-4

Designed by Barbara Bert

Preface

The *Reference Manual for Stenographers and Typists* is intended for anyone who writes, transcribes, or types. It presents the basic rules that apply in virtually every piece of business writing as well as the fine points that occur infrequently but cause trouble when they do. It offers an abundance of examples and illustrations so that users can quickly find a model on which to pattern a solution to a specific problem. It also provides the rationale underlying specific rules so that users can manipulate the principles of style with intelligence and taste.

The *Reference Manual* has undergone a substantial change in this fourth edition. It has been greatly expanded so as to provide guidance on virtually every problem that is likely to occur in ordinary written communications. It has been updated to reflect the significant changes in style that have occurred over the last few years. And it has been restructured to enhance its effectiveness as a reference tool.

The manual now consists of 20 sections, organized as follows:

Part One (Sections 1–11) deals with grammar, usage, and the chief aspects of style—punctuation, capitalization, numbers, abbreviations, plurals and possessives, spelling, compound words, and word division.

Part Two (Sections 12–17) deals with techniques and procedures for producing all kinds of written communications in business—letters, memos, telegrams, reports, manuscripts, and tabular matter.

Part Three (Sections 18–20) provides three appendixes for fast reference: a listing of model forms of address, a glossary of grammatical terms, and a bibliography of useful reference works.

While a reference manual is not intended to be read from cover to cover, an hour or two devoted at the outset to scanning the manual will enhance its usefulness later on as specific problems occur. The following comments provide a brief orientation to the manual and highlight features of each section that warrant special attention.

Section 1 (¶¶ 101–198) deals with the major marks of punctuation—the period, the question mark, the exclamation point, the comma, the semicolon, and the colon. As you scan Section 1, give especially close attention to the rules on the comma and the semicolon, since they treat punctuation problems that commonly occur in all business writing. Also note paragraphs such as ¶ 133, which provides an extensive list of model sentences for all the varied applications of the basic rule.

Section 2 (¶¶ 201–298) deals with the other marks of punctuation—the dash, parentheses, quotation marks, the underscore, the apostrophe, ellipsis marks, the asterisk, the diagonal, and brackets. Of special note are the model sentences provided for quotation marks (particularly those in ¶¶ 258–259) and the rules in ¶ 298, which indicate the typewriter spacing to be used with all marks of punctuation.

Section 3 (¶¶ 301–352) covers capitalization. Give particular attention to the introduction and the basic rules (¶¶ 301–309). If you grasp the function of capitalization, you not only will have a better perspective on all the specific rules that follow but will be better equipped to resolve capitalization problems on your own.

Section 4 (¶¶ 401–466) discusses number style. For an explanation of the concepts that underlie all aspects of number style, read the introduction and the basic rules (¶¶ 401–407). If you understand the functional difference between expressing numbers in figures and in words, you can solve many specific style questions without having to refer to the manual.

Section 5 (¶¶ 501–538) deals with abbreviations. Since most of the problems concerning abbreviations involve punctuation and spacing, scan ¶¶ 531–538, which summarize these rules.

Section 6 (¶¶ 601–650) covers plurals and possessives. Because of the frequency with which these forms occur, give special attention to the basic rules that govern their formation and usage.

Section 7 (¶¶ 701–715) provides a number of spelling guides that could help you reduce your dependence on the dictionary. For fast assistance on words that look alike or sound alike, consult ¶ 715, which provides a 12-page guide to these troublesome combinations.

Section 8 (¶¶ 801–834) deals with all kinds of compound words and provides guides as to whether they should be spaced, solid, or hyphenated. Note in particular ¶¶ 808–823 on compound adjectives, which offer an extensive series of patterns and examples to clarify the applications of the basic rule.

Section 9 (¶¶ 901–922) discusses word division in terms of a few absolute rules and a number of preferred practices. In addition, Section 9 offers a number of hints on determining correct syllabication without reference to a dictionary.

Section 10 (¶¶ 1001–1075) offers a compact survey of all the rules of grammar that the user is likely to need. The coverage ranges from subject-verb agreement to proper sentence structure, with special attention given to problems involving verbs, pronouns, adjectives, adverbs, prepositions, and the use of negatives.

Section 11 (¶ 1101) deals with problems of usage. Individual entries are provided for a wide range of troublesome words and phrases and are listed alphabetically for fast reference.

Section 12 (¶¶ 1201–1227) provides a useful summary of proper dictation and transcription techniques.

Section 13 (¶¶ 1301–1329) describes a variety of typing techniques—for example, how to make corrections, how to prepare carbon copies and duplicating masters, and how to type on cards. A full-page illustration on page 193 shows how to construct symbols not on the typewriter.

Section 14 (¶¶ 1401–1482) is a key unit for anyone who writes or types letters and memos. It provides extensive styling notes on every element in a letter—from the letterhead to the postscript; it discusses letter styles, punctuation patterns, and effective placement, with the aid of extensive illustrations and tables; it treats the preparation of envelopes and gives up-to-date instruction on ZIP Code placement and the new two-letter state abbreviations; and it provides special guides on memos and social-business correspondence.

Section 15 (¶¶ 1501–1510) provides the most current information on telegraph services, including a discussion of the new Western Union form.

Section 16 (¶¶ 1601–1627) provides guides and illustrations on the preparation of reports, manuscripts, footnotes, and bibliographies. Note in particular ¶ 1612, which offers a series of easy-to-follow patterns for constructing footnotes.

Section 17 (¶¶ 1701–1713) offers detailed guidelines and sample layouts for the arrangement of tabular matter.

Section 18 (¶ 1801) lists the correct forms of address and appropriate salutations for a wide range of officials and dignitaries.

Section 19 (¶ 1901) provides an alphabetized glossary of grammatical terms for the user who wants to quickly check the meaning of a particular term or who wants a fast review of grammatical terminology as a whole.

Section 20 (¶ 2001) offers a recommended bibliography of reference books that are useful on any office bookshelf.

The foregoing notes are only a preliminary guide to what you can discover more effectively at first hand. As you make your own survey of the text, you will want to single out the key rules that deserve further study; these are the rules that deal with everyday situations, the rules you need to have at your command. You may also want to develop a passing acquaintance with the fine points of style. It is sufficient simply to know that such rules exist; then, when you need them, you will know where to find them. Finally, you will want to take note of special word lists, sentence patterns, and illustrations that could be useful to you later on. If you find out now what aids the manual provides, you will know what kind of help you can count on in the future. And what is more important, you will be able to find what you are looking for faster.

How to Look Things Up

Suppose you were writing the following paragraph to someone in another department:

> I understand you are doing a confidential study of the Bronson matter. May I please get an advance copy of your report [At this point you hesitate. Should this sentence end with a period or a question mark?]

This is the kind of problem that continually comes up in any type of written communication. How do you find a fast answer to such questions? In this manual there are several ways to proceed.

Using the Index. The surest approach, perhaps, is to check the detailed index at the back of the manual (11 pages, with over 1,600 entries). For example, any of the following entries will lead you to the right punctuation for the problem sentence above:

Period, **101–108**　　　　Question mark, **109–117**　　Request, punctuation
　. . .　　　　　　　　　　. . .　　　　　　　　　　of, **103**
　　at end of request, **103**　　at end of request, **103**

In each entry the boldface number refers to the proper rule, ¶ 103. (If you look up ¶ 103, you will find that a question mark is the right punctuation for the sentence in question.)

In almost all of the index entries, references are made to specific rule numbers so that you can find what you are looking for fast. In a few cases, where a page reference will provide a more precise location (for example, when a rule runs on for several pages), a page number is given in lightface type. Suppose you were confronted with the following problem:

> If you compare the performance records of Catano, Harris, and Williams, you won't find much difference (*between/among*) them.

The index will show the following entries:

among–between, 175　　**OR**　　*between–among,* 175

The actual rule on page 175 indicates that *between* is the right answer for this situation.

Using a Fast-Skim Approach. Many users of reference manuals have little patience with detailed indexes; they would rather open the book and skim through the pages until they find what they are looking for. If you are the kind of person who prefers this approach, you will find the brief topical index on the front cover especially helpful, since it indicates (by page number) where each major topic begins. Moreover, extensive cross-references have been provided throughout the manual so that you can quickly locate related rules that could prove helpful. Suppose the following problem came up:

> The only point still at issue is whether or not new *Federal* [or is it *federal?*] legislation is required.

The index on the front cover indicates that the topic of capitalization starts on page 59. A fast skim from that point on will lead you to ¶ 326, which indicates that *federal* is the proper form in this sentence.

Playing the Numbers. There is still a third way to find the answer to a specific problem—and this is an approach that will grow in appeal as you become familiar with the organization and the content of the manual. From a fast inspection of the rule numbers, you will observe that they all carry a section number as a prefix. Thus Section 3 (on capitalization) has a "300" series of rules—from 301 to 352; Section 4 (on number style) has a "400" series—from 401 to 466; and so on. Once you become familiar with the section numbers and the section titles, you can find your way around fairly quickly, without reference to either index. For example, you are about to write the following sentence:

> *43* percent of the questionnaires have now been returned. [Or should it be, "*Forty-three* percent of the questionnaires . . .*"*?]

If you know that matters of number style are treated in Section 4, you can quickly turn to the "400" series of rules, where a fast skim will lead you to the answer in ¶ 408. (*Forty-three percent* is the right answer in this instance.)

A familiarity with the rule-numbering system and its relationship to the section titles will prove useful in other respects. For one thing, it can suggest whether or not you ought to pursue a cross-reference. The rule in ¶ 408 reads as follows:

> Always spell out a number that begins a sentence. (See ¶¶ 830–833.)

If you know that Section 8 indicates whether compound words should be hyphenated, spaced, or solid, you are not likely to pursue this cross-reference.

A familiarity with the section numbers and section titles can also save you time when you are using the index. If your index entry lists several different paragraph numbers, you can often anticipate what the paragraphs will deal with. For example, if you want to know whether to type *5 lb.* or *5 lbs.* on a purchase order and you check the index, you might encounter the following entry:

> Weights, **429-430, 520-521, 620**

If you know that Section 6 deals with plurals, you will try ¶ 620 first.

Looking Up Specific Words. Many of the problems that arise deal with specific words. For this reason the index provides as many entries for such words as space will permit. For example, in the following sentence, should *therefore* be set off by commas or not?

It is(,) *therefore*(,) essential that operations be curtailed.

A check of the index will show the following entry:

therefore, punctuation with, **141–143, 145**

A reading of the rules in ¶ 141 will indicate that no commas should be used in this sentence. If you asked the same question about another specific word and did not find it listed as a separate entry in the index, your best approach would be to check the index under "Comma" and investigate the most promising references or make a direct scan of the comma rules in Section 1 until you find the answer you are looking for.

If you are having difficulty with words that look alike and sound alike—*jibe* and *gibe* or *affect* and *effect*—turn directly to ¶ 715 and consult the alphabetized list of troublesome combinations for guidance.

For other troublesome words and phrases, consult the alphabetical sequence of entries in ¶ 1101.

Contents

PART TWO. TECHNIQUES AND PROCEDURES

PART THREE. REFERENCES AND RESOURCES

Section 1
PUNCTUATION:
MAJOR MARKS

Punctuation marks are the mechanical means for making the meaning of a sentence easily understood. They indicate the proper relationships between words, phrases, and clauses when word order alone is not sufficient to indicate these relationships.

One important caution about punctuation: If you find it particularly difficult to determine the appropriate punctuation for a sentence you have written, the chances are that the sentence is improperly constructed. To be on the safe side, recast your thought in a form you can handle with confidence. In any event, do not try to save a badly constructed sentence by means of punctuation.

Section 1 deals with the three marks of terminal punctuation (the period, the question mark, and the exclamation point) plus the three major marks of internal punctuation (the comma, the semicolon, and the colon). All other marks of punctuation are covered in Section 2.

THE PERIOD

AT THE END OF A SENTENCE

101 Use a period to mark the end of a sentence that makes a statement or expresses a command.

> I was very happy to hear about your promotion.
>
> I question the wisdom of Jones's recommendation.
>
> You can count on quick service when you order from Lyons, Inc.
>
> Be sure to answer Mrs. Andrews' letter promptly.

102 Use a period to mark the end of an *elliptical* (condensed) expression that represents a complete statement or command. These elliptical expressions frequently occur as answers to questions or as transitional phrases.

> Yes.   By all means.   No.
>
> Now, to answer your closing question.

NOTE: Do not confuse sentences of this type with *sentence fragments,* which are incomplete sentences. Fragments should never be treated as separate sentences.

> The shipment arrived yesterday, after we had waited for six weeks.
>
> (**NOT:** The shipment arrived yesterday. After we had waited for six weeks.)
>
> If you prefer, we can fill the order in genuine leather.
>
> (**NOT:** If you prefer. We can fill the order in genuine leather.)

1

103   Requests, suggestions, and commands are often phrased as questions out of politeness. End this kind of sentence with a period if you expect your reader to respond *by acting* rather than by giving you a yes-or-no answer.

> Will you please let us have your decision as soon as possible.
>
> Would you kindly send my order to this address.
>
> May I suggest that you call in advance to be sure of prompt service.
>
> If you would like a free ticket to the exhibition, would you please send us your name and address.

If your reader might think your request presumptuous when presented as a statement, use a question mark instead. The question mark offers your reader a chance to say no to your request and preserves the politeness of the situation.

> May I have an appointment to see you next week?
>
> May I make a suggestion?
>
> Will you please handle the production reports for me while I'm away?

NOTE: If you are not sure whether to use a question mark or a period, re-phrase the sentence so that it is clearly a question or a statement and then punctuate it accordingly.

> Would you be willing to handle the production reports for me while I'm away?
>
> I would appreciate your handling the production reports for me while I'm away.

104   Use a period to mark the end of an indirect question.

> The marketing director has asked whether the sales figures for March are ready.
>
> The only question I have is whether the job will be completed on schedule.
>
> Who the new vice president will be has not yet been decided.
>
> The problem is clear; the question is what to do about it.

WITH DECIMALS

105   Use a period (without space before or after) to separate a whole number from a decimal fraction; for example, *33.33%, $5.50.*

IN OUTLINES AND DISPLAYED LISTS

106   Use periods after numbers or letters that enumerate items in an outline or a displayed list—unless the numbers or letters are enclosed in paren-theses. (See ¶¶ 107, 223 for illustrations.)

107   Use periods after independent clauses, dependent clauses, or long phrases that are displayed on separate lines in a list. No periods are needed after short phrases unless the phrases are essential to the grammatical completeness of the statement introducing the list.

Please order the following items:	BUT: Capitalize the first word of:
1. Paper clips	a. Every sentence.
2. Rubber bands	b. Direct quotations.
3. No. 10 envelopes	c. Lines of poetry.
4. Red ball-point pens	d. Items displayed in a list.

A FEW DON'TS

108 Don't use a period:

a. After roman numerals (for example, *Volume I, Queen Elizabeth II*). EXCEPTION: Periods follow roman numerals that enumerate items in an outline. (See ¶ 223.)

b. After displayed headings, titles of tables and charts, etc., unless they are run-in headings followed by reading matter. This rule is illustrated by the headings that occur throughout this text.

c. After letters used to designate persons or things (for example, *Miss A, Class B, Grade C*). EXCEPTION: Use a period when the letter is the actual initial of a person's last name (for example, *Mr. A.* for *Mr. Abbott*).

d. After contractions. (See ¶ 502.)

e. After ordinals expressed in figures (*1st, 2d, 3d*).

▶ Periods with dashes: see ¶¶ 213, 214, 215a.
Periods with parentheses: see ¶¶ 224c, 225a, 225c, 226c.
Periods with quotation marks: see ¶¶ 248, 258, 259.
Three spaced periods (ellipsis marks): see ¶¶ 275–280, 291.
Typewriter spacing: see ¶ 298.
Periods in abbreviations: see ¶¶ 531–535.

THE QUESTION MARK

TO INDICATE INDEPENDENT QUESTIONS

109 Use a question mark at the end of a direct question. (See ¶ 104 for the punctuation of indirect questions.)

Where are the records for Frasier, Inc.?

Why not see your dealer today?

NOTE: Be sure to place the question mark at the *end* of the question.

Have you read my latest article, which appeared in the September issue of *Transportation*? (NOT: Have you read my latest article? which appeared in the September issue of *Transportation*.)

How do you account for this entry: "Paid to E. M. Johnson, $300"? (NOT: How do you account for this entry? "Paid to E. M. Johnson, $300.")

110 Use a question mark at the end of an *elliptical* (condensed) question—that is, a word or phrase that represents a complete question.

[Continued on page 4.]

Frank tells me that you are still opposed to the plan. Why? (The complete question is, "Why are you still opposed to the plan?")

NOTE: Punctuate complete and elliptical questions separately, according to your meaning.

When will the job be finished? In a week or two? (NOT: When will the job be finished in a week or two?)

Where shall we meet? At the airport? (As punctuated, the writer allows for the possibility of meeting elsewhere.)

Where shall we meet at the airport? (As punctuated, the writer simply wants to pinpoint a more precise location.)

111 Use a question mark at the end of a sentence that is phrased like a statement but spoken with the rising intonation of a question.

They still doubt his ability?

These figures are correct?

112 A request, suggestion, or command phrased as a question out of politeness may not require a question mark. (See ¶ 103.)

TO INDICATE QUESTIONS WITHIN SENTENCES

113 When a short direct question falls *within a sentence,* set off the question with commas and put a question mark at the end of the sentence.

You have the authority, *do you not,* to make this decision yourself?

When a short direct question falls *at the end of a sentence,* use a comma before it and a question mark after.

I can count on your support, *can't I?*

114 When an independent question comes *at the end of a sentence,* it starts with a capital letter and is preceded by a comma or a colon. The question mark that ends the question also serves to mark the end of the sentence.

We now come to the important question, What profit can we expect?

This is the important question: What profit can we expect? (Use a colon if the introductory matter is an independent clause.)

BUT: We now come to the important question of what profit we can expect. (Indirect question; no special punctuation or capitalization is needed.)

115 When an independent question comes *at the beginning of a sentence,* it should be followed by a question mark (for emphasis) or simply a comma.

How can we achieve these goals? is the next question.

OR: How can we achieve these goals, is the next question.

BUT: How we can achieve these goals is the next question. (Indirect question; no special punctuation is needed.)

116 A series of brief questions at the end of a sentence may be separated by commas or (for emphasis) by question marks. Do not capitalize the individual questions.

Can you estimate the cost of the roofing, the tile work, and the painting?

OR: Can you estimate the cost of the roofing? the tile work? the painting?

NOTE: Do not confuse these brief questions (which are all related to a common subject and verb) with a series of independent questions. Each independent question must start with a capital and end with a question mark.

Consider the following points: Is the plan adequate? Is it financially feasible? Is it acceptable to management?

Independent questions in a series are often elliptical. (See ¶ 110.)

Has Walter's loan been approved? When? By whom? For what amount?

(NOT: Has Walter's loan been approved, when, by whom, and for what amount?)

TO EXPRESS DOUBT

117   A question mark enclosed in parentheses may be used to express doubt or uncertainty about a word or phrase within a sentence.

He was graduated from Oberlin in 1942(?).

▶   Question marks with dashes: see ¶¶ 214, 215a.
Question marks with parentheses: see ¶¶ 224d, 225a, 225d, 226c.
Question marks with quotation marks: see ¶¶ 250, 258, 259.
Typewriter spacing: see ¶ 298.

THE EXCLAMATION POINT

The exclamation point is most often found in advertising copy and sales correspondence. However, in all business writing it should be used sparingly and avoided wherever possible.

NOTE: If your typewriter does not carry the exclamation point as a standard character, you can construct it by typing the apostrophe, backspacing once, and then typing the period. On some machines it is not necessary to backspace if the space bar is held down while both characters are typed.

TO EXPRESS STRONG FEELING

118   Use an exclamation point at the end of a sentence (or an expression that stands for a sentence) to indicate enthusiasm, surprise, incredulity, urgency, or strong feeling.

Yes! Dresses, jackets, and coats are selling at 50 percent off!

No! It can't be true!   How could it have happened!   Just a minute!

NOTE: The exclamation point may be enclosed in parentheses and placed directly after a word that the writer wants to intensify.

Did you know that Erskine's is selling genuine(!) mink coats for $500?

119   A single word may be followed by an exclamation point to express intense feeling. The sentence that follows it is punctuated as usual.

> Wait! We can't let that mistake pass.

When such words are repeated for emphasis, an exclamation point follows each repetition.

> Hush! Hush! Don't let our competitors hear this.

120   When exclamations are mild, a comma or a period is sufficient.

> Well, well, so we've come to the end of that story.
> No. There's no use in vain regrets.

WITH OH AND O

121   The exclamation *oh* may be followed by either an exclamation point or a comma, depending on the emphasis required. It is capitalized only when it starts a sentence. The capitalized *O*, the sign of direct address, is not usually followed by any punctuation.

> Oh! I didn't expect that!   "O for a Muse of fire, that would ascend
> Oh, what's the use?   The brightest heaven of invention . . ."

▶   Exclamation point with dashes: see ¶¶ 214, 215a.
Exclamation point with parentheses: see ¶¶ 224d, 225a, 225d, 226c.
Exclamation point with quotation marks: see ¶¶ 250, 258, 259.

THE COMMA

The comma has two primary functions: it *separates* elements within a sentence whose relationship to one another would otherwise be unclear, and it *sets off* parenthetical elements that interrupt the flow of thought from subject to verb to object or complement. It takes only a single comma to "separate," but it typically requires two commas to "set off."

SOME BASIC CAUTIONS

In the process of separating or setting off words, commas create pauses. However, not every pause within a sentence requires a comma. The diagonal marks in the examples in ¶¶ 122–124 indicate points at which commas are often incorrectly inserted.

122   Do not use a *single* comma to separate a subject and its verb, a verb and its object (or complement), an adjective and a noun, or a noun and a prepositional phrase.

> The *woman with red hair/ is* Mrs. Potter. (Subject and verb.)
> *That he is one of the outstanding scientists in America/ has* long been recognized. (Subject and verb.)

On his first day in office the mayor *dismissed/ the police chief.* (Verb and object.)

During the war he *had been/ an enlisted man.* (Verb and complement.)

She *seems/ honest, sincere, and capable.* (Verb and complement.)

He is not afraid of working long, *hard/ hours.* (Adjective and noun.)

The *president/ of the company* will address the staff this afternoon. (Noun and prepositional phrase.)

BUT: The woman with red hair, *I believe,* is Mrs. Potter. (Use *two* commas to set off an interrupting expression.)

123 Do not use a *single* comma to separate a coordinating conjunction (*and, but, or,* or *nor*) and the following word.

I tried to convince him, *but/ he* wouldn't listen.

You can read it now *or/ when* you get home tonight.

BUT: You can read it now or, *if you prefer,* when you get home tonight. (Use two commas to set off an interrupting expression.)

124 Do not use a *single* comma to separate two items joined by a coordinating conjunction.

The letters in the tray/ and those in these folders are all to be filed. (Two subjects.)

The critic *reviewed the book/ and then answered questions.* (Two predicates. See also ¶ 126*b*.)

We hope *that you will visit our store soon/* and *that you will like our merchandise.* (Two objects of the verb *hope.*)

He may go on to graduate school at *Stanford/* or *Harvard.* (Two objects of the preposition *at.*)

BUT: *Miller will handle the tickets,* and *Powers will be responsible for publicity.* (A comma separates two independent clauses joined by a coordinating conjunction. See ¶ 125.)

IN COMPOUND SENTENCES

125 When a compound sentence consists of two independent clauses joined by *and, but, or,* or *nor,* a "separating" comma should precede the conjunction. (See also ¶ 127.)

Judson spoke for twenty minutes, *and* then he answered questions from the audience.

Take this message to Mrs. Jackson, *and* please wait for her answer. (See ¶ 126*c*.)

Please send your remittance at once, *or* we shall be obliged to put your account in the hands of our attorneys for collection.

The material in this dress is not the right color, *nor* is it the quality ordered.

Not only must a secretary be an accurate typist, *but* she must also be a rapid one.

BUT: A secretary not only must be an accurate typist *but* must also be a rapid one. (See ¶ 126*b*.)

[*Continued on page 8.*]

EXCEPTION: When a sentence starts with a dependent clause that applies to both independent clauses that follow, no comma separates the independent clauses. (A comma would make the introductory dependent clause seem to apply only to the first independent clause.)

> If you want to become an executive, you must understand accounting *and* you must know your product. (The *if* clause applies equally to the two independent clauses; hence no comma before *and*.)
>
> BUT: If you want to become an executive, you must understand accounting, *but* don't think your preparation ends there.

126 Do not confuse a true compound sentence with a sentence having a *compound predicate.*

a. A compound sentence contains at least two independent clauses, and each clause contains a subject and a predicate. (See ¶ 125.)

> He *was graduated in May with honors,* and he *began working for a bank in June.*

b. A sentence may contain one subject with two predicates connected by a conjunction. In such sentences no comma separates the predicates.

> He *was graduated in May* and *began working for a bank in June.*
> The critic *reviewed the book* and *then answered questions.*
> Mr. Adams not only *criticized the report* but also *recommended that it be revised.*

c. When one or both verbs are in the imperative, treat the sentence as a compound sentence and use a comma between the clauses.

> You may take as much time as you need to reach a decision, but *don't overlook* the advantages of acting promptly.
> *Send* this letter to Mrs. Phillips, and please *attach* a copy of Invoice 43011.
> Please *sign* both copies of the contract where indicated, and *return* the original copy to us.

127 If the two clauses of a compound sentence are short, the comma may be omitted before the conjunction.

> Their prices are low and they offer good service.
> Please initial these forms and return them by Monday.

128 When a compound sentence consists of three or more independent clauses, punctuate this series of clauses like any other series. (See ¶ 147.)

> Mary can do the typing, Pam can handle the duplicating, and Jean and I can do the rest.

129 Do not use a comma between two independent clauses that are not joined by a coordinating conjunction. This error of punctuation is known as a *comma splice* and produces a *run-on sentence.* Use a semicolon, a colon, or a dash (whichever is appropriate), or start a new sentence.

Mark top-priority letters *RUSH;* transcribe these first.

OR: Mark top-priority letters *RUSH.* Transcribe these first.

IN COMPLEX SENTENCES

130   A complex sentence contains one independent clause and one or more dependent clauses. *After, although, as, because, before, if, since, unless, when,* and *while* are among the words most frequently used to introduce dependent clauses. (See ¶ 133 for a longer list.)

a. When a dependent clause *precedes* a main clause, separate the two clauses with a comma.

Before we can make a decision, we must have all the facts.

When a child is tired and pale, the cause is often lack of nutritious food.

If, however, they had been more conservative in their investments, the partnership would have remained financially sound.

b. Be sure to recognize an introductory dependent clause, even if some of the essential words are omitted from the clause. (Such constructions are known as *elliptical clauses.*)

Whenever possible, he leaves his office by six. (Whenever it is possible, . . .)

If so, I will call you tomorrow. (If that is so, . . .)

Should you be late, just call to let me know. (If you should be late, . . .)

c. When a dependent clause serves as the subject of the sentence, do not follow it with a comma.

Whomever you nominate will have a good chance of being elected.

Whether the job is finished by Friday or Monday will make no difference.

How you solve the problem is entirely up to you.

That the department must be reorganized is no longer questioned.

131   The sentences illustrated in ¶ 130 often occur in indirect discourse, where they are introduced by an expression such as *he said that, he believes that,* or *he knows that.* In such cases use the same punctuation prescribed in ¶ 130:

Jack believes that *before we can make a decision,* we must have all the facts.

Doctors will tell you that *when a child is tired and pale,* the cause is often lack of nutritious food.

Frank says that *whenever possible,* he leaves his office by six.

Everyone thinks that *whomever you nominate* will have a good chance of being elected.

132   When a dependent clause *follows* the main clause or *falls within* the main clause, commas are used or omitted depending on whether the dependent clause is essential (restrictive) or nonessential (nonrestrictive).

a. An *essential* clause is necessary to the meaning of the sentence. Because it *cannot be omitted,* it should not be set off by commas.

[Continued on page 10.]

Political leaders *who are responsive to the wishes of their constituents* will support the bill. (Tells which political leaders.)

This ruling applies to everyone *who works in the plant.* (Tells which persons.)

The airport limousine arrived *before I was ready to leave.* (Tells when.)

The fact *that he arrived on time today* is some sign of improvement. (Tells which fact.)

Tom said *that he would wait.* (Tells what was said.)

Give this letter to *whoever is at the front desk.* (Tells which person.)

b. A *nonessential* clause provides additional descriptive or explanatory detail. Because it *can be omitted* without changing the meaning of the sentence, it should be set off by commas.

He stopped off in Chicago to see his father, *who is an eminent lawyer.* (Simply adds information about the father.)

Green's first book, *which sold a million copies,* is now out of print. (Gives additional information about Green's book but is not needed to establish *which* book is meant.)

The airport limousine arrived at ten, *before I was ready to leave.* (Gives additional information but is not essential to establish *when* the limousine arrived.)

Jim's last suggestion, *that we send Torres to the meeting in Miami next month,* is a good one. (Gives additional information but is not essential to establish *which* suggestion.)

c. A dependent clause occurring within a sentence must always be set off by commas when it interrupts the flow of the sentence.

I can set up the meeting for tomorrow or, *if that is inconvenient,* for Friday.

Please include customer's full address and, *whenever possible,* his ZIP Code number. (The complete dependent clause is *whenever it is possible.*)

He is the kind of person who, *if you understand him,* will be a devoted employee.

If, *when you have tried our product,* you are not satisfied with it, please return it for a full refund of the purchase price.

BUT: He said that *when he had the time,* he would help us with the report. (See ¶ 131 for dependent clauses following *that* in indirect discourse.)

133   The following list presents the words and phrases most commonly used to introduce dependent clauses. For most of these expressions, two sentences are given: one containing an essential clause and one a nonessential clause. In a few cases, only one type of clause is possible. If you cannot decide whether a clause is essential or nonessential (and therefore whether commas are required or not), compare it with the related sentences below.

After. ESSENTIAL: The telegram came *after you left last evening.* (Tells *when.*) NONESSENTIAL: The telegram came this morning, *after the decision had been made.* (The phrase *this morning* clearly tells when; the *after* clause provides additional but nonessential information.)

All of which. ALWAYS NONESSENTIAL: The rumors, *all of which were unfounded,* brought about the defeat of the candidate.

Although and **though.** ALWAYS NONESSENTIAL: She bought a new dress for the party, *although I do not believe she will wear it.* (Clause of concession.)

As. ESSENTIAL: The results of the mailing are *as you prophesied they would be.*
NONESSENTIAL: The results of the mailing are disappointing, *as you prophesied they would be.*

As . . . as. ALWAYS ESSENTIAL: He talked *as* well at the meeting *as* he did over the telephone.

As if and **as though.** ESSENTIAL: The man walked *as if* (or *as though*) *he were in a hurry.*
NONESSENTIAL: The man walked fast, *as if* (or *as though*) *he were in a hurry.*

As soon as. ESSENTIAL: We will fill your order *as soon as we receive new stock.*
NONESSENTIAL: We will fill your order next week, *as soon as we receive new stock.*

At, by, for, in, and **to which.** ESSENTIAL: I went to the floor *to which I had been directed.*
NONESSENTIAL: I went to the tenth floor, *to which I had been directed.*

Because. ESSENTIAL: He left *because he had another appointment.*
NONESSENTIAL: This report must be on his desk tonight, *because he is leaving tomorrow.*

Before. ESSENTIAL: The shipment was sent *before your letter was received.*
NONESSENTIAL: The shipment was sent on Tuesday, *before your letter was received.*

For. ALWAYS NONESSENTIAL: He read the book, *for he was interested in psychology.* (Clause of reason.)

If. ESSENTIAL: Let us hear from you *if you are interested.*
NONESSENTIAL: She promised to write from Toronto, *if I remember correctly.* (Clause added loosely.)

In order that. Essential or nonessential, depending on closeness of relation.
ESSENTIAL: Please notify your instructor promptly *in order that a makeup examination may be scheduled.*
NONESSENTIAL: Please notify your instructor promptly if you will be unable to attend the examination on Friday, *in order that a makeup examination may be scheduled.*

No matter what (why, how, etc.). ALWAYS NONESSENTIAL: The order cannot be ready by Monday, *no matter what the manager says.*

None of which. ALWAYS NONESSENTIAL: We received five boxes of candy for Christmas, *none of which have been opened.*

None of whom. Refers to persons. ALWAYS NONESSENTIAL: We interviewed ten applicants, *none of whom were satisfactory.*

Since. ESSENTIAL: We have taken no applications *since we received your instructions.*
NONESSENTIAL: We are taking no more applications, *since our lists are now closed.* (Clause of reason.)

So . . . as. ALWAYS ESSENTIAL: The second dress was not *so* well made *as* the first one.

So that. Essential or nonessential, depending on closeness of relation.
ESSENTIAL: Examine all shipments *so that any damage may be detected promptly.*
NONESSENTIAL: Examine all shipments as soon as they arrive, *so that any damage may be detected promptly.*

So . . . that. ALWAYS ESSENTIAL: The man was *so* tired *that* he could not finish the job.

Some of whom. Refers to persons. ALWAYS NONESSENTIAL: The agency has sent us five applicants, *some of whom seem promising.*

Than. ALWAYS ESSENTIAL: The employees were more disturbed by the rumor *than they cared to admit.*

That. Used in referring to things; also to persons when a class or type is meant. Some writers prefer *that* (instead of *which*) for introducing essential clauses: This is the house *that he owns today.* He is the kind of candidate *that I prefer.* (See also ¶ 1054a and b.)

Though. See *Although.*

Unless. ESSENTIAL: The item will be discontinued *unless customers begin to show an interest in it.*

NONESSENTIAL: I shall start transferring the files, *unless you have other work for me.* (Clause added loosely as an afterthought.)

When. ESSENTIAL: The company will accept bids *when Mr. Polk returns from his vacation.*

NONESSENTIAL: The company will accept bids next Monday, *when Mr. Polk returns from his vacation.*

Where. ESSENTIAL: Please tell me *where you put the paste.*

NONESSENTIAL: It is on the top shelf, *where it always is.*

Whereas. ALWAYS NONESSENTIAL: The figures for last year include rural areas only, *whereas those for this year include large cities as well.* (Clause of contrast.)

Which. Used in referring to animals, things, and ideas. Always use *which* (instead of *that*) to introduce nonessential clauses: The bay, *which was full of small sailing craft,* was very rough. (See also ¶ 1054b.)

While. ESSENTIAL: The workers struck *while negotiations were still going on.* (*While* meaning "during the time that.")

NONESSENTIAL: The workers at the Union Company struck, *while those at the Powers Company remained at work.* (*While* meaning "whereas.")

Who. Refers to persons. ESSENTIAL: All students *who are members of the Student Council* will be excused at two o'clock today.

NONESSENTIAL: John Cranshaw, *who is a member of the Student Council,* will be excused at two o'clock today.

Whom. Refers to persons. ESSENTIAL: This package is for the friend *whom I am visiting.*

NONESSENTIAL: This package is for my cousin Amy, *whom I am visiting.*

Whose. ESSENTIAL: The prize will be awarded to the student *whose essay shows the most originality.*

NONESSENTIAL: The prize was awarded to Eunice, *whose story showed the most originality.*

IN COMPOUND-COMPLEX SENTENCES

134 A compound-complex sentence typically consists of two independent clauses and one or more dependent clauses. To punctuate a sentence of this kind, first place a comma before the coordinating conjunction that joins the two independent clauses; this serves to break the sentence into two parts. Then consider each half of the sentence alone and provide additional punctuation as necessary.

Frank Swanson, Eastwood's treasurer, promised to call me *as soon as he arrived in town,* but I have not yet heard from him.

In May, 1968, the merger was first proposed, but Harold Johnson, *who was then Allied's chief executive officer,* refused to make a firm commitment.

I thought their offices were in Canton, Ohio, but *when my letter came back undelivered,* I realized they must be in Canton, Massachusetts.

a. If a misreading is likely or a stronger pause is desired, use a semicolon rather than a comma to separate the two main clauses. (See ¶ 177.)

b. If the dependent clause comes at the beginning of the sentence and applies equally to the two independent clauses that follow, omit the comma between the independent clauses. (See also ¶ 125, exception.)

Before you begin to type this manuscript, review the style sheet and check Mr. Foster's specific directions.

WITH PARTICIPIAL, INFINITIVE, AND PREPOSITIONAL PHRASES

135   When a participial, an infinitive, or a prepositional phrase comes *at the beginning of a sentence,* the following rules apply:

a. Use a comma after an *introductory participial phrase.*

Speaking in a loud voice, the chairman called the meeting to order.
Pleased by the unusual service, the woman has become a steady customer.
Having made the correction, I no longer worried.

NOTE: Do not confuse a participial phrase with a gerund phrase that is the subject of a sentence. No comma should follow a gerund phrase serving as the subject.

Speaking before a large audience always frightens me.

b. Use a comma after an *introductory infinitive phrase* unless the phrase is the subject of the sentence. (Infinitive phrases are introduced by the word *to.*)

To obtain the best results from the camera, follow these directions.

To have displayed the goods more effectively, he should have consulted a lighting specialist.

BUT: *To have displayed the goods more effectively* would have been an expensive project. (Infinitive phrase used as subject.)

c. Use a comma after an *introductory prepositional phrase* unless the phrase is short and no misunderstanding is likely to result from the omission of the comma. (Some writers consistently insert the comma after an introductory prepositional phrase to avoid having to analyze each situation.)

In response to the many requests of our customers, we are opening a suburban branch. (Comma required after a long phrase.)

On Monday morning the mail is always late. (No comma required after a short phrase.)

In 1967 our entire inventory was destroyed by fire. (No comma required after a short phrase.)

[Continued on page 14.]

CONFUSING: After all you have gone through a great deal.

CLEAR: After all, you have gone through a great deal. (Comma required after a short phrase to prevent misreading.)

NOTE: Always use a comma after an introductory prepositional phrase that contains a verb form, even if the phrase is short.

At the time you called, I was tied up in a meeting.

In preparing your report, be sure to include last year's figures for the sake of comparison.

136 When a participial, infinitive, or prepositional phrase occurs *at the beginning of a clause within the sentence,* insert or omit the comma following, just as if the clause were at the beginning of the sentence. (See ¶ 135.)

The chairman strode to the platform, and *speaking in a loud voice,* he called the meeting to order. (A comma follows the participial phrase just as if the sentence began with the word *Speaking.* No comma precedes the phrase because there is no need to treat the phrase parenthetically.)

The salesclerk explained that *to get the best results from the camera,* you should follow the directions.

We should like to announce that *in response to the many requests of our customers,* we are opening a suburban branch.

Last year we had a number of thefts, and *in 1967* our entire inventory was destroyed by fire. (No comma is needed after a short introductory prepositional phrase.)

He was a man who, *in the best tradition of the company,* did what the job demanded. (Here the phrase is set off by two commas because it interrupts the flow between the dependent clause subject *who* and the verb *did.*)

If, *in the interest of time,* you decide to fly to Detroit, I'll be glad to help you make your plane reservations.

137 When a participial, infinitive, or prepositional phrase occurs *at some point other than the beginning of a sentence or the beginning of a clause,* commas are omitted or used, depending on whether the phrase is essential or nonessential.

a. An *essential* participial, infinitive, or prepositional phrase is necessary to the meaning of the sentence and cannot be omitted. Therefore, do not use commas to set it off.

The instructions *printed in italics* are the most important. (Participial.)

It is a pleasure *to recommend Miss Brown.* (Infinitive.)

The copy *with the signatures* should be retained. (Prepositional.)

b. A *nonessential* participial, infinitive, or prepositional phrase can be omitted without changing the meaning of the sentence. Set off such phrases with commas.

Our entire collection of dining room furniture, *created by one of Denmark's outstanding designers,* will be on sale throughout this month. (Participial.)

I found that the brake linings were worn, *to mention only one defect.* (Infinitive.)

He has extraordinary talents, *in my opinion.* (Prepositional.)

138   When a business letter is referred to by date, any related phrases or clauses that follow are usually nonessential.

> Thank you for your letter of May 8, *in which you reported receiving damaged shipments.* (The date is sufficient to identify which letter is meant; the *in which* clause simply provides additional but nonessential information.)

However, no comma is needed after the date if the following phrase is short and closely related.

> Thank you for your letter of May 8 *about the damaged shipment.*

WITH INTRODUCTORY, PARENTHETICAL, OR TRANSITIONAL EXPRESSIONS

139   Use commas to set off parenthetical elements—that is, words, phrases, or clauses that are not necessary to the completeness of the structure or the meaning of the sentence. Such expressions either provide a transition from one thought to the next or reflect the writer's attitude toward the meaning of the sentence. Here is a list of the expressions most frequently used in this way:

accordingly	for example	meanwhile	personally
actually	for instance	moreover	respectively
after all	for the time being	namely	say
again	furthermore	naturally	still (see ¶ 145)
also	hence (see ¶ 145)	needless to say	strictly speaking
apparently	however	nevertheless	that is
as a matter of fact	if any	next	then (see ¶ 145)
as a result	in addition	no	theoretically
as a rule	in any case	no doubt	therefore
as you know	in fact	obviously	thus (see ¶ 145)
at any rate	in my opinion	of course	to begin with
besides	in other words	of necessity	to say the least
better yet	in short	on the contrary	to tell the truth
certainly	in the first place	on the other hand	too (see ¶ 146)
consequently	in turn	on the whole	well
finally	inclusive	otherwise	without doubt
first	indeed	perhaps	yes

140   Use one comma to set off a parenthetical element *at the beginning or end of a sentence.*

> *After all,* you have done more for him than he had any right to expect.
>
> *However,* you look at the letter yourself and see whether you interpret it as I do.
>
> *Obviously,* the toastmaster was moved by the reception the audience gave him.
>
> We shall take all appropriate measures, *of course.*

[Continued on page 16.]

If the expression is essential to the *structure* or the *meaning* of the sentence, do not set it off with a comma.

> *After all* you have done for him, he has no right to expect more.
>
> *However* you look at the letter, there is only one possible interpretation.
>
> *Obviously* moved by the reception the audience gave him, the toastmaster gave an excellent speech.
>
> We shall take all appropriate measures as a matter *of course.*

▶ See also ¶ 145.

141 Use two commas to set off the expression when it occurs as a parenthetical element *within the sentence.*

> It is generally understood, *however,* that he will accept the position.
>
> You, *too,* will be pleased with the materials used in our products.

If, however, the expression is used as an essential element, omit the commas.

> **PARENTHETICAL:** There is, *no doubt,* a reasonable explanation for his behavior.
>
> **ESSENTIAL:** There is *no doubt* about his honesty.
>
> **PARENTHETICAL:** Let me say, *to begin with,* that I have always thought highly of him.
>
> **ESSENTIAL:** If you want to improve your English, you ought *to begin with* a good review of grammar.

IMPORTANT NOTE: In many sentences the only way you can tell whether an expression is parenthetical or essential is by the way you say it. If your voice tends to *drop* as you utter the expression, it is parenthetical and should be set off by commas.

> It is understood, *nevertheless,* that he will accept the position.
>
> He is willing, *certainly,* to do the job over.
>
> It is important, *therefore,* that we check the files at once.

If your voice tends to *rise* as you utter the expression, it is essential and should not be set off by commas.

> It is *nevertheless* understood that he will accept the position.
>
> He is *certainly* willing to do the job over.
>
> It is *therefore* important that we check the files at once.

If commas are inserted in the previous example, the entire reading of the sentence will be changed. The voice will rise on the word *is* and drop on *therefore.*

> It is, *therefore,* important that we check the files at once.

142 When the expression occurs *at the beginning of the second independent clause* in a compound sentence and is *preceded by a semicolon,* use one comma following the expression.

> I never met him formally; *however,* I know him by sight.
>
> My schedule on Friday has eased up considerably; *therefore,* I can see you any time after two.

143   When the expression occurs *at the beginning of the second independent clause* in a compound sentence and is *preceded by a comma and a coordinating conjunction,* use one comma following the expression.

> The job seemed to have no future, and *to tell the truth,* the salary was pretty low.
>
> In the first place, I think the budget for the project is unrealistic, and *in the second place,* the deadlines are almost impossible to meet.

NOTE: If the expression is a simple adverb like *therefore* or *consequently,* the comma following the expression is usually omitted.

> The matter must be resolved by Friday, and *therefore* our preliminary conference must be held no later than Thursday.

144   If the expression occurs *at the beginning of a dependent clause,* either treat it as parenthetical (and set it off with two commas) or treat it as essential (and omit the commas).

> If, *moreover,* they do not meet the next interim deadline, we have the right to cancel the contract.
>
> If *indeed* they are interested in settling the dispute, why don't they agree to submit the issues to arbitration?
>
> He is a man who, *in my opinion,* will make a fine marketing director.
>
> He is a man who *no doubt* knows how to run a department smoothly and effectively.
>
> The situation is so serious that, *strictly speaking,* bankruptcy is the only real solution.
>
> The situation is so serious that *perhaps* bankruptcy may be the only solution.

145   When the one-syllable connectives *hence, still, then,* and *thus* occur at the beginning of a sentence or an independent clause, the comma following is omitted unless the connective requires special emphasis or a pause is desired at that point.

> Melt the butter over high heat; *then* add the egg.
>
> **BUT:** Melt the butter over high heat; *then,* when the foam has subsided, add the egg.

NOTE: Some writers also omit the comma after longer connectives (such as *therefore, moreover, furthermore,* and *consequently*) at the beginning of a sentence or an independent clause.

146   When the adverb *too* (in the sense of "also") occurs at the end of a clause or a sentence, the comma preceding is omitted unless the connective requires special emphasis.

> If you want to bring your wife along *too,* I'll make the necessary arrangements.

[*Continued on page 18.*]

Paul expected a bonus *too,* but I told him it was out of the question.

You should try to improve your math *too.*

When *too* (in the sense of "also") occurs elsewhere in the sentence, particularly between subject and verb, set it off with two commas.

You, *too,* can save by shopping at Feder's.

NOTE: When *too* is used as an adverb meaning "excessively," it is never set off with commas.

I am *too* busy to participate in the session.

The package arrived *too* late to be delivered.

IN A SERIES

147 When the last member of a series of three or more items is preceded by *and, or,* or *nor,* place a comma before the conjunction as well as between the other items. (See also ¶ 128.)

Study the rules for the use of the comma, the semicolon, *and* the colon.

They hiked to the summit, ate their lunch, rested for an hour, *and* were home by nightfall.

The critics agreed that the book was well written, that the facts were accurate, *and* that the conclusions were sound.

148 Do not, however, use a comma before the & sign in a company name.

The machine is manufactured by Ames, Wright & Company.

149 When *etc.* (abbreviation for *et cetera,* meaning "and so forth") closes a series, a comma precedes and follows the abbreviation (unless, of course, the abbreviation falls at the end of a sentence).

The sale of suits, coats, hats, *etc.,* will start tomorrow.

At nine o'clock tomorrow we shall start our sale of suits, coats, hats, *etc.*

150 Do not insert a comma after the last item in a series unless the sentence structure demands a comma at that point.

January 15, March 3, and May 20 are the dates of the three letters.

January 15, March 3, and May 20, 1969, are the dates of the three letters. (The comma following the year is one of the pair that sets off the year. See ¶ 167.)

151 When *and, or,* or *nor* is used to connect all the items in a series, do not separate the items by commas.

Invitations are being sent to parents *and* alumnae *and* faculty.

152 If a series consists of only two items, do not separate the items with a comma. (See also ¶ 124.)

I can reach the office quickly either *by bus* or *by subway.*

NOTE: Use a comma, however, to separate two independent clauses joined by *and, but, or,* or *nor.* (See ¶ 125.)

▶ See ¶¶ 184–185 for the use of the semicolon in a series.

WITH ADJECTIVES

153   When two or more consecutive adjectives modify the same noun, separate the adjectives by commas.

> The employer described him as a *quiet, efficient* worker. (A worker who is quiet and efficient.)

NOTE: Do *not* use a comma between adjectives if they are connected by *and, or,* or *nor.*

> The employer described him as a *quiet* and *efficient* worker.

154   When the last adjective in the series is closely connected in thought with the noun so that the first adjective modifies the combined idea of the last adjective plus the noun, do not separate the adjectives by a comma.

> The house was surrounded by an *old stone* wall. (A stone wall that is old.)
>
> Mr. Howard is working on the *annual financial* statement. (A financial statement that is annual.)

NOTE: To decide whether consecutive adjectives should be separated by commas or not, try reversing their order and inserting *and* between them. If they read smoothly and sensibly in that position, they should be separated by commas in their actual position.

> We need an *intelligent, enterprising* man for the job. (One can speak of "an enterprising and intelligent man"; hence a comma is correct in the original wording.)
>
> He was wearing an *old winter coat.* (One cannot speak of "a winter and old coat"; hence no comma should be used in the actual sentence.)

155   Do not use a comma between the final adjective in a series and the following noun.

> I put in a long, hard, *demanding* day on Monday.
>
> (NOT: I put in a long, hard, *demanding,* day on Monday.)

156   When two or more adjectives occur out of their normal order in a sentence, the series as a whole should be set off by commas.

> NORMAL ORDER: The *sleek and shimmering* ocean liner entered the bay and headed toward the Narrows.
>
> BUT: The ocean liner, *shimmering and sleek,* entered the bay and headed toward the Narrows.
>
> NORMAL ORDER: Miss Hershey looked *delighted and amused* as she blew out the candles on the cake.
>
> BUT: *Delighted and amused,* Miss Hershey blew out the candles on the cake.

WITH IDENTIFYING, APPOSITIVE, OR EXPLANATORY EXPRESSIONS

157 Words, phrases, and clauses that identify or explain other terms should be set off by commas. (See ¶ 169 for expressions indicating residence or business connections.)

> Mr. Clark, *the president,* is retiring on Monday, *June 30.*
>
> His latest interest is etymology, *that is, the study of the history of words.* (See also ¶¶ 181–183.)
>
> Our first thought, *to run to the nearest exit,* would have resulted in panic.
>
> Mr. Green, *the salesman who led the group,* is to be the new manager.
>
> Business transacted on credit is based on two factors, *sales and collections.*
>
> She enjoys outdoor sports, *such as tennis and golf.*
>
> His latest book, *Color and Design,* sells for $3.

158 No commas are required when a noun and its appositive are so closely related that they are read as a unit without an intervening pause. (The appositive in this case is considered an *essential appositive.*)

> My sister *Nancy* was graduated from high school in June.
>
> **BUT:** My sister, *Nancy Lask,* will be visiting us with her family.
>
> The poet *Richard Wilbur* will give a reading tomorrow night at the college.
>
> Mary *herself* made all the arrangements for the luncheon.
>
> The year *1950* marked the end of the first half of the twentieth century.
>
> The word *accommodate* is often misspelled.
>
> She enjoys such outdoor sports *as tennis and golf.*
>
> The book *Color and Design* sells for $3.

159 When *or* introduces a word or a phrase that identifies or explains the preceding word, set off the explanatory expression with commas.

> Set off parenthetical, *or nonessential,* elements with commas.

However, if *or* introduces an alternative thought, the expression is not parenthetical and should not be set off by commas.

> The punctuation depends on whether the item is parenthetical *or essential.*

WITH INTERRUPTIONS OF THOUGHT AND AFTERTHOUGHTS

160 Use commas to set off words, phrases, or clauses that interrupt the flow of a sentence or that are loosely added at the end as an afterthought.

> She has received, *so I was told,* a letter of commendation from the mayor.
>
> The exhibit contained only modern art, *if I remember correctly.*
>
> Our lighting equipment, *you must admit,* is most inadequate.
>
> His record is outstanding, *particularly in the field of electronics.*
>
> This book is as well written as, *though less exciting than,* his other books.
>
> This course of action is the wisest, *if not the most expedient,* one under the circumstances.

CAUTION: When enclosing an interrupting expression with two commas, be sure the commas are inserted accurately.

WRONG: That is the best, *though not the cheapest method,* of rebuilding your garage.

RIGHT: That is the best, *though not the cheapest,* method of rebuilding your garage.

WRONG: Frank has a deep interest in, *as well as a great fondness,* for oriental art.

RIGHT: Frank has a deep interest in, *as well as a great fondness for,* oriental art.

WITH ADDITIONAL CONSIDERATIONS

161 A phrase introduced by *as well as, in addition to, besides, accompanied by, together with,* and similar expressions should be set off by commas when it falls between the subject and the verb.

Our executives, *as well as our staff,* acclaimed the decision.

When the phrase occurs elsewhere in the sentence, commas may be omitted if the phrase is closely related to the preceding words.

The decision was acclaimed by our executives *as well as our staff.*

BUT: He is leaving for Chicago on Friday morning, *together with his assistant and two marketing consultants.*

WITH CONTRASTING EXPRESSIONS

162 Contrasting expressions should be set off by commas. (Such expressions often begin with *but* or *not.*)

Jones is willing to sell, *but only on his terms.*

He had changed his methods, *not his objectives,* we noticed.

The more even your typing touch, the more pleasing the results.

Fred, *rather than Al,* was chosen for the job.

NOTE: When such phrases fit smoothly into the flow of the sentence, no commas are required.

They have chosen Fred *rather than Al.*

It was a busy *but enjoyable* trip.

TO INDICATE OMITTED WORDS

163 Use a comma to indicate the omission of a word or words that are clearly understood from the context. (The omitted words are usually verbs.)

The English test was given to all students; the history test, to a selected group.

Something is wrong. What, we don't know.

A payment of half the purchase price is due on delivery of the goods; the balance, in three months.

FOR CLARITY

164   Note how the use of the comma prevents misreading.

> As you know, nothing came of the meeting. (**NOT**: As you know nothing came of the meeting.)
>
> Prescriptions filled reasonably, accurately. (Meaning reasonably *and* accurately. **NOT**: Prescriptions filled reasonably accurately.)

165   Sometimes, for clarity, it is necessary to separate even a subject and a verb.

> All any insurance policy is, is a contract for services.

IN DIRECT ADDRESS

166   Names and titles used in direct address must be set off by commas.

> You cannot deny, *Mr. Monroe,* that you made that statement.
>
> No, *sir,* I did not see him.
>
> *Mr. Chairman,* I rise to a point of order.

IN DATES

167   Use two commas to set off the year when it follows the month and day or the month alone.

> He began work on January 2, 1970, under the terms of the contract.
>
> It was in March, 1965, that the breakthrough occurred.

▶   See ¶ 418 for commas and other punctuation in dates.

WITH STATES AND COUNTRIES

168   Use two commas to set off the name of a state, a country, a county, etc., that directly follows a city name.

> You can fly from Miami, *Florida,* to Bogotá, *Colombia,* in under four hours.
>
> Show your address as Verona, *Essex County, New Jersey,* when you fill out the form.
>
> He moved to Franklin Square, *Long Island,* in the late fifties.

WITH RESIDENCE AND BUSINESS CONNECTIONS

169   Use commas to set off a *long phrase* denoting a person's residence or his business connections.

> Mr. Lee, *of the Hansford Company in Clarksville, Tennessee,* will be in town next Thursday.
>
> Mr. Lee *of Clarksville, Tennessee,* will be in town next Thursday. (Omit the comma before *of* to avoid too many breaks in a short phrase. The state name must always be set off by commas when it follows a city name.)

Mr. Lee *of the Hansford Company* will be in town next Thursday. (Short phrase; no commas.)

Mr. Lee *of Clarksville* will be in town next Thursday. (Short phrase; no commas.)

WITH JR., SR., ETC.

170 Use commas to set off designations following a person's name, such as *Jr., Sr., Esq.,* and abbreviations signifying academic degrees or religious orders.

Mr. L. B. Kelly, *Jr.,* sailed for Europe today. (A growing trend in business correspondence is to omit the commas with *Jr.* and *Sr.*)

Mr. L. B. Kelly, *Jr.'s* family sailed for Europe today. (Always omit the second comma when a possessive ending is attached to *Jr., Sr.,* etc.)

We were represented in court by Henry E. Stevens, *Esq.,* of New York.

Roger Farrier, *LL.D.,* will address the Elizabethan Club on Wednesday.

The Reverend James Hanley, *S.J.,* will serve as moderator of the panel.

171 Commas are not used to set off roman or arabic numerals following a name.

Henry Ford II   David Weild 3d   King George V

WITH INC. AND LTD.

172 Insert a comma before *Inc.* and *Ltd.* in company names unless you know that the official name of the company is written without a comma. Within a sentence, a comma must follow the abbreviation if a comma also precedes it.

Field Hats, Ltd.   **BUT:** Time Inc.

Field Hats, *Ltd.,* should be notified of the mistake.

Time *Inc.* has expanded its operations beyond magazine publishing.

IN FIGURES

173 When numbers run to four or more figures, use commas to separate thousands, hundreds of thousands, millions, etc.

$2,375.88   147,300 $11,275,478   4,300,000,000

NOTE: Some writers leave out the commas in four-digit numbers unless these numbers occur together with larger numbers that require commas.

174 Do not use commas in year numbers, page numbers, house or room numbers, telephone numbers, serial numbers (for example, invoice, style, model, or lot numbers), and decimals.

1973   8760 Sunset Drive   846-0462   Lot 6913
page 1246   Room 1804   Invoice 38162   64.9999

EXCEPTION: Patent numbers are written with commas; for example, *Patent No. 680,181.*

175   Some serial numbers (such as social security numbers) are written with hyphens, spaces, or other devices. Follow the style of the source.

    Social Security No. 152-22-8285   License No. SO14 785 053

▶   Commas with questions within sentences: see ¶¶ 113-116.
    Commas with parentheses: see ¶ 224a.
    Commas inside quotation marks: see ¶ 248.
    Commas at end of a quotation: see ¶¶ 254-256.
    Commas preceding a quotation: see ¶ 257.
    Commas with quotations within a sentence: see ¶¶ 260-262.
    Commas to set off interruptions in quoted matter: see ¶¶ 263-264.

THE SEMICOLON

BETWEEN INDEPENDENT CLAUSES—AND, BUT, OR, OR NOR OMITTED

176   When a coordinating conjunction (*and, but, or,* or *nor*) is omitted between two independent clauses, use a semicolon—not a comma—to separate the clauses.

    The union was willing to compromise; the management was not.

    (NOT: The union was willing to compromise, the management was not.)

NOTE: If the clauses are not closely related, treat them as separate sentences.

    WEAK: Thank you for your letter of March 16; we are sorry about the error in the shipment and are rushing the correct items to you by air express.

    BETTER: Thank you for your letter of March 16. We are sorry about the error in the shipment and are rushing the correct items to you by air express.

BETWEEN INDEPENDENT CLAUSES—AND, BUT, OR, OR NOR INCLUDED

177   A comma is normally used to separate two independent clauses joined by a coordinating conjunction. However, under certain circumstances, a semicolon is appropriate.

    a. Use a semicolon in order to achieve a stronger break between clauses than a comma provides.

    NORMAL BREAK: Everyone is convinced that he could personally solve the problem if given the authority to do so, but no one will come forward with a clear-cut plan that we can evaluate in advance.

    STRONG BREAK: Everyone is convinced that he could personally solve the problem if given the authority to do so; but no one will come forward with a clear-cut plan that we can evaluate in advance.

b. Use a semicolon when one or both clauses contain internal commas and a misreading might occur if a comma were also used to separate the clauses.

> CONFUSING: I sent you an order for bond letterheads, onionskin paper, carbons, and envelopes, and shipping tags, cardboard cartons, stapler wire, and binding tape were sent to me instead.

> CLEAR: I sent you an order for bond letterheads, onionskin paper, carbons, and envelopes; and shipping tags, cardboard cartons, stapler wire, and binding tape were sent to me instead.

c. If no misreading is likely, a comma is sufficient to separate the clauses, even though commas are also used internally within the clauses.

> On May 19, 1972, I wrote to Mr. Harold McGee, your sales manager, but I have not yet had an answer to my letter.

> On the whole, his progress has been good, and considering his medical history, I think he will make a complete recovery.

NOTE: If a stronger break is desired between clauses in the two examples above, use a semicolon.

WITH TRANSITIONAL EXPRESSIONS

178 When independent clauses are linked by transitional expressions (see partial list below), use a semicolon between the clauses. (If the second clause is long or requires special emphasis, treat it as a separate sentence.)

accordingly	however	so (see ¶ 179)
besides	moreover	that is (see ¶ 181)
consequently	namely (see ¶ 181)	then
for example (see ¶ 181)	nevertheless	therefore
furthermore	on the contrary	thus
hence	otherwise	yet (see ¶ 179)

> The motion was voted down; *moreover,* it was voted down by a large majority.

> Let's plan to work till one; *then* we can break for lunch.

> Our costs have increased; our prices, *however,* have not.

NOTE: Use a comma after the transitional expression when it occurs at the start of the second clause. (EXCEPTION: No comma is needed after the one-syllable connectives *hence, so, still, then, thus,* and *yet* unless a strong pause is wanted at that point.)

▶ See ¶¶ 140–141, 143–145 for the use of commas when the transitional expression occurs elsewhere in the sentence.

179 An independent clause introduced by *so* (in the sense of "therefore") or *yet* may be preceded by a comma or a semicolon. Use a comma if the two clauses are closely related and there is a smooth flow from the first clause to the second. Use a semicolon if the clauses are long and complicated or if the transition between clauses calls for a long pause or a strong break.

. [Continued on page 26.]

Sales have been good, *yet* profits are low.

His report explains why production has slowed down; *yet* it does not indicate how to avoid future delays.

These sale-priced toasters are going fast, *so* don't delay if you want one.

We have been getting an excessive number of complaints during the last few months about our service; *so* I would like each of you to review the operations in your department and indicate what steps you think ought to be taken.

180   If both the coordinating conjunction and the transitional expression occur at the start of the second clause, use a comma before the conjunction.

The site has a number of disadvantages, *and furthermore* the asking price is quite high.

REMEMBER: A semicolon is needed to separate independent clauses, not so much because a transitional expression is present, but because a coordinating conjunction is absent.

WITH FOR EXAMPLE, THAT IS, NAMELY, ETC.

181   **Before an Independent Clause**

a. In general, when two independent clauses are linked by a transitional expression such as *for example* (abbreviated *e.g.*), *namely,* or *that is* (abbreviated *i.e.*), use a semicolon before the expression and a comma afterward.

He is highly qualified for the job; *for example,* he has had ten years' experience in the field.

b. If the first independent clause serves to anticipate the second clause and the full emphasis is to fall on the second clause, use a colon before the transitional expression.

Your proposal covers all but one point: *namely,* who is going to foot the bill?

c. For a stronger but less formal break between clauses, the semicolon or the colon may be replaced by a dash.

Hammer says he will help—*that is,* he will help if you ask him to.

182   **At the End of a Sentence**

When *for example, namely,* or *that is* introduces words, phrases, or a series of clauses *at the end of a sentence,* the punctuation preceding the expression may vary as follows:

a. If the first part of the sentence expresses the complete thought and an explanation is added on almost as an afterthought, use a semicolon before the transitional expression.

Always use figures with abbreviations; *for example,* 4 p.m., 6 ft., 9 sq. in. (Here the examples are not anticipated by the earlier part of the sentence.)

b. If the first part of the sentence suggests that an explanation or an illustration will follow, use a colon before the transitional expression.

My assistant has three important duties: *namely,* attending all meetings, writing the minutes, and sending out notices. (The word *three* anticipates the enumeration following *namely.*)

c. If the expression introduces an appositive that explains a word or phrase immediately preceding, a comma should precede the transitional expression.

Do not use quotation marks to enclose an indirect quotation, *that is, a restatement of a person's exact words.*

d. The semicolon, the colon, and the comma in the examples above may be replaced by a dash or by parentheses. The dash provides a stronger but less formal break; the parentheses serve to subordinate the explanatory element.

183 Within a Sentence

When these expressions introduce words, phrases, or clauses *within a sentence,* treat the entire construction as parenthetical and set it off with commas, dashes, or parentheses.

Many of the components, *for example, the motor,* are manufactured by outside suppliers.
Many of the components—*for example, the motor*—are manufactured by . . .
Many of the components (*for example, the motor*) are manufactured by . . .

NOTE: Commas are suitable to set off the parenthetical element so long as it contains no internal punctuation (other than the comma after the introductory expression). If the parenthetical element is internally punctuated with several commas, set it off with either dashes (for emphasis) or parentheses (for subordination).

Many of the components—*for example, the motor, the batteries, and the cooling unit*—are manufactured by outside suppliers. (Use dashes for emphasis.)
OR: Many of the components (*for example, the motor, the batteries, and the cooling unit*) are manufactured by outside suppliers. (Use parentheses for subordination.)

IN A SERIES

184 Use a semicolon to separate items in a series if any of the items already contain commas.

Attending the conference in Washington were John Osgood, executive vice president; Donald Hays, marketing director; Charles Lindstrom, advertising manager; and Paul Hingle, sales promotion manager.

185 Avoid starting a sentence with a series punctuated with semicolons. Try to recast the sentence so that the series comes at the end.

[Continued on page 28.]

AWKWARD: Our sales managers in Portland, Oregon; Seattle, Washington; Salt Lake City, Utah; and Los Angeles, California, have been sent invitations.

IMPROVED: Invitations have been sent to our sales managers in Portland, Oregon; Seattle, Washington; Salt Lake City, Utah; and Los Angeles, California.

WITH SUBORDINATE CLAUSES

186   Use semicolons to separate a series of parallel subordinate clauses if they are long or contain internal commas. (However, a simple series of dependent clauses requires only commas, just like any other kind of series.)

> He promised that he would review the existing specifications, costs, and sales estimates for the project; that he would analyze Merkle's alternative figures; and that he would prepare a detailed comparison of the two proposals.

> If you have tried special clearance sales but have not raised the necessary cash; if you have tried to borrow the money and have not been able to find a lender; if you have offered to sell part of the business but have not been able to find a partner, then your only course of action, in my judgment, is to go out of business.

▶   Semicolons with parentheses: see ¶ 224a.
Semicolons with quotation marks: see ¶ 249.

THE COLON

BETWEEN INDEPENDENT CLAUSES

187   Use a colon between two independent clauses when the second clause explains or illustrates the first clause and there is no coordinating conjunction or transitional expression linking the two clauses.

> The job you have described sounds very attractive: the salary is good and the opportunities for advancement seem excellent.

> **BUT:** The job you have described sounds very attractive; for example, the salary is good and the opportunities for advancement seem excellent. (Use a semicolon when a transitional expression links the clauses.)

> The job you have described sounds very attractive; it is the kind of job I have been looking for. (Use a semicolon when the second clause does not explain the first clause.)

BEFORE LISTS AND ENUMERATIONS

188   Place a colon before such expressions as *for example, namely,* and *that is* when they introduce words, phrases, or a series of clauses anticipated earlier in the sentence. (See ¶ 182 for examples.)

189   When a clause contains an anticipatory word (such as *the following, as follows, thus,* and *these*) and leads to a series of explanatory words, phrases, or clauses, use a colon between the clause and the series.

These are the job requirements: a college degree, three years' experience in the field, and freedom to travel abroad.

The following rules should be observed in writing checks:
1. Write them in ink.
2. Leave no empty spaces on lines that are to be filled in.
3. Make no changes or erasures in an amount of money.

190   Use the colon even if the anticipatory expression is only implied and not stated.

The house has attractive features: cross ventilation in every room, a two-story living room, and two terraces.

191   Do not use the colon in the following cases:

a. If the sentence in which the anticipatory expression occurs is a long sentence and if the expression occurs near the beginning of that sentence.

We are sorry to be obliged to set the *following* restrictions on the return of merchandise, because many customers have abused the privilege. Goods cannot be returned after five days, and price tags must not be removed.

BUT: The *following* students were absent today: Davis, Hale, and Lloyd.

b. If the sentence containing the anticipatory expression is followed by another sentence.

Campers will find that the *following* small items will add much to their enjoyment of the summer. These articles may be purchased from a store near the camp.

Flashlight	Hot-cold food bag
Camera	Fishing gear

c. If an explanatory series follows a preposition or a verb.

The panel consists of Miss Halsey, Mrs. Finch, and Mr. Martin. (**NOT:** The panel consists of: Miss Halsey, Mrs. Finch, and Mr. Martin.)

This set of china includes 12 dinner plates, 12 salad plates, and 12 cups and saucers. (**NOT:** This set of china includes: 12 dinner plates, 12 salad plates, and 12 cups and saucers.)

NOTE: Retain the colon if the items in the series are listed on separate lines.

This set of china includes:
    12 dinner plates
    12 salad plates
    12 cups and saucers

IN EXPRESSIONS OF TIME AND PROPORTIONS

192   When hours and minutes are expressed in figures, separate the figures by a colon, as in the expression *8:25*. (No space precedes or follows this colon.)

193   A colon is used to represent the word *to* in proportions, as in the ratio 2:1. (No space precedes or follows this colon.)

AFTER SALUTATIONS

194   In business letters, use a colon after the salutation (see also ¶ 1431). In social letters, use a comma (see also ¶ 1481*b*).

CAPITALIZING AFTER A COLON

195   Do not capitalize after a colon if the material cannot stand alone as a sentence.

> The essentials are as follows: shorthand, typing, and English. (Words following a colon.)
>
> All cash advances must be countersigned by the general manager, with one exception: when the amount is less than $50. (Dependent clause following a colon.)

196   Do not capitalize the first word of an independent clause after a colon if the clause explains, illustrates, or amplifies the thought expressed in the first part of the sentence.

> There is a simple explanation for the high morale of our employees: we pay well.
>
> Essential and nonessential elements require altogether different punctuation: the former should be set off by commas, whereas the latter should not.

197   Capitalize the first word of an independent clause after a colon if it requires special emphasis or is presented as a formal rule. (In such cases the independent clause expresses the main thought; the first part of the sentence usually functions only as an introduction.)

> Let me say this: If the company is to recover from its present difficulties, we must immediately devise an entirely new marketing strategy.
>
> Here is the key principle: Parenthetical elements must be set off by commas; essential elements should not be set off.

198   Also capitalize the first word after a colon under these circumstances:

a. When the material following the colon consists of two or more sentences.

> There are several drawbacks to this proposal: First, it will tie up a good deal of capital for the next five years. Second, the likelihood of a significant return on the investment has not been shown.

b. When the material following the colon is a quoted sentence.

> Mr. Korman had this to say: "No single person can take full credit for the success of the show."

c. When the material following the colon starts on a new line (for example, the body of a letter following the salutation, or the individual items displayed on separate lines in a list).

Dear Mr. Frank:

Thank you for your letter of
May 3. I have talked to Hal . . .

Capitalize the first word of:
a. Every sentence.
b. Direct quotations.

d. When the material *preceding* the colon is a short introductory word such as *Note, Caution,* or *Wanted.*

> *Note:* All expense reports must be submitted no later than five days after the end of the accounting period.

▶ Colons with parentheses: see ¶ 224a.
Colons with quotation marks: see ¶ 249.

Section 2
PUNCTUATION: OTHER MARKS

Section 2 covers the following punctuation marks: the dash, parentheses, quotation marks, the underscore, the apostrophe, ellipsis marks, the asterisk, the diagonal, and brackets. In addition, it indicates the proper typewriter spacing to be used with all punctuation marks.

THE DASH

Although the dash has a few specific functions of its own, it most often serves in place of the comma, the semicolon, the colon, or parentheses. When used as an alternative to these other marks, it creates a much more emphatic separation of words within a sentence. Because of its versatility, careless writers are tempted to use a dash to punctuate almost any break within a sentence. However, the indiscriminate use of dashes is inappropriate; moreover, it serves to destroy the special forcefulness of this mark. Use the dash sparingly—and then only for deliberate effect.

IN PLACE OF COMMAS

201   Use dashes in place of commas to set off a parenthetical element that requires special emphasis.

> We intend to see to it that our agents—as well as the transportation companies and the public—receive a fair decision in the matter.
> There is a typographical error in one of the paragraphs—the second one.

202   If a parenthetical element already contains internal commas, use dashes in place of commas to set the element off. (If dashes provide too emphatic a break, use parentheses instead. See ¶¶ 183, 219.)

> All large appliances—refrigerators, stoves, washing machines, and dryers—will be on sale throughout the first week of March.
>
> The storm extended the entire length of the Eastern Seaboard—from Eastport, Maine, to Key West, Florida—in hurricane force.

203   To give special emphasis to the second independent clause in a compound sentence, use a dash rather than a comma before the coordinating conjunction.

> Carroll's proposal will double the tax burden on property owners—and I can prove it!

IN PLACE OF A SEMICOLON

204   For a stronger but less formal break, use a dash in place of a semicolon between closely related independent clauses.

> I do the work—he gets the credit!
> The job needs to be done—moreover, it needs to be done well.
> Wilson is totally unprepared for a promotion—for example, he still does not grasp the basic principles of good management.

IN PLACE OF A COLON

205   For a stronger but less formal break, use a dash in place of a colon to introduce explanatory words, phrases, or clauses.

> I need only a few items for my meeting with Kaster—specifically, a copy of his letter of May 18, a copy of the contract under dispute, and a bottle of aspirin.
>
> My arrangement with Gene is a simple one—he handles sales and promotion, and I take care of production.

IN PLACE OF PARENTHESES

206   Use dashes instead of parentheses when the parenthetical element requires strong emphasis. (See ¶¶ 183, 219.)

> Call Frank Spenser—he's with Jax Electronics—and get his opinion.

TO INDICATE AN ABRUPT BREAK OR AN AFTERTHOUGHT

207   Use a dash to show an abrupt break in thought or to set off an afterthought.

> Here's gourmet food in a jiffy—economical too!
> I believe he said the convention would be held in Portland, Oregon—or was it Portland, Maine?

208   If a *question* or an *exclamation* is broken off abruptly before it has been completed, use a dash followed by a question mark or an exclamation point as appropriate. If the sentence is a *statement,* however, use a dash alone, followed by two spaces.

> Where can I find—? Never mind, I found it!
> If only— Yet there's no point in talking about what might have been.
> (**NOT:** If only—. Yet there's no point in talking about what might have been.)

▶ See ¶ 291*b* for the use of ellipsis marks to indicate an abrupt break in thought.

TO SHOW HESITATION

209 Use a dash to indicate hesitation, faltering speech, or stammering.

> The work on the Lawson dam was begun—oh, I should say—well, about May 1—certainly no later than May 15.

TO EMPHASIZE SINGLE WORDS

210 Use dashes to set off single words that require special emphasis.

> Money—that is all he thinks about.
> He cares about only one thing—success.

WITH REPETITIONS AND RESTATEMENTS

211 Use dashes to set off and emphasize words that repeat or restate a previous thought.

> Right now—at this very moment—our showrooms are crammed with bargains.
> Sometime next week—say, Wednesday—let's plan to meet for lunch.
> That is the folder—the folder he said I had lost.

BEFORE SUMMARIZING WORDS

212 Use a dash before such words as *these, they,* and *all* when these words stand as subjects summarizing a preceding list of details.

> A lawn mower, a rake, and a spade—these are the only tools you will need.
> Juniors, seniors, and graduate students—all are invited to the Symington lecture on Tuesday.
> **BUT:** Juniors, seniors, and graduate students are all invited . . . (No dash is used when the summarizing word is not the subject.)

PUNCTUATION PRECEDING AN OPENING DASH

213 An opening dash should not be preceded by a comma, a semicolon, a colon, or a period (except a period following an abbreviation).

> We do a good job—and we do it fast!
> (**NOT:** We do a good job,—and we do it fast!)
> The shipment was sent c.o.d.—as you requested.

PUNCTUATION PRECEDING A CLOSING DASH

214   When a *statement* or a *command* is set off by dashes within a sentence, do not use a period before the closing dash.

> John Edgecroft—he used to head up the sales force at Marker's—now has his own consulting firm.
>
> (**NOT:** John Edgecroft—He used to head up the sales force at Marker's.—now has his own consulting firm.)

When a *question* or an *exclamation* is set off by dashes within a sentence, use a question mark or an exclamation point before the closing dash.

> The representative of the Hitchcock Company—do you know the one I mean?—has called again for an appointment.
>
> The new sketches—I can't wait to show them to you!—should be ready by Monday.

NOTE: When a complete sentence is set off in dashes, do not capitalize the first word unless it is a proper noun, a proper adjective, the pronoun *I*, or the first word of a quoted sentence.

PUNCTUATION FOLLOWING A CLOSING DASH

215   When the sentence construction requires some mark of punctuation following a closing dash, either retain the dash or use the sentence punctuation—but do not use both marks together.

a. When a closing dash falls at the end of a sentence, it should be replaced by the punctuation needed to end the sentence—a period, a question mark, or an exclamation point. (See ¶ 208 for exceptions.)

> Wheeler's Transport delivers the goods—on time!

b. When a closing dash occurs at a point where the sentence requires a comma, retain the closing dash and omit the comma.

> The situation has become critical—indeed dangerous—but no one seems to care. (Here the closing dash is retained, and the comma before the coordinating conjunction is omitted.)
>
> If you feel you are qualified for the job—and you may very well be—you ought to take the employment test. (Here the closing dash is retained, and the comma that separates a dependent clause from an independent clause is omitted.)
>
> Brophy said—and you can check with him yourself—"This office must be vacated by Friday." (Here the closing dash is retained, and the comma before the quotation is omitted.)

c. If a closing dash occurs at a point where the sentence requires a semicolon, a colon, or a closing parenthesis, drop the closing dash and use the required sentence punctuation.

> Please try to get your sales projections to us by Wednesday—certainly by Friday at the latest; otherwise, they will be of no use to us in planning next year's budget.

Here is what Marshall had to say—or at least the gist of it: look for new opportunities for expansion and then move in fast.

You need a volunteer (someone like John Borden, for example—he's always cooperative) to play the part of the customer.

TYPING DASHES

216   The dash is constructed by striking the hyphen key *twice,* with no space before, between, or after the hyphens.

Improve your English—today!   (**NOT:** Improve your English — today!)

BUT: If he would only try— (Two spaces follow a dash when a statement breaks abruptly. See ¶ 208.)

217   A dash should follow the last word typed on a line (rather than start a new line).

Let's set the date for June 30—   **NOT:** Let's set the date for June 30
a Wednesday, I believe.   —a Wednesday, I believe.

PARENTHESES

Parentheses and dashes serve many of the same functions, but they differ in one significant respect: parentheses can set off only nonessential elements, whereas dashes can set off essential and nonessential elements. In setting off elements, dashes emphasize; parentheses *de-emphasize.*

WITH EXPLANATORY MATTER

218   Use parentheses to enclose explanatory material that is independent of the main thought of the sentence. The material within parentheses may be a single word, a phrase, or even an entire sentence.

We are disappointed at the very small number of people (five) who have accepted our invitation. (A single word.)

Bids are requested for repaving Sutton Avenue (formerly Lombard Street) in the town of Chester. (A phrase.)

We regret that from now until the end of the year (our fiscal year starts January 1) we can make no further loans. (A sentence.)

NOTE: Be sure that the parentheses enclose only what is truly parenthetical and not words essential to the construction of the sentence.

WRONG: I merely said I was averse (not violently opposed *to*) your suggestion.

RIGHT: I merely said I was averse (not violently opposed) *to* your suggestion.

219   Use parentheses to set off a parenthetical element when dashes would be too emphatic and commas would be inappropriate or might prove confusing.

[Continued on page 36.]

He is the manager of our Portland (Oregon) branch.

BETTER THAN: He is the manager of our Portland, Oregon, branch. (Parentheses are clearer than commas when a "city-state" expression occurs as an adjective.)

All the classes on this list meet three days a week (Mondays, Wednesdays, and Fridays). (Parentheses are clearer than commas when the parenthetical element already contains commas within it.)

WITH REFERENCES

220   Use parentheses to set off references and directions.

Because of unusually heavy expenses to date (see the financial report attached), we are not in a position to make further changes this year.

When references fall *at the end of a sentence,* they may be treated as part of the sentence or as a separate sentence.

The statistics that support these conclusions are given in the appendix (see pages 314–316).

OR: The statistics . . . are given in the appendix. (See pages 314–316.)

▶   See also the note at the end of ¶ 225.

WITH DATES

221   Dates that accompany a person's name or an event are enclosed in parentheses.

Thomas Jefferson (1743–1826) was the third President of the United States.

At the time of the merger (1948), both parties agreed to establish new headquarters in St. Louis.

WITH ENUMERATED ITEMS

222   Use parentheses to enclose numbers or letters that accompany enumerated items within a sentence.

We need the following information to complete our record of Mr. Rice's experience: (1) the number of years he worked for your company, (2) a description of his duties, and (3) the number of promotions he received.

3. Please include these items in your expense account: (*a*) the cost of your hotel room; (*b*) the cost of meals, including tips; and (*c*) the amount spent on transportation. (Letters are used to enumerate items within a sentence when the sentence itself is part of a *numbered* sequence.)

NOTE: If the enumerated items appear on separate lines, the letters or numbers are usually followed only by periods. (See ¶ 223.)

223   Subdivisions in outlines are often enclosed in parentheses. When there are many gradations, it is sometimes necessary to use a single closing parenthesis to provide another grade.

1. Basic weaves	I. . . . .
a. Plain	A. . . . .
(1) Basket	1. . . . .
(2) Ribbed	*a.* . . . .
b. Twill	(1) . . . .
etc.	(*a*) . . . .
	1) . . . .
	a) . . . .

PARENTHETICAL ITEMS WITHIN SENTENCES

224 If the item in parentheses falls *within a sentence:*

a. Make sure that any punctuation needed at that point (such as a comma, a semicolon, a colon, or a dash) falls *outside* the closing parenthesis.

> If you will call me tomorrow (Thursday), I can give you more precise data.
>
> I wrote to him promptly (as I said I would); however, he has not answered.
>
> There is only one thing he cares about (and he admits it): himself!
>
> Your boss's name is mentioned in this week's issue of *Time* (see page 43)—and won't he be delighted!

NOTE: Never insert a comma, a semicolon, a colon, or a dash *before* an opening parenthesis.

b. Do not capitalize the first word of the item in parentheses, even if the item is a complete sentence. **EXCEPTIONS:** Proper nouns, proper adjectives, the pronoun *I,* and the first word of a quoted sentence. (See examples in *c* and *d* below.)

c. Do not use a period before the closing parenthesis except with an abbreviation.

> Mrs. Andrews' letter (please be sure to answer it promptly) makes me question the effectiveness of our order fulfillment procedures.
>
> Fred Trynor (our public relations man in Washington, D.C.) could give you that information.
>
> I want you to meet Ed Ferguson (he's our new sales manager) when you come to Omaha.
>
> **NOT:** I want you to meet Ed Ferguson (He's our new sales manager.) when you come to Omaha.

d. Do not use a question mark or an exclamation point before the closing parenthesis unless it applies solely to the parenthetical item and the sentence ends with a different mark of punctuation.

> At the coming meeting (will you be able to make it on the 19th?), let's plan to discuss next year's budget.
>
> May I still get tickets to the exhibition (and may I bring a friend), or is it now too late?
>
> **NOT:** May I still get tickets to the exhibition (and may I bring a friend?), or is it now too late?

PARENTHETICAL ITEMS AT THE END OF SENTENCES

225   If the item in parentheses is to be incorporated *at the end of a sentence:*

a. Make sure that the punctuation needed to end the sentence goes *outside* the closing parenthesis.

> The meeting will be held on March 31 (Friday).
> Have you met John Duff (he's with the Peabody Company)?
> Delivery has been put off again (till next Friday)!

b. Do not capitalize the first word of the item in parentheses, even if the item is a complete sentence. EXCEPTIONS: Proper nouns, proper adjectives, the pronoun *I*, and the first word of a quoted sentence. (See examples in *c* and *d* below.)

c. Do not use a period before the closing parenthesis except with an abbreviation.

> I waited at the airport for hours (until 3 a.m.).
> I waited at the airport for hours (I was there until three).
> **NOT:** I waited at the airport for hours (I was there until three.).

d. Do not use a question mark or an exclamation point before the closing parenthesis unless it applies solely to the parenthetical element and the sentence ends with a different mark of punctuation.

> My new assistant is Bill Ellsworth (didn't you meet him once before?).
> Be sure to send the letter to Portland, Oregon (not Portland, Maine!).
> Then he walked out and slammed the door (can you believe it?)!
> Do you know Don Smyth (or is it Smythe)?
> **NOT:** Do you know Don Smyth (or is it Smythe?)?
> I'm through with the job (and I mean it)!
> **NOT:** I'm through with the job (and I mean it!)!

NOTE: When a complete sentence occurs within parentheses at the end of another sentence, it may be incorporated into the sentence (as in the examples above) so long as it is fairly short and closely related. If the sentence in parentheses is long or requires special emphasis, it should be treated as a separate sentence (see ¶ 226).

PARENTHETICAL ITEMS AS SEPARATE SENTENCES

226   If the item in parentheses is to be treated as a *separate sentence:*

a. The preceding sentence should close with its own punctuation mark.

b. The item in parentheses should begin with a capital.

c. A period, a question mark, or an exclamation point (whichever is appropriate) should be placed before the closing parenthesis.

d. No other punctuation mark should follow the closing parenthesis.

Local businessmen charge that the proposed bond issue will raise the tax rate. (They present no proof of this, however.) Moreover, they claim that new industry will be discouraged.

He spoke at length on his favorite topic. (How could I stop him?) At the end of an hour, a number of people began to walk out.

▶ Parentheses around question marks: see ¶ 117.
Parentheses around exclamation points: see ¶ 118, note.
Parentheses around confirming figures: see ¶ 428.

QUOTATION MARKS

Quotation marks have three main functions: to indicate the use of someone else's exact words (see ¶¶ 227–233), to set off words and phrases for special emphasis (see ¶¶ 234–241), and to display the titles of literary and artistic works (see ¶¶ 242–244).

WITH DIRECT QUOTATIONS

227 Use quotation marks to enclose a *direct quotation,* that is, the exact words of a speaker or a writer.

> "I don't like the last paragraph in that letter," said Mr. Williams.
>
> When asked if she planned to attend, Mrs. Wilson simply said "No." (See ¶¶ 232, 257a.)

228 Do not use quotation marks for an *indirect quotation,* that is, a restatement or a rearrangement of a person's exact words. (An indirect quotation is often introduced by *that* or *whether* and usually differs from a direct quotation in person, verb tense, or word order.)

> **DIRECT QUOTATION:** Prescott asked his boss, "Am I still being considered for the transfer?"
>
> **INDIRECT QUOTATION:** Prescott asked his boss whether he was still being considered for the transfer.

NOTE: In some cases a person's exact words may be treated as either a direct or an indirect quotation, depending on the kind of emphasis desired.

> Brody said, "Thompson should be notified at once." (The use of quotation marks emphasizes that these are Brody's exact words.)
>
> Brody said Thompson should be notified at once. (Without quotation marks, the emphasis falls on the message itself. The fact that Brody used these particular words is not important.)

229 When only a word or phrase is quoted from another source, be sure to place the quotation marks around only the words extracted from the original source and not around any rearrangement of those words.

[Continued on page 40.]

> Bryant said he would decide when he had "all the facts." (Bryant's exact words were, "I will decide when I have all the facts.")
>
> **NOT:** Bryant said he would decide "when he had all the facts."

230 Be particularly sure not to include such words as *a* and *the* at the beginning or *etc.* at the end of the quotation unless these words were actually part of the original material.

> Joe said you turned in a "first-rate" report. (Joe's exact words were, "The report you turned in was first-rate.")
>
> Then end the letter with "I hope to hear from you soon," etc.

231 When quoting a series of words or phrases in the exact sequence in which it originally appeared, use quotation marks before and after the complete series. However, if the series of quoted words or phrases did not appear in this sequence in the original, use quotation marks around each word or phrase.

> According to Selby, the latest issue of the magazine looked "fresh, crisp, and appealing." (Selby's actual words were, "I think the new issue looks fresh, crisp, and appealing.")
>
> **BUT:** Selby thinks the magazine looks "fresh" and "crisp."

232 As a rule, the individual words *yes* and *no* should not be quoted unless heavy emphasis is desired. (Without quotation marks, these words are treated as indirect quotations; with quotation marks, these words emphatically represent what a person actually said or is asked to say or is likely to say.)

> Please don't say no until you have heard all the terms of the proposal. (**FOR EMPHASIS:** Please don't say "No" until . . .)
>
> Once the firm's board of directors says yes, we can proceed to draft the final specifications. (**FOR EMPHASIS:** . . . says "Yes," we can proceed . . .)
>
> When asked if he would accept a reassignment, Frank thought for a moment; then, without any trace of emotion, he said "Yes." (The context suggests this was Frank's exact comment.)

NOTE: When quoting these words, capitalize them if they represent a complete sentence.

> Please answer the question "Yes" or "No."
>
> I would have to answer that question by saying "Yes and no."
>
> **BUT:** That question requires something more than a yes-or-no answer.

233 Do not use quotation marks with well-known proverbs and sayings. They are not direct quotations.

> After that experience he surely knows that all that glitters is not gold.

FOR SPECIAL EMPHASIS

234 In nontechnical material, technical or trade terms should be enclosed in quotation marks when they are first introduced.

The use of "bleed" illustrations gives the book a handsome graphic effect.

235   Words used humorously or ironically are enclosed in quotation marks.

They serve "fresh" vegetables all right—fresh out of the tin!

236   Slang or poor grammar that is purposely used is enclosed in quotation marks.

Whatever the true facts are, Jeff "ain't sayin'."
When vacation comes, I'm going to head for the beach and "hang ten."

NOTE: Quotation marks are not needed for colloquial expressions.

I thought you were putting me on.

237   Words and phrases introduced by such expressions as *so-called, marked, signed,* and *entitled* are enclosed in quotation marks.

The carton was marked "Fragile."
He received a message signed "A Friend."
The article entitled "Write Your Senator" was in that issue.

NOTE: Titles of complete published works following the expression *entitled* require underscoring rather than quotation marks. (See ¶ 288 for titles to be underscored; ¶¶ 242–244 for titles to be quoted.)

238   A word referred to as a word may be enclosed in quotation marks but is now more commonly underscored. (See ¶ 285.)

239   When a word or an expression is formally defined, the word to be defined is usually underscored (italicized in print) and the definition is usually quoted so that the two elements may be easily distinguished. (See ¶ 286.)

240   The translation of a foreign expression is enclosed in quotation marks; the foreign word itself is underscored. (See ¶ 287.)

241   The *individual* names of ships, airplanes, and trains may be quoted (or underscored) for special display, but increasingly they are written simply with initial caps.

The S.S. "Ballou" will dock at Pier 34.   OR: The S.S. Ballou . . .

BUT: I flew to Miami on an Electra. (No special display is needed for the name *Electra,* because it identifies the class of aircraft but is not the individual name of the plane.)

WITH TITLES OF LITERARY AND ARTISTIC WORKS

242   Use quotation marks around titles that represent only *part* of a complete published work—for example, chapters, lessons, topics, sections, parts, tables, and charts within a book; articles and feature columns in newspapers and magazines; and essays, short poems, lectures, and sermons. (See ¶ 288 for titles of *complete* published works.)

[Continued on page 42.]

When you read Chapter 5, "The Effective Business Letter," give particular attention to the section headed "The Objectives of All Letter Writing."

His most recent article, "Who Speaks for You?" appeared last month. (See ¶¶ 261–262 for the use of commas with quoted titles.)

Could you recite the poem "The Boy Stood on the Burning Deck" if you were asked to?

NOTE: The titles *Preface, Contents, Appendix,* and *Index* are not quoted, even though they represent parts within a book. They are often capitalized, however, for special emphasis.

All the supporting data is given in the Appendix. (Often capitalized when referring to another section within the same work.)

BUT: You'll find that the most interesting part of his book is contained in the appendix. (Capitalization not required when reference is made to a section within another work.)

243 Use quotation marks around the titles of *complete but unpublished* works, such as manuscripts, dissertations, and reports.

I would like to get a copy of Johnson's special study, "Criteria for Evaluating Staff Efficiency."

244 Use quotation marks around titles of songs and other short musical compositions, titles of paintings and pieces of sculpture, and titles of television and radio series and programs.

Everyone sang "Happy Birthday" to Mr. Parrott.
Did you see the "Mona Lisa" when it was displayed in New York?
He will appear on "Face the Nation" next Sunday.

QUOTATIONS WITHIN QUOTATIONS

245 A quotation within another quotation is enclosed in single quotation marks. On a typewriter, use the apostrophe key for a single quotation mark.

"Tanned skin became a fashionable 'must' about twenty or twenty-five years ago."

246 If a quotation appears within the single-quoted matter, revert to double quotation marks for the inner portion.

Mrs. Walker then remarked, "I thought it a bit strange when Mr. Fowler said, 'Put these checks in an envelope marked "Personal Funds" and set them aside for me.'" (When single and double quotation marks occur together, do not insert any extra space between them in typewritten material.)

247 Be particularly careful in positioning sentence punctuation in relation to a single quotation mark. See ¶ 248, note, for placement of periods and commas; ¶ 249, note, for placement of semicolons and colons; ¶ 250, note, for placement of question marks and exclamation points; ¶ 251*b* for placement of dashes.

WITH OTHER MARKS OF PUNCTUATION

The following rules (¶¶ 248–252) indicate how to position certain marks of sentence punctuation with regard to the closing quotation mark— that is, *inside* or *outside*. For more specific guidance on *when* to use punctuation with quoted matter and *what kind* of punctuation to use, refer to the following paragraphs:

► Quotations standing alone: see ¶ 253.
Quotations at beginning of a sentence: see ¶¶ 254–256.
Quotations at end of a sentence: see ¶¶ 257–259.
Quotations within a sentence: see ¶¶ 260–262.
Quotations with interrupting expressions: see ¶¶ 263–264.
Long quotations and extracts: see ¶¶ 265–266.
Quoted letters and telegrams: see ¶ 267.
Quoted poetry: see ¶¶ 268–269.
Quoted dialogues and conversations: see ¶¶ 270–271.

248 *Periods* and *commas* always go *inside* the closing quotation mark. (This placement is dictated solely on grounds of typographical appearance.)

> Just as I was leaving his office, Mr. Brown called, "Miss Ward, I need five copies of that agreement."
>
> Mr. Chalmers drew a draft on Mr. Stuart, payable "six months after date."
>
> Canceled checks are checks that have been paid by the bank and stamped "Paid."
>
> Retain all copies marked "A."
>
> "I will call you tomorrow," he said.
>
> "Please try to arrive by 9:30 a.m.," she announced.
>
> His most recent article, "Systems Management and Education," appeared last January.
>
> "Witty," "clever," "vastly amusing," and "hilarious" are only a few of the adjectives that are being applied to your new book.
>
> The package was clearly labeled "Fragile," but apparently labels mean nothing to your delivery crew.

NOTE: Periods and commas also go *inside* the single closing quotation mark.

> Mr. Poston said, "Please let me see all the orders marked 'Rush.'"
>
> "Please answer the question 'Yes' or 'No,'" said the attorney.

249 *Semicolons* and *colons* always go *outside* the closing quotation mark.

> Last Tuesday he said, "I will mail you a check today"; however, it has not yet arrived.
>
> When the announcement of the changeover was made, my reaction was "Why?"; John's only reaction was "When?"
>
> Please get these supplies from the shelf marked "Editorial": 20 blue file folders, 12 No. 2 pencils, and 3 typewriter erasers.

NOTE: Semicolons and colons also go *outside* the single quotation mark.

> Mrs. Fennel said, "Please get these supplies from the shelf marked 'Editorial': 20 blue file folders, 12 No. 2 pencils, and 3 typewriter erasers."

250   **a.** A *question mark* or an *exclamation point* goes *inside* the closing quotation mark when it applies only to the quoted material.

> He asked, "Did you enjoy that book?" (Quoted question at the end of a statement.)
>
> My boss's favorite remark is, "This is a rush job!" (Quoted exclamation at the end of a statement.)

b. A question mark or an exclamation point goes *outside* the closing quotation mark when it applies to the entire sentence.

> Why did Harry say, "Don't expect to see me tomorrow"? (Quoted statement at the end of a question.)
>
> Don't keep saying, "Take it easy"! (Quoted statement at the end of an exclamation.)

c. If the quoted material and the entire sentence each require the same mark of punctuation, use only one mark—the one that comes first. (See also ¶¶ 258–259.)

> Have you seen the advertisement that starts, "Why pay more?" (Quoted question at the end of a question.)
>
> Don't anyone panic and yell "Fire!" (Quoted exclamation at the end of an exclamation.)

NOTE: These same principles govern the placement of a question mark or an exclamation point in relation to a single quotation mark.

> What prompted George to say, "Please be particularly careful in handling documents marked 'Confidential'"? (Quoted phrase within a quoted statement within a question.)
>
> Mr. Marks asked, "Was the check marked 'Insufficient Funds'?" (Quoted phrase within a quoted question within a statement.)
>
> Mrs. Parsons then said, "How did you answer him when he asked you, 'How do you know?'" (Quoted question within a quoted question within a statement.)

251   **a.** A *dash* goes *inside* the closing quotation mark to indicate that the speaker's or writer's words have broken off abruptly.

> Mr. Mills said, "When I see Malone—" We could all guess what he would say to Malone.

b. A dash goes *outside* the closing quotation mark when the sentence breaks off abruptly *after* the quotation.

> If one more person speaks to me about "innovation"—
>
> BUT: Mr. Ballard said, "If one more person speaks to me about 'innovation'—"

c. A closing dash goes *outside* the closing quotation mark when the quotation itself is part of the parenthetical matter being set off by a pair of dashes.

> Get the latest draft—it's the one with the notation "Let's go with this"—and take it to Mr. Pomeroy.

252   **a.** The closing *parenthesis* goes *inside* the closing quotation mark when the parenthetical element is part of the quotation.

> The meeting was to be held "on May 15 (Wednesday)" according to the memo.

b. The closing parenthesis goes *outside* the closing quotation mark when the quotation is part of the parenthetical element.

> Joe Elliott (the one everyone calls "Harper's fair-haired boy") will probably get the job.

PUNCTUATING QUOTATIONS STANDING ALONE

253   When a quoted sentence stands alone, put the appropriate mark of terminal punctuation—a period, a question mark, or an exclamation point—*inside* the closing quotation mark.

> "I can recommend John Porter without any reservation."
>
> "May I see you for about a half hour tomorrow?"
>
> "This transcript is worse than the one before!"

PUNCTUATING QUOTATIONS AT THE BEGINNING OF A SENTENCE

254   When a quoted *statement* occurs at the beginning of a sentence and is followed by an expression such as *he said* (indicating the source of the quotation), omit the period before the closing quotation mark and use a comma instead.

> "I can recommend John Porter without any reservation," he said.
>
> (**NOT:** . . . reservation.," he said.)

EXCEPTION: Retain the period if it accompanies an abbreviation.

> "By next May I expect to have my Ph.D.," he said.

255   When a quoted *question* or *exclamation* occurs at the beginning of the sentence, retain the question mark or the exclamation point before the closing quotation mark and do not insert a comma.

> "May I see you for about half an hour tomorrow morning?" he asked.
>
> (**NOT:** . . . morning?," he asked.)
>
> "This transcript is worse than the one before!" he said.
>
> (**NOT:** . . . before!," he said.)

256   When a quoted *word* or *phrase* occurs at the beginning of a sentence, no punctuation should accompany the closing quotation mark unless required by the overall construction of the sentence.

> "A smash hit" was the phrase used by more than one critic.
>
> "How to Get a Job," the last chapter in the manuscript, does not read as well as the rest of the material you have submitted. (The comma that follows the chapter title is the first of a pair needed to set off a nonessential appositive.)

PUNCTUATING QUOTATIONS AT THE END OF A SENTENCE

257   **a.** When a quoted *sentence* (a statement, a question, or an exclamation) occurs at the end of a sentence and is introduced by an expression such as *he said*, a comma usually precedes the opening quotation mark.

> Mr. Bryant said, "We'll close early on Friday."
>
> In his letter he said, "I plan to arrive on Thursday at 6 p.m."

NOTE: If the quotation is quite short, the comma may be omitted.

> All he said was "No."
>
> OR: All he said was, "No." (The comma creates a slight pause and throws greater emphasis on the quotation.)

b. Use a colon in place of a comma if the introductory expression is an independent clause.

> George did tell me this: "I'm willing to sign the contract with Harry if you'll guarantee that he will perform."
>
> This is what he said in his letter: "I plan to arrive on Thursday at 6 p.m."

c. Also use a colon in place of a comma if the quotation is long.

> Mr. Frost said: "In this case there is not much point in trying to fix the blame for what happened. The important thing is to establish procedures and safeguards to ensure that there are no recurrences."

d. Use a colon in place of a comma if the quotation is set off on separate lines as an extract. (See also ¶ 266.)

> Harold's letter said in part:
>> I have always valued your assistance on our various projects. You have acted as if you were actually part of our staff, with our interests in mind, and not as a manufacturer's representative who wanted to sell us everything in his kit.

e. Do not use either a comma or a colon before an indirect quotation.

> Harold wrote Bob that he had always valued Bob's assistance on various projects.

258   When a quoted *sentence* (a statement, a question, or an exclamation) falls at the end of a larger sentence, do not use double punctuation— that is, one mark to end the quotation and another to end the sentence. Choose the stronger mark. (REMEMBER: *A question mark is stronger than a period; an exclamation point is stronger than a period or a question mark.*) If the same mark of punctuation is required for both the quotation and the sentence as a whole, use the first mark that occurs—the one within quotation marks.

> **Quoted Sentences at the End of a Statement**
> Fred said, "Let's make the best of the situation." (Not ."".)
> Miss Harris asked, "Shall I put through that call now?" (Not ?".)
> Mr. Fennock exclaimed, "This gossiping must stop!" (Not !".)

Quoted Sentences at the End of a Question
Did you say, "I'll help out"? (Not .'"?)
Why did Mary ask, "Will Joe be there?" (Not ?"?)
Who yelled "Watch out!" (Not !"?)

Quoted Sentences at the End of an Exclamation
How could you forget to follow up when you were specifically told, "Give this order special attention"! (Not .'"!)
Stop saying "How should I know"! (Not ?"!)
How I'd like to walk into his office and say, "I quit!" (Not !"!)

NOTE: When a quoted sentence ends with an abbreviation, retain the abbreviation period even though a question mark or an exclamation point follows as the terminal mark of punctuation.

> The interviewer asked, "How long did you work for Pierson, Inc.?"
> Didn't Fred say, "I am now working for an LL.B."?

However, if a period is required as the terminal mark of punctuation, use only one period to mark the end of the abbreviation and the end of the sentence.

> Blum said, "The conference will begin at 9:30 a.m." (Not .".)

▶ See ¶ 248 for placement of periods; ¶ 250 for placement of question marks and exclamation points.

259 When a quoted *word* or *phrase* occurs at the end of a sentence, punctuate according to the appropriate pattern shown below. (NOTE: If the quoted word or phrase represents a complete sentence, follow the patterns shown in ¶ 258.)

Quoted Words and Phrases at the End of a Statement
He says he is willing to meet "at your convenience." (Not ".)
I thought his letter said he would arrive "at 10 p.m." (Not .".)
I've been meaning to read "Who Pays the Bill?" (Not ?".)
Critics have praised his latest article, "Freedom Now!" (Not !".)

Quoted Words and Phrases at the End of a Question
Why is he so concerned about my "convenience"?
Didn't he clearly state he would arrive "at 10 p.m."?
Have you had a chance to read "Who Pays the Bill?" (Not ?"?)
What did you think of the article "Freedom Now!"?

Quoted Words and Phrases at the End of an Exclamation
He couldn't care less about my "convenience"!
You're quite mistaken—he clearly said "at 10 a.m."!
Don't waste your time reading "Who Pays the Bill?"!
What a reaction he got with his article "Freedom Now!" (Not !"!)

PUNCTUATING QUOTATIONS WITHIN A SENTENCE

260 Neither a comma nor a colon is used before a quotation when it is woven into the flow of the sentence.

> Don't say "I can't do it" without trying.
>
> No considerate person would say "Why should I care?" under those circumstances.
>
> The audience shouted "Bravo!" and "Encore!" at the end of the concerto.

NOTE: Do not use a period at the end of a quoted statement, but retain the question mark or the exclamation point at the end of a quoted question or exclamation.

261 Do not set off a quotation that occurs within a sentence as an *essential* appositive. (See also ¶ 158.)

> The famous words "Don't give up the ship" have been attributed to several people.
>
> The chapter entitled "Factors of Production" should help you answer that question.

262 When a quotation occurs within a sentence as a *nonessential* appositive, a comma precedes the opening quotation mark and precedes the closing quotation mark.

> His parting words, "I hardly know how to thank you," were sufficient.
>
> The next chapter, "The Role of Government," further clarifies the answer.

However, if the quoted matter requires a question mark or an exclamation point before the closing quotation mark, omit the comma at that point.

> Your last question, "How can we improve communications between departments?" can best be answered by you.
>
> The final chapter, "Where Do We Go From Here?" shows how much remains to be accomplished.

NOTE: If omitting the second comma is likely to cause confusion, use a pair of dashes or parentheses to set off the quoted matter.

> Your last question—"How can we improve communications between departments?"—can best be answered by you.

PUNCTUATING QUOTED SENTENCES WITH INTERRUPTING EXPRESSIONS

263 When a quoted sentence is *interrupted* by an expression such as *he said*, a comma and a closing quotation mark precede the interrupting expression and another comma follows it. The quotation continues with an opening quotation mark and the first word in small letters.

> "For the fifth successive week," the report began, "we have chalked up increased sales in our New England territory."

264 If the interrupting expression ends the sentence and the quotation continues in a new sentence, the interrupting expression is followed by a period and the new sentence is started with an opening quotation mark and a capital letter.

> "We'll be late for the ceremonies," he said. "However, late or not, we have to attend."

PUNCTUATING LONG QUOTATIONS

265 If a quotation consists of more than one sentence without any interrupting elements, use quotation marks only at the beginning and at the end of the quotation. Do not put quotation marks around each sentence within the quotation.

> Here is what he wrote in his letter: "I hereby tender my resignation. I have reached what is considered a good age to retire. It is time for a younger man to take over."

266 Quoted extracts that will make four or more typewritten lines may be handled in one of the following ways:

a. Type the extract single-spaced in a shorter line length than is used for the remainder of the material. (Indent five spaces from each side margin.) Do not enclose the extract in quotation marks. This style is preferred by many. (See Letter Style 1, page 212.)

b. Type the extract using the same line length and spacing as the remainder of the material.

(1) If the extract consists of one paragraph only, place quotation marks before and after the paragraph.

(2) If the extract consists of two or more paragraphs, place a quotation mark at the start of each paragraph but after the last one only.

(3) Change any quotation marks within the extract to single quotation marks. (See ¶¶ 245–247.)

> "When writing a letter that grants a request, the writer usually follows this pattern:
>
> "First, he expresses appreciation for the writer's interest in the company's product or service.
>
> "Next, he gives the exact information requested and, if possible, additional information that may be of interest.
>
> "Finally, he expresses willingness 'to be of further help.'"

QUOTING LETTERS AND TELEGRAMS

267 Letters and telegrams that are to be copied word for word may be handled in one of the following ways:

a. Copy the letter or telegram on a separate sheet of paper headed *COPY*. In this case no quotation marks are used. This is the preferred method for handling long letters and telegrams.

[*Continued on page 50.*]

b. A short letter or telegram may be treated as an extract (see ¶ 266). If it is typed on a shorter line length, no quotation marks are used. If it is typed on the same line length as other material on the page, then type the opening quotation mark before the date line and type the closing quotation mark after the last word in the signature block.

QUOTING POETRY

268 When quoting a complete poem (or an extended portion of one) in a letter or a report, type it line for line, single-spaced (except for stanza breaks). If the line length is shorter than that of the normal text above and below the poem, no quotation marks are needed; the poem will stand out sufficiently as an extract. If, however, quotation marks are needed to indicate the special nature of the material, place a quotation mark at the beginning of each stanza and at the end of only the last stanza (see also ¶ 284*b*).

269 A short extract from a poem is sometimes woven right into a sentence or a paragraph. In such cases use quotation marks at the beginning and end of the extract and a diagonal line to indicate where each line would break in the original arrangement of the poem.

> As Alexander Pope put it, "A little learning is a dang'rous thing; / Drink deep, or taste not the Pierian spring . . . ."

QUOTING DIALOGUES AND CONVERSATIONS

270 When quoting dialogues and conversations, start the remarks of each speaker as a new paragraph, no matter how brief.

> "Are those the only styles you can show me?" the customer inquired.
>
> "I'm afraid so," replied the salesman, "but I can order anything shown in this catalog for you."
>
> "How long would it take to get the items?"
>
> "Two weeks."

271 In plays and court testimony, where the name of the speaker is indicated, quotation marks are not needed.

> George: What you say is impossible!
>
> Henry: I tell you it's true!
>
> George: I must have more proof than your word before I'll believe it.

STYLE IN QUOTED MATTER

272 In copying quoted matter, follow the style of the extract exactly in punctuation, spelling, capitalization, hyphenation, and number style. (See ¶ 283 for the use of [*sic*] to indicate errors in the original.)

CAPITALIZATION IN QUOTED MATTER

273   Capitalize the first word of every complete sentence in quotation marks.

> I heard John say, "Anyone could do that job!"

274   When quoting a word or phrase, do not capitalize the first word unless it meets *one* of these conditions:

a. It is a proper noun, a proper adjective, or the pronoun *I.*

> Mr. Sewara paid tribute to "American know-how."

b. It was capitalized in its original use.

> He wrote "Paid" across the face of the bill.
> The package came back stamped "Addressee unknown."

c. It represents a complete sentence.

> Frank flatly said "No"; George said "Maybe."
>
> **BUT:** Thompson said he would not pay the bill "until certain adjustments are made." (Thompson's exact words were, "I won't pay until certain adjustments are made.")

d. The quoted word or phrase occurs at the beginning of a sentence.

> "Electrifying" was the word one critic applied to Caliano's new play. (Even if the expression was uncapitalized in the original material, it must be capitalized here to mark the start of the sentence.)

OMISSIONS IN QUOTED MATTER

275   If one or more words are omitted *within* a quoted sentence, use ellipsis marks (three spaced periods, with one typewriter space before and after each period) to indicate the omission.

> "During the last few years . . . we have been witnessing a change in buying habits, particularly with respect to food."

276   If one or more words are omitted *at the end of a sentence,* use three spaced periods followed by the necessary terminal punctuation for the sentence as a whole.

> "Can anyone explain why . . . ?" (The original question read, "Can anyone explain why this was so?")
>
> "During the last few years . . . we have been witnessing a change in buying habits . . . ." (The first three periods represent the omitted words "particularly with respect to food"; the fourth period marks the end of the sentence.)

NOTE: Omit any internal sentence punctuation (a comma, a semicolon, a colon, or a dash) that occurs at the point where the spaced periods start. (Compare "habits . . ." in the example above with "habits," in the example in ¶ 275.)

277   If one or more sentences are omitted between other sentences within a long quoted extract, use three spaced periods *after* the terminal punctuation of the preceding sentence.

> "During the last few years, starting in the late 1950s, we have been witnessing a change in buying habits, particularly with respect to food. . . . How far this pattern of change will extend cannot be estimated." (The first of the four periods marks the end of a sentence. The remaining three periods signify the omission of one or more complete sentences. Two spaces follow before the next sentence.)

278   If only a fragment of a sentence is quoted, it is not necessary to signify the omission of words before or after the fragment.

> According to Robertson's report, there has been "a change in buying habits" during the last few years.

279   If one or more words are omitted at the beginning of a quoted sentence, use three spaced periods after the opening quotation mark. The three spaced periods signify the omission of the capitalized word (and possibly other words) at the beginning of the quoted sentence.

> According to Robertson's report, ". . . we have been witnessing a change in buying habits" during the last few years.

280   If a quoted extract starts with a complete sentence and ends with a complete sentence, it is not necessary to use three spaced periods following the opening quotation mark or preceding the closing quotation mark unless you wish to emphasize that the quotation has been extracted from a larger body of material.

281   If one or more paragraphs are omitted, the omission may be indicated by three asterisks typed on a line by themselves.

*   *   *

INSERTIONS IN QUOTED MATTER

282   For clarity it is sometimes necessary to insert explanatory words or phrases within quoted matter. Enclose such insertions in brackets. (See also ¶¶ 296–297.)

> Mr. Rawlings added, "At the time of the first lawsuit [1956], there was clear-cut evidence of an intent to defraud."

283   When the original wording contains a misspelling, a grammatical error, or a confusing expression of thought, the quoter should insert the term *sic* in brackets to indicate that the error is not his but existed in the original material.

▶   See ¶¶ 263–264 for simple interruptions such as *he said.*

TYPING QUOTATION MARKS

284 **a.** In a list, any opening quotation mark should clear the left margin, so that the first letter of the item will align with other items.

> I need the following stationery items:
>> Paper clips
>> Rubber bands
>> "Fragile" labels
>> White cord

b. In poems, opening quotation marks at the beginning of stanzas should clear the left margin so that the first letters of rhyming lines will be in alignment. (See also ¶ 268.)

THE UNDERSCORE

Underscoring in typewritten material is the counterpart of using *italics* in printed material.

FOR SPECIAL EMPHASIS

285 A word referred to as a word is usually underscored, but it may be enclosed in quotation marks instead. A word referred to as a word is often introduced by the expression *the term* or *the word*.

> The words carton and cartoon have quite different meanings. (**ALSO:** The words "carton" and "cartoon" have quite different meanings.)

> If you used fewer compound sentences, you wouldn't have so many ands in your writing.

> **BUT:** He refused to sign the contract because he said it had too many ands, ifs, and buts. (No underscores are required for the phrase *ands, ifs, and buts* because the writer is not referring literally to these words as words. The phrase means "too many conditions and qualifications.")

286 In a formal definition the word to be defined is usually underscored and the definition is usually quoted. In this way the two elements may be easily distinguished.

> The term psychosomatic has an interesting derivation: the prefix psycho means "of the mind"; the root word soma refers to the body.

> **NOTE:** An informal definition does not require any special punctuation.

> A chandler is a person who makes candles.

287   Underscore foreign expressions that are not considered part of the English language. (Use quotation marks to set off translations of foreign expressions.)

> A faux pas literally means "a false step."

NOTE: Once an expression of foreign origin has become established as part of the English language, underscoring is no longer necessary. (Most dictionaries offer guidance on this point.) Here are some frequently used expressions that no longer require underscoring or any other special display:

a la carte	habeas corpus	pro tem
ad hoc	ibid.	rendezvous
bona fide	per annum	repertoire
et al.	per se	résumé
etc.	prima facie	status quo
ex officio	pro rata	vice versa

WITH TITLES OF LITERARY AND ARTISTIC WORKS

288   Underscore titles of *complete* works that are published as separate items—for example, books, pamphlets, long poems, magazines, and newspapers. Also underscore titles of movies, plays, musicals, operas, and long musical compositions.

> Every secretary will find Etiquette in Business helpful.
> We find it beneficial to advertise occasionally in The New York Times.
> Next Saturday they are going to hear the opera La Traviata.

a. Titles of complete works may be typed in all capitals as an alternative to underscoring.

> Every secretary will find ETIQUETTE IN BUSINESS helpful.

NOTE: The use of all capitals is acceptable (1) in business correspondence where titles occur frequently (as in the correspondence of a publishing house) and (2) in advertising and sales promotion copy where the use of all capitals is intended to have an eye-catching effect. In ordinary circumstances, however, underscoring is preferable.

b. In typewritten material, titles of complete works are sometimes enclosed in quotation marks. However, to maintain a clear and consistent distinction between the title of a complete work and the title of a subordinate part of that work, it is preferable to use underscoring for the complete work and reserve the use of quotes for parts of the complete work.

c. In typewritten material that is *to be set in type,* titles of complete works *must* be underscored. The underscoring indicates to the printer that the title should be set in italics.

> Every secretary will find *Etiquette in Business* helpful.

TYPING UNDERSCORES

289   Underscore as a unit whatever should be stressed as a unit—individual words, titles, phrases, or even whole sentences.

a. When underscoring a unit consisting of two or more words, be sure to underscore the space between words.

> I plan to read <u>War and Peace</u> next summer.
>
> **BUT:** Do you understand the meaning of such terms as <u>quasi</u>, <u>ergo</u>, <u>ipso facto</u>, and <u>quid pro quo</u>? (Only the individual units are underscored, not the series as a whole.)

NOTE: When typing a stencil, do not underscore the space between words. Reason: A long underscore may cause the stencil to tear.

b. Do not underscore a mark of *sentence punctuation* that comes directly after the underscored matter. (However, underscore all punctuation marks that are an integral part of the underscored matter.)

> This week the Summertime Playhouse is presenting <u>My Fair Lady</u>; next week, <u>Hello, Dolly!</u>; and the following week, <u>How Now, Dow Jones</u>.

290   Techniques in underscoring:

a. For five or fewer characters, use the backspacer to draw the carriage back before underscoring.

b. If more than five characters are to be underscored consecutively, draw the carriage back by hand.

c. If underscoring will appear in several places in one typewritten line, type the entire line and then draw the carriage back by hand and underscore the appropriate portions in the line.

d. With an electric typewriter, use the mechanism for repeating underscores automatically instead of typing the underscore strokes individually.

THE APOSTROPHE (')

The use of the apostrophe is covered in the following paragraphs:

▶   As a single quotation mark, see ¶¶ 245–247.
To indicate the omission of figures in dates, see ¶ 420.
As a symbol for *feet*, see ¶ 432.
To form contractions, see ¶ 502.
To form plurals of figures, letters, etc., see ¶¶ 622–625.
To form possessives, see ¶¶ 629–650.

ELLIPSIS MARKS (. . .)

291   **a.** Ellipsis marks (three spaced periods with one typewriter space before and after each period) are often used, especially in advertising, to display individual items or to connect a series of loosely related phrases.

> The Inn at the End of the Road . . . where you may enjoy the epicure's choicest offerings . . . by reservation only . . . closed Tuesdays.
>
> Where can you match these services—
> . . . Free ticket delivery
> . . . Flight insurance
> . . . On-time departures

b. Ellipsis marks are also used to indicate that a sentence trails off before the end. The three spaced periods create an effect of uncertainty or suggest an abrupt suspension of thought. (No terminal punctuation is used with ellipsis marks in this kind of construction.)

> He could easily have saved the situation by . . . But why talk about it.

▶   See ¶¶ 275–280 for the use of ellipsis marks to indicate omissions in quoted matter.

THE ASTERISK (*)

292   The asterisk is used to refer the reader to a footnote, which usually is placed at the foot of a page.

> "Because they won't let you wear it unless it fits."*
> _____
> *Reg. U.S. Pat. Off.

a. When the asterisk and some other mark of punctuation fall at the same point in a sentence, the asterisk *follows* the punctuation mark, with no intervening space.

b. In the footnote itself, leave no space after the asterisk.

293   Asterisks are used to replace words that are considered unprintable.

> We were shocked to hear Mr. Scott refer to Mr. Frost as a ***.

▶   See also ¶ 281 for the use of asterisks to indicate omissions.

NOTE: If your typewriter does not have an asterisk key, a fair substitute can be made by typing a capital *A* over a small *v*. (See ¶ 1305 for illustration.)

THE DIAGONAL (/)

294   The diagonal occurs (without space before or after) in certain abbreviations and symbols.

> B/L   bill of lading   D/W   dock warrant   c/o   care of

295   The diagonal is also used in writing fractions (for example, *4/5*) and in some code and serial numbers (for example, *25/394756*).

▶   See ¶ 269 for the use of the diagonal when quoting poetry; also see entry for *and/or* in ¶ 1101.

BRACKETS ([ ])

296   A correction or an insertion in a quoted extract should be enclosed in brackets.

> "During the height of the storm, winds exceeded 55 miles an hour [the local weather station recorded 60 miles an hour], with gusts up to 65 miles an hour."

> "We cannot allow this situation to continue. [Extended applause.] The time for action is now."

297   If brackets do not appear on the typewriter keyboard, you may either construct them (as shown in the illustration below) or leave a space at the point where each mark should appear and insert the marks in pen after the paper has been removed from the machine.

> "We returned to Salem /Massachusetts/ the following year."

TYPEWRITER SPACING WITH PUNCTUATION MARKS

298   **Period**
Two spaces *after* the end of a sentence.
One space *after* an abbreviation within a sentence. (See also ¶ 536.)
No space *after* a decimal point.
No space when another mark of punctuation immediately follows the period (for example, a closing quotation mark, a closing parenthesis, or a comma following an "abbreviation" period).

Question Mark and Exclamation Point
Two spaces *after* either at the end of a sentence.
No space *after* either if another mark of punctuation immediately follows.

Comma
No space *before*—ever.
One space *after*, unless a closing quotation mark immediately follows the comma.
No space *after* commas within a number.

Semicolon
No space *before*; one space *after*.

Colon

No space *before.*

Two spaces *after* within a sentence.

No space *before* or *after* in expressions of time (*8:20 p.m.*) or proportions (*2:1*).

Dash

No space *before, between,* or *after* two hyphens used to represent a dash.

Two spaces *after* a dash at the end of a statement that breaks off abruptly.

Opening Parenthesis or Bracket

One space *before* when parenthetic matter is within a sentence.

Two spaces *before* when parenthetic matter follows a sentence. In this case the parenthetic matter starts with a capital and closes with its own sentence punctuation. (See ¶¶ 226, 296.)

No space *after.*

Closing Parenthesis or Bracket

No space *before.*

One space *after* when parenthetic matter is within a sentence.

Two spaces *after* when parenthetic matter is itself a complete sentence and another sentence follows. (See ¶¶ 226, 296.)

No space *after* if another mark of punctuation immediately follows.

Opening Quotation Mark

Two spaces *before* when quoted matter starts a new sentence or follows a colon.

No space *before* when a dash or an opening parenthesis precedes.

One space *before* in all other cases.

No space *after.*

Closing Quotation Mark

No space *before.*

Two spaces *after* when quoted matter ends the sentence.

No space *after* when another mark of punctuation immediately follows (for example, a semicolon or a colon).

One space *after* in all other cases.

Single Quotation Mark

No space between single and double quotation marks. (See also ¶ 246.)

Apostrophe (')

No space *before,* either within a word or at the end of a word.

One space *after* only if it is at the end of a word within a sentence.

Ellipsis Marks (. . .)

One space *before* and *after* each of the three periods within a sentence. (See ¶¶ 275–276.)

No space *before* when an *opening* quotation mark precedes the ellipsis marks. (See example in ¶ 279.)
No space *after* when a *closing* quotation mark follows the ellipsis marks. (See example in ¶ 276, note.)
Two spaces *after* ellipsis marks that follow a period, question mark, or exclamation point at the end of a sentence. (See example in ¶ 277.)

Asterisk (*)
No space *before* an asterisk following a word or punctuation mark within a sentence.
Two spaces *after* an asterisk at the end of a sentence.
One space *after* an asterisk following a word or punctuation mark within a sentence.
No space *after* an asterisk in a footnote. (See ¶ 292.)

Diagonal (/)
No space *before* or *after* a diagonal line. (See ¶ 269 for an exception in poetry.)

Section 3
CAPITALIZATION

The function of capitalization is to give distinction, importance, and emphasis to words. Thus the first word of a sentence is capitalized to indicate distinctively and emphatically that a new sentence has begun. Moreover, proper nouns like *George, Chicago, Dun & Bradstreet, the Parthenon, January,* and *Friday* are capitalized to signify the special importance of these words as the official names of particular persons, places, and things. A number of words, however, may function either as proper nouns or as common nouns—for example, terms like *the board of directors* or *the company.* Here capitalization practices vary widely, but the variation merely reflects the relative importance each writer assigns to the word in question.

Despite disagreements among authorities on specific rules, there is a growing consensus against the heavy use of capitalization that has characterized the style of business correspondence in the past. When too many words stand out, none stand out. The current trend, then, is to use capitalization more sparingly—to give importance, distinction, or emphasis only when and where it is warranted.

The following rules of capitalization are written with the ordinary business office in mind. If you work in a specialized situation, such as a government office or an advertising agency, you might be asked to capitalize some of those terms that would not be capitalized ordinarily. Whenever your office has a particular preference, be sure to follow that style.

IMPORTANT NOTE: ¶¶ 301–309 represent the basic rules of capitalization. The remaining paragraphs in this section provide more detailed coverage of specific topics.

FIRST WORDS

301   Capitalize the first word of:

a. Every sentence. (See also ¶ 302.)

> Up-to-date sales reports will be released tomorrow.
> Will the computations be ready by then?
> The news is unbelievable!

b. An expression used as a sentence. (See also ¶¶ 102, 110, 119.)

> So much for that.   Really?   No!

c. A quoted sentence. (See also ¶¶ 273–274.)

> Mr. Jarvis said, "The estimates will be submitted on Monday."

d. An independent question within a sentence. (See also ¶¶ 114–116.)

> The question is, Will this policy reduce staff turnover?

e. Each item displayed in a list or an outline. (See ¶ 107.)

f. Each line in a poem. (Always follow the style of the poem itself, however.)

> When to the sessions of sweet silent thought
> I summon up remembrance of things past,
> I sigh the lack of many a thing I sought,
> And with old woes new wail my dear time's waste.
> —William Shakespeare

302   Do not capitalize the first word of a sentence when it is set off by *dashes* or *parentheses* within another sentence. (See ¶¶ 214, 224–225 for examples.) Moreover, do not capitalize the first word of a sentence following a colon except under certain circumstances. (See ¶¶ 195–198.)

PROPER NOUNS

303   Capitalize every proper noun, that is, the official name of a particular person, place, or thing. Also capitalize adjectives derived from proper nouns.

> George (n.), Georgian (adj.)   South America (n.), South American (adj.)
>
> **EXCEPTIONS:** Congress, congressional; the Constitution (U.S.), constitutional

304 Capitalize imaginative names and nicknames that designate particular persons, places, or things. (See ¶ 339 for imaginative names of historical periods.)

the First Lady	the Granite State (for New Hampshire)
the Windy City (for Chicago)	the Stars and Stripes

305 Some words that were originally proper nouns or adjectives are now considered common nouns and should not be capitalized.

plaster of paris	venetian blind	ampere	roman numeral
manila envelope	morocco leather	watt	(**BUT:** Roman history)

NOTE: Check an up-to-date dictionary to determine capitalization for words of this type.

COMMON NOUNS

306 A common noun names a class of things (for example, *books*), or it may refer indefinitely to one or more things within that class (a *book, several books*). Nouns used in this way are considered general terms of classification and are often modified by indefinite words such as *a, any, every,* or *some.* Do not capitalize nouns used as general terms of classification.

a company	every board of directors
any corporation	some senators

307 A common noun may also be used to name a particular person, place, or thing. Nouns used in this way are often modified by *the, this, these, that,* or *those,* or by possessive words such as *my, your, his, our,* or *theirs.* Do not capitalize a general term of classification, even though it refers to a particular person, place, or thing.

COMMON NOUN:	the instructor	that secretary	our supervisor
PROPER NOUN:	Mr. Patterson	Sandra Nelson	Mrs. Halliday

308 Capitalize a common noun when it is an actual part of a proper name. As a rule, however, do not capitalize the common-noun element when it is used alone in place of the full name. (See ¶ 309 for exceptions.)

Professor Burke	**BUT:** the professor
the Chase Corporation	the corporation
the Easton Municipal Court	the court
Elston Avenue	the avenue
the Clayton Antitrust Act	the act

309 Some *short forms* (common-noun elements replacing the complete proper name) are capitalized when they are intended to carry the full significance of the complete proper name. It is in this area, however, that the danger of overcapitalizing most often occurs. Therefore, do not capitalize a short form unless it clearly warrants the importance, distinction, or emphasis that capitalization conveys. The following kinds of short forms are commonly capitalized:

PERSONAL TITLES: Capitalize titles replacing names of high-ranking national, state, and international officials (but not ordinarily local officials or company officers). (See ¶ 311.)

ORGANIZATIONAL NAMES: Capitalize short forms of company names *but only* in formal or legal writing. (See ¶¶ 319–320.)

GOVERNMENTAL NAMES: Capitalize short forms of names of national and international bodies (but not ordinarily state or local bodies). (See ¶¶ 324–325, 330–331.)

PLACE NAMES: Capitalize only well-established short forms. (See ¶¶ 329, 331.)

NOTE: Do not use a short form to replace a full name unless the full name has been mentioned earlier or will be clearly understood from the context.

PERSONAL NAMES

▶   See ¶ 1407 for the capitalization of personal names.

PERSONAL TITLES

310   Capitalize all official titles of honor and respect when they *precede* personal names.

EXECUTIVE TITLES:

President Arthur Orwell of Cromwell University   Chairman Stevens

PROFESSIONAL TITLES:

Professor George Hamilton Booth   Dr. Morgan (see ¶ 506)

CIVIC TITLES:

Governor Nelson Rockefeller   Ambassador Bunker

MILITARY TITLES:

General Martin O. Johnson   Commander Wilkinson

RELIGIOUS TITLES:

the Reverend John S. Wyman   Rabbi Silverman

a. Do not capitalize such titles when the personal name that follows is in apposition and is set off by commas.

The *president*, Arthur Orwell, will address the faculty tomorrow afternoon.
BUT: *President* Arthur Orwell will address the faculty tomorrow afternoon.

b. Do not capitalize occupational designations preceding a name, such as *author, surgeon, publisher, oilman, lawyer,* and *businessman.*

Among those attending the opening of the exhibit was *banker* John French, who has been the chief sponsor of the new art museum.

NOTE: Occupational designations can be distinguished from professional or executive titles in that only real titles can be used with a last name alone. Since one would not address a person as "Oilman Jones" or "Publisher Johnson," these are not titles and should not be capitalized.

311   In general, do not capitalize titles of honor and respect when they *follow* a personal name or are used *in place of* a personal name. (As indicated below, exceptions are made for important officials and dignitaries.)

> Dr. Arthur Orwell, *president* of Cromwell University, will speak tomorrow night at eight. The *president's* topic is . . .

a. Retain the capitalization in titles of high-ranking national, state, and international officials when they *follow* or *replace* a specific personal name. Below are examples of titles that remain capitalized.

> NATIONAL OFFICIALS: the *President,* the *Vice President,* Cabinet members (such as the *Secretary of State* and the *Attorney General*), the heads of government agencies and bureaus (such as the *Director* or the *Commissioner*), the *Chief Justice,* the *Ambassador,* the *Senator,* the *Representative.*
>
> STATE OFFICIALS: the *Governor,* the *Lieutenant Governor.* (BUT: the *attorney general,* the *senator.*)
>
> FOREIGN DIGNITARIES: the *Queen of England,* the *King,* the *Prime Minister,* the *Premier.*
>
> INTERNATIONAL FIGURES: the *Pope,* the *Secretary General of the United Nations.*

b. Titles of local governmental officials and those of lesser federal and state officials are not usually capitalized when they follow or replace a personal name. However, these titles are sometimes capitalized in writing intended for a limited readership (for example, in a local newspaper, in internal communications within an organization, or in correspondence coming from or directed to the official's office), where the person in question would be considered to have very high rank by the intended reader.

> The *Mayor* announced today that the strike had been settled. (Item in a local newspaper.)
>
> BUT: John Norton, *mayor* of Waterville, Pennsylvania, was interviewed in New York today before leaving for Europe. The *mayor* indicated . . . (From a national news service release.)
>
> I would like to request an appointment with the *Attorney General.* (In a letter sent to the state attorney general's office.)
>
> BUT: I have written for an appointment with the *attorney general* and expect to hear from his office soon.

c. Titles of *company officials* (for example, the *president,* the *chairman*) should not be capitalized when they follow or replace a personal name. Exceptions are made in formal minutes of meetings and in rules and bylaws.

> The *chairman* will visit thirteen countries in his tour of company installations abroad. (Normal style.)
>
> The *Secretary's* minutes were read and approved. (In formal minutes.)

NOTE: Some companies choose to capitalize these titles in all their communications because of the great respect the officials command within the company. However, this practice confers excessive importance on people who are neither public officials nor eminent dignitaries, and it should be avoided.

312 Do not capitalize titles when used as general terms of classification. (See ¶ 306.)

a United States senator   every king
a state governor   any ambassador

EXCEPTION: Because of the special regard for the office of the President of the United States, this title is capitalized even when used as a general term of classification (for example, a *President,* every *President*).

313 Capitalize any title (even if not of high rank) when it is used in *direct address* (that is, quoted or unquoted speech made directly to another person).

DIRECT ADDRESS: Tell me, *Professor,* what you think of Allen's work.

INDIRECT ADDRESS: I asked the *professor* to tell me what he thought of Allen's work.

NOTE: In direct address, do not capitalize *miss* or *sir* if it stands alone without a proper name following.

Please tell me, *sir,* how we can help you.

314 In the *inside address* of a letter, in the *signer's identification block,* and on an *envelope,* capitalize all titles whether they precede or follow the name. (See ¶¶ 1408–1412.)

315 Do not capitalize *former* and *late* used with titles, nor *ex-* and *-elect* joined to titles. (See ¶ 352 for the style in headings.)

the late President Roosevelt   ex-President Johnson   Governor-elect Ott

FAMILY TITLES

316 Capitalize words such as *mother, father, aunt, uncle,* etc., when they stand alone or are followed by a personal name.

I spoke to *Mother* and *Dad* on the phone last night.
Let's invite *Uncle John* and *Aunt Eleanor.*
I know that *Grandmother Morrison* will help us if we ask her.

317 Do not capitalize such words when they are preceded by possessives (*my, your, his, our, their,* etc.) and simply describe a family relationship.

I spoke to both my *mother* and my *uncle* on the phone last night.
We have often heard Edith speak of her *sister* Kate.

NOTE: If the words *Uncle, Aunt,* or *Cousin* form a unit when used together with a first name, capitalize these titles, even when they are preceded by a possessive.

Frank wants us to meet his *Uncle John.* (Here *Uncle John* is a unit.)

BUT: Frank wants us to meet his *uncle,* John Cunningham. (Here *uncle* simply describes a family relationship.)

I hope you can meet my *Cousin May.* (The writer thinks of her as *Cousin May.*)

BUT: I hope you can meet my *cousin* May. (Here the writer thinks of her as *May;* the word *cousin* merely indicates relationship.)

NAMES OF ORGANIZATIONS

318 Capitalize the names of companies, associations, societies, independent committees and boards, schools, political parties, conventions, fraternities, clubs, and religious bodies. (Follow the style established by the organization itself, as shown in the letterhead or some other written communication from the organization.)

the Anderson Hardware Company
the Young Women's Christian Association
the Committee for Economic Development
the Board of Realtors of Morris County, Inc.
the League of Women Voters

the Farmington Chamber of Commerce
the University of Montana
the Democratic and Liberal Parties
the Republican National Convention
the Glen Ridge Country Club
the American Red Cross
St. Luke's Episcopal Church

319 When the common-noun element is used in place of the full name (for example, *the company* in place of *the Anderson Hardware Company*), do not capitalize the short form unless special emphasis or distinction is required (as in legal documents, minutes of a meeting, bylaws, and other formal communications, where the short form is intended to invoke the full authority of the organization). In most cases, however, capitalization is unnecessary because the short form is used only as a general term of classification (see ¶¶ 306–307).

The *company*, in my opinion, has always made a conscientious effort to involve itself in community affairs. (As used here, *company* is a general term of classification.)

BUT: On behalf of the *Company,* I am authorized to accept your bid. (Here the full authority of the company is implied; hence the capital *C.*)

Mr. Harris has just returned from a visit to Haverford College. He reports that the *college* is planning a new fund-raising campaign.

BUT: The *College* hopes to raise an additional $10,000,000 this year to finance the construction of the new instructional resource center. (Announcement in the alumni bulletin.)

NOTE: Do not capitalize the short form if it is modified by a word other than *the.* In constructions such as *our company, this company, every company,* etc., the noun is clearly a general term of classification. (See also ¶ 307.)

320 Common organizational terms such as *advertising department, manufacturing division, finance committee,* and *board of directors* are ordinarily

capitalized when they are the actual names of units within the writer's own organization. These terms are not capitalized when they refer to some other organization, unless the writer has reason to give these terms special importance or distinction.

> The *Board of Directors* will meet next Thursday at 2:30. (From a company memorandum.)
>
> **BUT:** Edward Perez has been elected to the *board of directors* of the Kensington Trade Corporation. (From a news release intended for a general audience.)
>
> The *Finance Committee* will meet all week to review next year's budget. (Style used by insider.)
>
> **BUT:** Gilligan says his company can give us no encouragement until the *finance committee* has reviewed our proposal. (Style normally used by outsider.)
>
> I would like to learn more about the position you have open in the *Advertising Department*. (Outsider may capitalize name of department to indicate the special importance he assigns to it.)

NOTE: These terms should not be capitalized when modified by a word other than *the*; for example, *this credit department, their credit department*. (See also ¶ 319, note.) When *our* is used as a modifier, the preferred form is *our credit department*. However, the form *our Credit Department* may be used to give special emphasis to the name of a unit within one's own organization.

321 Capitalize such nouns as *marketing, advertising,* or *promotion* when they are used alone to designate a department within an organization.

> Ann Heller of *Customer Relations* is the person to see.
>
> I want to get a reaction from our people in *Marketing* first.
>
> **BUT:** I want to talk to our *marketing* people first. (Here *marketing* is simply a descriptive adjective.)

322 Capitalize *the* preceding the name of an organization only when it is part of the legal name of the organization.

> The Investment Company   The Associated Press   The New York Times
> of America

Do not capitalize *the* when the name is used as a modifier or is abbreviated.

> the Associated Press report   the AP   the Times

NAMES OF GOVERNMENT BODIES

323 Capitalize the names of countries and international organizations as well as national, state, county, and city bodies and their subdivisions.

> the Republic of Panama   the Ohio Legislature
> the United Nations   the Court of Appeals of the State
> the Ninety-first Congress   of Wisconsin
> the Nixon Administration   the New York State Board of Education

▶ See ¶¶ 330-331 for city and state names.

324   Capitalize short forms of names of national and international bodies and their major divisions.

> the House (referring to the House of Representatives)
>
> the Department (referring to the Department of Defense, the State Department, etc.)
>
> the Bureau (referring to the Bureau of the Budget, the Federal Bureau of Investigation, etc.)
>
> the Court (referring to the United States Supreme Court, the International Court of Justice, etc.)

As a rule, do not capitalize short forms of names of state or local governmental groups, except when special circumstances warrant emphasis or distinction. (See ¶ 325.)

325   Common terms such as *police department, board of education,* and *county court* need not be capitalized (even when referring to a specific body) since they are terms of general classification. However, such terms should be capitalized when the writer intends to refer to the organization in all of its official dignity.

> The *Police Department* has announced the promotion of Robert Boyarsky to the rank of sergeant. (The short form is capitalized here because it is intended to have the full force of the complete name, the *Cranfield Police Department.*)
>
> **BUT:** The Cranfield *police department* sponsors a youth athletic program that we could well copy. (No capitalization is used here because the writer is referring to the department in general terms and not by its official name.)

NOTE: Do not capitalize the short form if it is not actually derived from the complete name. For example, do not capitalize the short form *police department* if the full name of the organization is *Department of Public Safety.*

326   Capitalize *federal* only when it is part of the official name of a federal agency, a federal act, or some other proper noun.

> the *Federal* Reserve Board   the *Federal* Insurance Contributions Act
>
> **BUT:** . . . subject to *federal,* state, and local laws.

327   The terms *federal government* and *government* (referring specifically to the United States government) are now commonly written in small letters because they are considered terms of general classification. In government documents and correspondence, and in other communications where these terms are intended to have the force of an official name, they are capitalized. (See also ¶ 511.)

328   Capitalize the words *union* and *commonwealth* only when they refer to a specific government.

> Ferguson has lectured on the topic in almost every state in the *Union.*

NAMES OF PLACES

329 Capitalize the names of places, such as streets, buildings, parks, monuments, rivers, oceans, and mountains. Do not capitalize short forms used in place of the full name.

Fulton Street	**BUT:** the street	the Rocky	**BUT:** the mountains
the Empire State Building	the building	Mountains	
Central Park	the park	the Statue of Liberty	the statue
the Ohio River	the river	Death Valley	the valley
Lake Superior	the lake	O'Hare Airport	the airport
the Atlantic and Pacific Oceans	the oceans	Hotel Plaza	the hotel
		Union Station	the station

EXCEPTIONS: A few short forms are capitalized because of clear association with one place.

the Coast (the West Coast)   the Channel (the English Channel)
the Continent (Europe)   the Canal (the Panama Canal)

330 Capitalize the word *city* only when it is a part of the corporate name of the city or part of an imaginative name.

Kansas City   the Eternal City (Rome)   **BUT:** the city of San Francisco

331 Capitalize *state* only when it follows the name of a state or is part of an imaginative name.

New York *State* is also called the Empire *State.*
The *state* of Alaska is the largest in the Union.
Several Canadian families have recently moved to the *States.* (Meaning the United States.)

NOTE: Do not capitalize *state* even when used in place of the actual state name.

He is an employee of the *state.* (People working for the state government, however, might write *State.*)

332 Capitalize *the* only when it is a part of the official name of a place.

The Bronx   The Hague   **BUT:** the Netherlands

POINTS OF THE COMPASS

333 Capitalize *north, south, east, west,* etc., when they designate definite regions or are an integral part of a proper name.

in the North	the Far North	North Dakota
back East	the Near East	the Eastern Seaboard
down South	the Deep South	the South Side
out West	the Middle West	the West Coast

Do not capitalize these words when they merely indicate direction or general location.

Many textile plants have moved from the *Northeast* and relocated in the *South.*
(Region.)

He maintains a villa in the *south* of France. (General location.)

Go *west* on Route 517 and then *south* on U.S. 9. (Direction.)

John is coming back *East* after three years on the *West Coast.* (Region.)
BUT: The *west coast* of the United States borders on the Pacific. (Referring only
to the shoreline, not the region.)

Most of his customers live on the *East Side.* (Definite locality.)
BUT: Most of his customers live on the *east side* of town. (General location.)

334   Capitalize such words as *Northerner, Southerner,* and *Midwesterner.*

335   Capitalize *northern, southern, eastern, western,* etc., when these words
pertain to the people in a region and to their political, social, or cultural
activities. Do not capitalize these words, however, when they merely
indicate general location or refer to the geography or climate of the
region.

Eastern bankers	**BUT:** the eastern half of Pennsylvania
Southern hospitality	southern temperatures
Western civilization	westerly winds
the Northern vote	a northern winter

The *Northern* states did not vote as they were expected to. (Political activities.)
BUT: The drought is expected to continue in the *northern* states. (Climate.)

John Banks of our *western* regional office will try to advise you. (General location.)

His sales territory takes in most of the *southeastern* states. (General location.)

336   When *northern, southern, eastern, western,* etc., precede a place name,
they are not capitalized because they merely indicate general location
within a region. In a few cases, where these words are actually part of the
place name, they must be capitalized. (Check an atlas or a gazetteer when
in doubt.)

Preceding a Place Name	**Part of a Place Name**
northern New Jersey	**BUT:** Northern Ireland
the southwestern United States	Southern Rhodesia
western Massachusetts	Western Australia

DAYS OF THE WEEK, MONTHS, HOLIDAYS, SEASONS, EVENTS, PERIODS

337   Capitalize names of *days, months, holidays,* and *religious days.*

Wednesday	Good Friday
February	Passover
New Year's Day	the Fourth of July
Veterans Day	Mother's Day

338   Capitalize the names of the seasons only when they are personified.

Come, gentle Spring.

BUT: Our order for *fall* merchandise was mailed today.

339   Capitalize the names of historical events and imaginative names given to historical periods.

the American Revolution	the Middle Ages
World War II	the Atomic Age
Fire Prevention Week	the Great Depression

340   Do not capitalize the names of decades and centuries.

during the thirties	in the twentieth century
in the nineteen-seventies	during the eighteen hundreds

NOTE: Decades are capitalized, however, in special expressions.

the Gay Nineties	the Roaring Twenties

ACTS, LAWS, BILLS, TREATIES

341   Capitalize formal titles of acts, laws, bills, and treaties, but do not capitalize common-noun elements that stand alone in place of the full name.

the Social Security Act	BUT: the act
Public Law 85-1	the law
the Treaty of Versailles	the treaty

RACES, PEOPLES, LANGUAGES, RELIGIONS

342   Capitalize the names of races, peoples, tribes, religions, and languages.

Chinese   Afro-American   Judaism   Sanskrit

HEAVENLY BODIES

343   Do not capitalize the words *sun, moon,* or *earth* unless they are used in connection with the capitalized names of other planets or stars.

The *sun* was hidden behind a cloud.

The *earth* revolves on its axis.

In our astronomy class we have been comparing the orbits of Mars, Venus, and *Earth.*

COURSES OF STUDY AND SUBJECTS; ACADEMIC DEGREES

344   Capitalize the names of specific courses of study. However, do not capitalize names of subjects or areas of study, except for any proper nouns or adjectives in such names.

American History 201 meets on Tuesdays and Thursdays. (Course title.)

Fred has decided to major in *American history.* (Area of study.)

345 Do not capitalize academic degrees used as general terms of classification (for example, a *bachelor of arts* degree). However, capitalize a degree used after a person's name (John Howard, *Doctor of Philosophy*).

COMMERCIAL PRODUCTS

346 Capitalize trademarks, brand names, proprietary names, names of commercial products, and market grades. The common noun following the name of a product should not ordinarily be capitalized; however, manufacturers and advertisers often capitalize such words in the names of their own products for special emphasis.

      Ivory soap   Hotpoint dishwasher   Choice lamb (market grade)

347 Capitalize all trade names except those that have become clearly established as common nouns. To be safe, check a dictionary, the *United States Government Printing Office Style Manual,* or (for the final authority) the trademark register in the U.S. Patent Office.

Coca-Cola, Coke	Teflon	Dacron	**BUT:** nylon
Pyrex	TelePrompTer	Teletype	cellophane
Photostat	Xerox	Mimeoscope	mimeograph

ADVERTISING MATERIAL

348 Words that are not ordinarily capitalized may be capitalized in advertising correspondence and advertising copy for special emphasis. (This style is inappropriate in all other kinds of written communication.)

    Save money now during our Year-End Clearance Sale.

    It's the event Luxury Lovers have been waiting for . . . from Whitehall's!

LEGAL CORRESPONDENCE

349 In legal documents many words that ordinarily would be written in small letters are written with initial capitals or all capitals—for example, references to parties, the name of the document, special provisions, and sometimes spelled-out amounts of money (see ¶ 428).

    Whereupon I, the said Notary, at the request of the aforesaid, did PROTEST, and by these presents do publicly and solemnly PROTEST, as well against Maker and Indorser of said note . . .

    THIS AGREEMENT, made this 31st day of January, 1972, . . .

    . . . hereinafter called the SELLER

    WHEREAS the Seller has this day agreed . . .

    WITNESS the signatures . . .

NOUNS WITH NUMBERS OR LETTERS

350   Capitalize a noun followed by a number or a letter that indicates sequence.
EXCEPTIONS: The nouns *line, note, page, paragraph, size,* and *verse* are not
capitalized.

Act I	Class 4	Lesson 20	Policy 394857
Appendix A	Column 1	line 4	Room 501
Article 2	Diagram 4	Lot 2	Section 1
Book III	Exercise 8	note 1	size 10
Bulletin T-119	Exhibit A	page 158	Table 7
Car 8171	Figure 9	paragraph 2a	Track 2
Chapter V	Flight 626	Part Three	Unit 2
Chart 3	Illustration 19	Plate XV	verse 3
Check 181	Invoice 270487	Platform 3	Volume II

NOTE: It is not necessary to use *No.* before the number.

Purchase Order 4713 (**RATHER THAN:** Purchase Order *No.* 4713)

TITLES OF LITERARY AND ARTISTIC WORKS; HEADINGS

351   In titles of literary and artistic works and in displayed headings, capitalize all words with *four or more* letters. Also capitalize words with
fewer than four letters except:

ARTICLES: *the, a, an*
SHORT CONJUNCTIONS: *and, as, but, if, or, nor*
SHORT PREPOSITIONS: *at, by, for, in, of, off, on, out, to, up*

> *How to Succeed in Business Without Really Trying*
> "Redevelopment Proposal Is Not Expected to Be Approved"

NOTE: Even articles, short conjunctions, and short prepositions should
be capitalized under the following circumstances:

a. Capitalize the first and last word of a title.

> "*A Man to Be Proud Of*"

CAUTION: Do not capitalize *the* at the beginning of a title unless it is actually
part of the title.

> For further details check the *Encyclopaedia Britannica.*
> This clipping is from *The New York Times.*

b. Capitalize the first word following a dash or colon in a title.

> *Abraham Lincoln—The Early Years*
> *The Treaty of Versailles: A Reexamination*

c. Capitalize short words like *in, out, off,* and *up* in titles when they
serve as adverbs rather than as prepositions. (These words may occur in
verb phrases or in hyphenated compounds derived from verb phrases.)

"IBM Chalks *Up* Record Earnings for the Year"
"Ellsworth Is Runner-*Up* in Election" (see also ¶ 352)
BUT: "Sailing *up* the Mississippi"

HYPHENATED WORDS

352 *Within a sentence,* capitalize only those elements of a hyphenated word that are proper nouns or proper adjectives. *At the beginning of a sentence,* capitalize the first element in the hyphenated word, but not other elements unless they are proper nouns or adjectives. *In a heading or title,* capitalize all the elements except articles, short prepositions, and short conjunctions (see ¶ 351).

Within Sentences	Beginning Sentences	In Headings
up-to-date	Up-to-date	Up-to-Date
Spanish-American	Spanish-American	Spanish-American
English-speaking	English-speaking	English-Speaking
mid-September	Mid-September	Mid-September
ex-President Johnson	Ex-President Johnson	Ex-President Johnson
Senator-elect Murray	Senator-elect Murray	Senator-Elect Murray
self-confidence	Self-confidence	Self-Confidence
de-emphasize	De-emphasize	De-Emphasize
follow-up	Follow-up	Follow-Up (see ¶ 351c)
Eighty-ninth Congress	Eighty-ninth Congress	Eighty-Ninth Congress
one-sixth	One-sixth	One-Sixth
post-World War II	Post-World War II	Post-World War II

► Capitalization of questions within sentences: see ¶¶ 114, 116.
Capitalization after a colon: see ¶¶ 195–198.
Capitalization after an opening dash: see ¶ 214, note.
Capitalization after an opening parenthesis: see ¶¶ 224–226.
Capitalization after an opening quotation mark: see ¶¶ 273–274.
Capitalization of abbreviations: see ¶ 530.

Section 4
NUMBERS

There is a significant difference between using figures and using words to express numbers. Figures are big (like capital letters) and compact and informal (like abbreviations); when used in a sentence, they stand out clearly from the surrounding words. By contrast, numbers expressed in words are unemphatic and formal; they do not stand out in a sentence. This functional difference between figures and words underlies all aspects of number style.

The rules for expressing numbers would be quite simple if writers would all agree to express numbers entirely in figures or entirely in words. But in actual practice the exclusive use of figures is considered appropriate only in tabulations and statistical matter, whereas the exclusive use of words to express numbers is found only in ultraformal documents (such as proclamations and social invitations). In writing that is neither ultraformal nor ultratechnical, most style manuals call for the use of both figures and words in varying proportions. Although authorities do not agree on details, there are two basic number styles in wide use: the *figure style* (which uses figures for most numbers above 10) and the *word style* (which uses figures for most numbers above 100). Unless you deal with a very limited type of business correspondence, you will want to know both styles and be prepared to use each appropriately as the situation demands.

FIGURE STYLE

The figure style is most commonly used in ordinary business correspondence (dealing with sales, production, advertising, and other routine commercial matters). It is also used in journalistic and technical material. In writing of this kind most numbers represent significant quantities or measurements that should stand out for emphasis or quick comprehension.

401   Spell out numbers from 1 through 10; use figures for numbers above 10. This rule applies to both exact and approximate numbers.

> We ordered *ten* cases of yarn, but they can ship only *four* or *five*.
> Please send us *35* copies of your latest bulletin.
> About *60* to *70* file folders have been lost or misplaced.
> I have received some *30-odd* letters about Tuesday's column.
> We have sold more than *1,200* tickets to date.
> This stadium can seat more than *110,000* people.

NOTE: Even the numbers 1 through 10 may be expressed in figures (as in this sentence) when emphasis and quick comprehension are essential. This is the style used in tabulations and statistical matter, and in some offices it is the style used in sales letters and interoffice correspondence.

402   Use the same style to express *related* numbers above and below 10. (If most of the numbers are below 10, put them all in words; if most are above 10, express all in figures.)

> Smoke damaged *five* dresses, *eight* suits, and *eleven* coats.
> Please order *28* chairs, *19* tables, and *9* desks.
> I have requisitioned *16* reams of bond paper, *120* scratch pads, and *8* boxes of envelopes for the *four* secretaries. (Figures are used for related items of stationery; the number of secretaries is not related.)

403 For fast comprehension, numbers in the *millions* or higher may be expressed as follows:

21 million (in place of 21,000,000)	14½ million (in place of 14,500,000)
3 billion (in place of 3,000,000,000)	2.4 billion (in place of 2,400,000,000)

a. This style may be used only when the amount consists of a whole number with nothing more than a simple fraction or decimal following. A number such as *4,832,067* must be written all in figures.

b. Treat related numbers alike.

Last year we sold *21,557,000* items; this year, nearly *23,000,000*. (**NOT:** 23 million.)

▶ See ¶ 424 for examples involving money.

WORD STYLE

The word style of numbers is used in executive-level correspondence and in nontechnical material, where the writing is of a more formal or literary nature and the use of figures would give numbers an undesired emphasis and obtrusiveness. Here are the basic rules for the word style.

404 Spell out all numbers, whether exact or approximate, that can be expressed in one or two words. (A hyphenated compound number like *twenty-one* or *ninety-nine* counts as one word.) In effect, spell out all numbers from 1 through 100 and all round numbers above 100 that require no more than two words (such as *sixty-two thousand* or *forty-five million*).

Mr. Ryan received *twenty-three* letters praising his talk at the Rotary Club.

Every week more than *twelve million* people watch the TV series we sponsor.

I have received *sixty-odd* phone calls today in response to my ad.

Over *two hundred* people attended the reception for Mr. Watson.

BUT: Over *250* people attended the reception. (Use figures when more than two words are required.)

NOTE: In writing of an ultraformal nature—proclamations, social invitations, and many legal documents—even a number that requires more than two words is spelled out (see ¶¶ 831–832). However, the word style, as a matter of practicality, ordinarily uses figures when more than two words are required.

405 Express related numbers the same way, even though some are above 100 and some below.

We sent out *three hundred* invitations and have already received over *one hundred* acceptances.

BUT: We sent out *300* invitations and have already received *125* acceptances. (**NOT:** three hundred . . . 125 . . .)

406 When spelling out large round numbers, use the shortest form possible.

We have distributed over *twelve hundred* copies of our prospectus. (**RATHER THAN:** one thousand two hundred.)

407   Numbers in the millions or higher *that require more than two words when spelled out* may be expressed as follows:

> 231 million (in place of 231,000,000)
> 9¾ billion (in place of 9,750,000,000)
> 671.4 million (in place of 671,400,000)

Even a two-word number such as *sixty-two million* should be expressed as *62 million* when it is related to a number such as *231 million* (which cannot be spelled in two words). Moreover, it should be expressed as *62,000,000* when it is related to a number such as *231,163,520.*

▶   The rules for the figure style (¶¶ 401–403) and the word style (¶¶ 404–407) are basic guidelines that govern in the absence of more specific principles. A number of situations (involving the expression of dates, money, measurements, etc.) require special rules, which are presented in the remainder of this section. *These rules apply whether you are following a figure style or a word style.* In a number of cases, where either figures or words may be used, your choice will depend on which basic style you are following.

AT THE BEGINNING OF A SENTENCE

408   Always spell out a number that begins a sentence. (See ¶¶ 830–833.)

> *Forty-six* glasses were broken.   *Five hundred* people attended.

409   For consistency, also spell out related numbers.

> *Twenty* to *thirty* percent of the goods received were defective. (**NOT:** Twenty to 30 percent.)

410   If the numbers are large (requiring more than two words when spelled out) or if figures are preferable (for emphasis or quick reference), rearrange the wording of the sentence.

> The company sent out *298* circulars. (**INSTEAD OF:** *Two hundred and ninety-eight* circulars were sent out by the company.)
> We had a good year in *1969.* (**INSTEAD OF:** *1969* was a good year for us.)
> Our mining operations provide *60* to *70* percent of our revenues. (**INSTEAD OF:** *Sixty* to *seventy* percent of our revenues come from our mining operations.)

INDEFINITE NUMBERS AND AMOUNTS

411   Always spell out indefinite numbers and amounts.

> a few hundred votes   hundreds of customers
> several thousand orders   thousands of questionnaires
> many millions of dollars (see ¶ 422)   millions of people

ORDINALS

412   Spell out all ordinals (*first, second, third,* etc.) that can be expressed in one or two words.

in the twentieth century	the Twenty-third Assembly District
the Ninety-first Congress	the ten millionth visitor to the United Nations
on his thirty-fifth birthday	the store's two hundredth anniversary

▶ See ¶¶ 830, 833 for the style of spelled-out ordinal numbers.

413 Figures are used to express ordinals in certain expressions of dates (see ¶ 414), in numbered street names above 10 (see ¶ 1419), and occasionally in displayed headings and titles for special effect.

NOTE: Ordinal figures are expressed as follows: *1st, 2d* or *2nd, 3d* or *3rd, 4th, 5th, 6th,* etc. Do not use an "abbreviation" period following an ordinal.

DATES

These rules apply to dates in sentences. See ¶¶ 1402–1404 for date lines in correspondence.

414 When the day *precedes* the month or *stands alone*, express it either in ordinal figures (*1st, 2d, 3d, 4th,* etc.) or in ordinal words (the *first,* the *twelfth,* the *twenty-eighth*).

Our meeting starts on the *25th* of July and continues until the *29th.* (Figure style.)

I will arrive on the *ninth* of March and stay until the *twenty-third.* (Word style.)

415 When the day *follows* the month, always express it in cardinal figures (1, 2, 3, etc.).

on March 6 (NOT: March 6th or March sixth)

416 Express complete dates in month-day-year sequence.

March 6, 1969

Do *not* use the following forms to express the complete date: March 6th, 1969; Mar. 6, 1969; 3/6/69; the 6th of March, 1969; the sixth of March, 1969.

417 In United States military correspondence and in letters from foreign countries, the complete date is expressed in day-month-year sequence.

15 September 1969

418 Note the correct use of commas and other punctuation with expressions of dates.

On *March 12, 1969,* construction began on our present headquarters. (Two commas set off the year following the month and day.)

In *April, 1969,* the format of our newsletter was changed. (Two commas set off the year following the month alone.)

The corporation was founded in *May, 1930*—or was it *May, 1931*? (Omit the second comma when stronger punctuation, such as a dash, is required at that point.)

[Continued on page 78.]

The *March 1969* issue of *Harper's* carried the article. (Omit both commas when the month and year are used together as one adjective.)

In *1965* Richardson and Hanlon were elected to the board. (No comma follows the year in a short introductory phrase.)

On *January 15* we met to review your proposal. (No comma follows the month and day in a short introductory phrase.)

BUT: On *January 15, 22* new employees will be added to the staff. (Insert a comma when another figure immediately follows. See ¶ 460.)

▶ See also ¶ 138 for the use or omission of a comma following dates.

419 In legal documents, proclamations, and formal invitations, spell out the day and the year. A number of styles may be used:

May twenty-first	nineteen hundred and sixty-nine
the twenty-first of May	one thousand nine hundred and sixty-nine
this twenty-first day of May	in the year of Our Lord one thousand nine hundred and sixty-nine

▶ See ¶¶ 830, 831a for the spelling of numbers.

420 Class graduation years and well-known years in history may appear in abbreviated form.

the class of '74   the blizzard of '88

▶ See ¶¶ 451–452 for the expression of centuries and decades; ¶¶ 462–464 for dates in a sequence.

MONEY

421 Use figures to express exact or approximate amounts of money. (See ¶ 428 for the style in legal documents.)

$5	about $200	over $1,000,000	a $20 bill
$9.75	nearly $1,000	a $15,000-a-year man	$2,000 worth

NOTE: An isolated, nonemphatic reference to money may be spelled out.

five hundred dollars	a twenty-dollar bill
nearly a thousand dollars	two thousand dollars' worth

422 Spell out indefinite amounts of money; for example, *a few million dollars, many thousands of dollars.*

423 Do not add a decimal point or ciphers to a whole dollar amount when it occurs in a sentence.

I am enclosing a check for *$125* as payment in full.

This model costs $12.50; that one costs *$10.*

In tabulations, however, if any amount in the column contains cents, add a decimal point and two ciphers to all *whole* dollar amounts to maintain a uniform appearance.

$150.50
25.00
8.05
$183.55

424   Money in round amounts of a million or more may be expressed partially in words.

$12 million	**OR**	12 million dollars
$10½ million	**OR**	10½ million dollars
$10.5 million	**OR**	10.5 million dollars

$6¼ billion	**OR**	6¼ billion dollars	**OR**	$6,250 million
$6.25 billion	**OR**	6.25 billion dollars	**OR**	6,250 million dollars

a. This style may be used only when the amount consists of a whole number with nothing more than a simple fraction or decimal following. An amount like *$10,235,000* must be written entirely in figures.

b. Express related amounts the same way.

from $500,000 to $1,000,000 (**NOT:** from $500,000 to $1 million)

c. Repeat the word *million* (*billion,* etc.) with each figure to avoid misunderstanding.

$5 million to $10 million (**NOT:** $5 to $10 million)

425   Fractional expressions of large amounts of money should be either completely spelled out or converted to an all-figure style.

one-quarter of a million dollars   **OR** $250,000

(**BUT NOT:** ¼ of a million dollars **OR** $¼ million)

half a billion dollars   **OR** $500,000,000

(**BUT NOT:** ½ billion dollars **OR** $½ billion)

426   For amounts under a dollar, use figures and the word *cents.*

I am sure that customers will not pay more than *50 cents* for this item.

NOTE: An isolated, nonemphatic reference to cents may be spelled out.

I wouldn't give *two cents* for that car.

a. Do not use the style *$.75* in sentences except when related amounts require a dollar sign.

Prices for the principal grains were as follows: wheat, $1.73; corn, $1.23; oats, $.78; rye, $1.58.

b. The symbol ¢ should be used only in technical and statistical matter containing many price quotations.

Yesterday's wholesale prices for food commodities were as follows: coffee, 42¢; cocoa, 23¢; sugar, 7¢; butter, 66¢.

427   When using the dollar sign or the cent sign with a price range or a series of amounts, use the sign with each amount.

$5,000 to $10,000	10¢ to 20¢	$10 million to $20 million

If the term *dollars* or *cents* is to be spelled out, use it only with the final amount.

10 to 20 cents	10 to 20 million dollars

428   In legal documents, amounts of money are often expressed first in words and then, within parentheses, in figures. (See also ¶ 831*b*.)

> One Hundred Dollars ($100)   NOT: One Hundred ($100) Dollars
> Three Hundred Twenty-five and 50/100 Dollars ($325.50)

NOTE: The capitalization of spelled-out amounts is optional. Sometimes only the first letter of the first word is capitalized (as on checks); sometimes the entire amount is given all in capitals.

MEASUREMENTS

429   Most measurements have a technical significance and should be expressed in figures for emphasis or quick comprehension. However, spell out a measurement that lacks technical significance.

> A higher rate is charged on parcels over *2 pounds.*
> BUT: I'm afraid I've gained another *two pounds* this week.
>
> Add *1 quart* of sugar for each *4 quarts* of strawberries.
> BUT: Last weekend we picked *four quarts* of strawberries from our own patch.
>
> There is no charge for delivery within a *30-mile* radius of Chicago.
> BUT: Last Sunday we took an *eighty-mile* drive through the countryside.

NOTE: Dimensions, sizes, and temperature readings are always expressed in figures.

> The dimensions of his office are *12* by *14 feet.* (See ¶ 432.)
> Your order for one pair of tennis shoes, *size 6,* has been delayed.
> The thermometer now stands at *98,* a rise of three degrees in the last hour.

430   When a measurement consists of several words, do not use commas to separate the words. The measurement is considered a single unit.

> The parcel weighed *6 pounds 14 ounces.*   I am *6 feet 2 inches* tall.
> The punch bowl holds *4 quarts 1 pint.*   He has *20/20* vision.

431   The unit of measure may be abbreviated or expressed as a symbol only in technical matter or tabular work. See ¶¶ 520–521 for abbreviations of units of measure; ¶ 459 for abbreviations and symbols in a range of numbers.

432   Dimensions may be expressed as follows:

> GENERAL USAGE: a room 15 by 30 feet   a 15- by 30-foot room
> TECHNICAL USAGE: ⎰a room 15 x 30 ft.   a 15- x 30-ft. room
>   ⎱a room 15′ x 30′   a 15′ x 30′ room
>
> GENERAL USAGE: 15 feet 6 inches by 30 feet 9 inches
> TECHNICAL USAGE: 15 ft. 6 in. x 30 ft. 9 in.   OR   15′ 6″ x 30′ 9″

FRACTIONS

433   A mixed number (a whole number plus a fraction) is written in figures except at the beginning of a sentence.

This year's sales are 3¾ times as great as they were five years ago.

Five and one-quarter (**OR** *Five and a quarter*) inches of snow fell last night. (Note the use of *and* between the whole number and the fraction.)

434 A fraction that stands alone (without a whole number preceding) should be expressed in words unless the spelled-out form is long and awkward or unless the fraction is used in technical writing. (See ¶¶ 832–833 for the hyphenation of such fractions.)

one-half the vote   three-fourths of the voters
a two-thirds majority   half an hour later

five thirty-seconds of an inch (**IN TECHNICAL MATTER:** 5/32 inch)

half-inch tubing (**IN TECHNICAL MATTER:** ½-inch tubing)

¾-yard lengths (**BETTER THAN:** three-quarter-yard lengths)

435 Fractions expressed in figures should not be followed by *st, ds, nds,* or *ths* or by an *of* phrase.

3/200 (**NOT:** 3/200ths)   9/64 inch (**NOT:** 9/64ths of an inch)

If a sentence requires the use of an *of* phrase following the fraction, spell the fraction out.

three-quarters of an hour (**NOT:** ¾ of an hour)

436 When constructing fractions that do not appear on the typewriter, use the diagonal (/). Separate a whole number from a fraction by a space (not by a hyphen).

The rate of interest was *3 7/8* percent.

437 In the same sentence, do not mix constructed fractions (7/8, 5/16) with those that appear on the typewriter (½, ¼).

The rate of interest has risen from *4 1/2* to *4 5/8* percent. (**NOT:** 4½ to 4 5/8 percent.)

DECIMALS

438 Always write decimals in figures. Never insert commas in the decimal part of a number.

665.3184368 (no comma in decimal part of the number)
8,919.23785 (comma used in whole part of the number)

439 When a decimal stands alone (without a whole number preceding the decimal point), insert a cipher before the decimal point unless the decimal itself begins with a cipher. (Reason: The cipher prevents the reader from overlooking the decimal point.)

0.55 inch   .08 gram   **EXCEPTIONS:** a Colt .45; a .36 caliber revolver

440 When a cipher occurs at the end of a decimal (for example, *2.7870*), it means either that the decimal is an exact number or has been rounded off from a longer computation.

441   Do not begin a sentence with a decimal figure.

> The temperature reading at 8 a.m. was 63.7.
>
> (NOT: 63.7 was the temperature reading at 8 a.m.)

PERCENTAGES

442   Express percentages in figures, and spell out the word *percent*. (See ¶¶ 408–410 for percentages at the beginning of a sentence.)

> He is willing to give us a discount of *15 percent*.
>
> We have had an *8 percent* increase in sales this year. (A compound modifier expressing percentage is not hyphenated.)
>
> Our terms are 2 percent 10 days, net 30 days. (On invoices these credit terms may be abbreviated as *2/10, n/30*.)

NOTE: The % symbol is used only in tabulations, business forms, interoffice memorandums, and statistical or technical matter.

443   **a.** Fractional percentages *under 1 percent* should be spelled out or expressed as a decimal figure.

> one-half of 1 percent   OR   0.5 percent

NOTE: The cipher before the decimal point in 0.5 percent prevents a misreading of the amount as *5 percent*.

b. Fractional percentages *over 1 percent* should be expressed in figures.

> 7½ percent   OR   7.5 percent   9¼ percent   OR   9.25 percent

444   In a range or series of percentages, the word *percent* follows the last figure only. The symbol %, if used, must follow each figure (see ¶ 442, note).

> Price reductions range from *20 to 50 percent*. (BUT: from 20% to 50%.)
>
> We give discounts of *10, 20, and 30 percent*. (BUT: 10%, 20%, and 30%.)

RATIOS AND PROPORTIONS

445   Always write ratios and proportions in figures.

> a 5 to 1 ratio   OR   a 5:1 ratio   a 100 to 1 shot
> a proportion of 5 to 1   7 parts of benzene to 3 parts of water
> the odds are 100 to 1   a 50-50 chance to recover

AGES AND ANNIVERSARIES

446   In general, spell out numbers designating ages and anniversaries.

> Mary is *nineteen* years old.   Sam is *sixty-eight* years of age.
> on her twenty-first birthday   their fortieth anniversary
> a five-year-old   a child five years old
> a man in his fifties   a woman in her mid-thirties
>
> I interviewed a man aged *ninety-six*. (Note the use of *aged*, not *age*.)

447   Use figures to express ages and anniversaries if they are used as technical measurements or as significant statistics (as in news releases, personal data sheets, and matters pertaining to employment, retirement, insurance, and the like). Also use figures when the number would require more than two words if spelled out.

> Ralph Thompson, *40,* has been promoted to professor of law.
>
> At the age of *50,* a policyholder may collect disability benefits; at *65,* he may begin to collect retirement benefits. (Avoid the abrupt construction *at age 50* in nontechnical writing.)
>
> The Hamden Corporation will be celebrating its *125th* anniversary next year.

448   Use figures for ages expressed in years, months, and days. Do not use commas to separate the elements; they are considered to make up a single unit.

> On June 13 he will be *19 years 4 months and 17 days old.* (The *and* linking months and days is often omitted.)

PERIODS OF TIME

449   In general, express periods of time in words.

> a twenty-minute wait   in twenty-four months
> eight hours later   in the last thirty years
> twelve days from now   three hundred years ago

450   Use figures to express periods of time when they are used as technical measurements or significant statistics (as in discounts, interest rates, and credit terms). Also use figures when the number would require more than two words if spelled out.

> a 5-minute warmup   a note due in 6 months
> an 8-hour day   a 30-year mortgage
> payable in 30 days   350 years ago

451   Centuries may be expressed as follows:

> the 1900s   **OR**   the nineteen hundreds
> the twentieth century
> nineteenth-century business customs

452   Decades may be expressed as follows:

> the 1930s   **OR**   the nineteen-thirties   **OR**   the thirties   **OR**   the '30s
> the mid-1940s   **OR**   the mid-forties   **OR**   the mid-'40s

NOTE: Decades are not capitalized except in special expressions such as *the Gay Nineties, the Roaring Twenties.*

CLOCK TIME

453   **With A.M., P.M., Noon, and Midnight**
a. Always use figures with *a.m.* or *p.m.*

> The boat sails at *11:30 a.m.*
> The train leaves at *7 p.m.,* CST. (See ¶ 519.)

[*Continued on page 84.*]

b. The abbreviations *a.m.* and *p.m.* are typed in small letters without spaces. (In printed matter they usually appear in small capitals: A.M., P.M.)

c. When expressing time "on the hour," do not add ciphers to denote minutes except in tables where other times are given in hours and minutes.

> Our store is open from 9:30 a.m. to 6 *p.m.*
> We always close from *12 noon* to 1:30 p.m.
> You can buy your tickets between 9 and *10 a.m.*

In tabulations, however, if other times are given in hours and minutes, add a colon and two ciphers to exact hours to maintain a uniform appearance.

ARR	DEP
8:45	9:10
9:00	9:25
9:50	10:00

d. Do not use *a.m.* or *p.m.* unless figures are used.

> this morning (**NOT:** this a.m.)   tomorrow afternoon (**NOT:** tomorrow p.m.)

e. Do not use *a.m.* or *p.m.* with *o'clock.*

> 6 o'clock   **OR**   6 p.m.   ten o'clock   **OR**   10 a.m.
> (**NOT:** 6 p.m. o'clock)   (**NOT:** 10 a.m. o'clock)

f. Do not use *a.m.* or *p.m.* with the expressions *in the morning, in the afternoon, in the evening,* or *at night.* The abbreviations themselves already convey one of these meanings.

> at 9 p.m.   **OR**   at nine in the evening   (**NOT:** at 9 p.m. in the evening)

g. Use a colon (without space before or after) to separate hours from minutes (as in *3:22*).

h. The times *noon* and *midnight* may be expressed in words alone. However, use the forms *12 noon* and *12 midnight* when these times are given with other times expressed in figures.

> The second shift ends at *midnight.*
> **BUT:** The second shift runs from *4 p.m.* to *12 midnight.*

454 **With O'Clock**

a. With *o'clock* use figures for emphasis or words for formality.

> 3 o'clock (figure style)   three o'clock (word style)

b. To express hours and minutes with *o'clock,* the correct form is *half after four o'clock* or *half past four o'clock* (but not *four-thirty o'clock*).

c. Expressions of time containing *o'clock* may be reinforced by such phrases as *in the morning, in the afternoon,* and the like.

> 10 o'clock at night   seven o'clock in the morning

However, for quick comprehension, the forms *10 p.m.* and *7 a.m.* are preferable.

455 · Without A.M., P.M., or O'Clock

a. When expressing time "on the hour" without *a.m., p.m.,* or *o'clock,* spell the hour out.

>He will arrive at *eight* tonight. (**NOT:** at 8 tonight.)

b. When expressing time in hours and minutes without *a.m., p.m.,* or *o'clock,* spell out the time or—for quick comprehension—convert the expression to an all-figure style.

>five after six   **OR**   6:05
>a quarter past ten   **OR**   10:15
>twenty of four   **OR**   3:40
>a quarter to five (**OR** of five)   **OR**   4:45
>half past nine   **OR**   nine-thirty   **OR**   9:30
>nine forty-two   **OR**   9:42

NOTE: A hyphen is used between hours and minutes (*seven-thirty*) but not if the minutes must be hyphenated (seven *thirty-five*).

SCORES AND VOTING RESULTS

456   Use figures (even for 1 through 10) to express scores and voting results.

>a score of 85 on the test   New York 8, Chicago 6   a vote of 17 to 6

SERIAL NUMBERS

457   Always use figures to express serial numbers (invoice, style, model, lot numbers, etc.), telephone numbers, house or room numbers, page numbers, and the like. Do not use commas to set off "thousands" in such numbers (see ¶ 174).

>Invoice 12693   Column 6   page 1112
>(516) 783-9097   Figure 9   line 367

▶   See ¶ 350 for the capitalization of nouns before numbers.

WITH ABBREVIATIONS AND SYMBOLS

458   Always use figures with abbreviations and symbols.

>$25   90¢   6 in. **OR** 6″   50%   9 a.m.   6:30 p.m.   No. 985

459   If a symbol is used in a range of numbers, it should be repeated with each number. A full word or an abbreviation used in place of the symbol is given only with the last number.

>65°–75° F.   65 to 75 degrees Fahrenheit   **OR**   65–75 deg. F.
>5½″ x 8″   5½ by 8 inches   **OR**   5½ x 8 in.
>9′ x 12′   9 by 12 feet   **OR**   9 x 12 ft.
>30%–40%   30 to 40 percent
>50¢–60¢   50 to 60 cents
>$70–$80   seventy to eighty dollars

ADJACENT NUMBERS

460   When two unrelated numbers come together in a sentence and both are in figures or both are in words, separate them with a comma.

> In *1968, 440* employees received bonuses.
> Out of *ten, two* were defective.
> On page *31, 90* cents is incorrectly given as the price.
> On Account *4613,* $*18.60* is the amount still due.

NOTE: No comma is necessary when one number is in figures and the other is in words.

> On *March 3 eight* cases of measles were reported.

461   When two numbers come together and one is part of a compound modifier (see ¶ 812), express one of the numbers in figures and the other in words. As a rule, spell the first number unless the second number would make a significantly shorter word.

> two 8-room houses   **BUT:** 500 four-page leaflets
> sixty $5 bills   150 five-dollar bills

NUMBERS IN A SEQUENCE

462   Use commas to separate numbers that do not represent a continuous sequence.

> on pages 18, 20, and 28   data for the years 1945, 1950, and 1955

463   A hyphen may be used in place of the word *to* to link two figures that represent a continuous sequence.

> on pages 18-28   in Articles I-III
> during the week of May 15-21   during the years 1945-1950

Do not use the hyphen if the sequence is introduced by the word *from* or *between.*

> from 1945 to 1950   between 1960 and 1965
> (**NOT:** from 1945-1950)   (**NOT:** between 1960-1965)

464   In a continuous sequence of figures connected by hyphens, the second figure may be expressed in abbreviated form. This style is used for sequences of page numbers or years only when they occur quite frequently. (In isolated cases, do not abbreviate.)

> 1960-65 (**OR** 1960-1965)   pages 110-12 (**OR** pages 110-112)
> 1901-2 (**OR** 1901-1902)   pages 101-2 (**OR** pages 101-102)

a. Do not abbreviate the second number when the first number ends in two zeros.

> 1900-1965   pages 100-101

b. Do not abbreviate the second number when it starts with different digits.

1890–1902	pages 998–1004

c. Do not abbreviate the second number when it is under 100.

46–48 A.D.	pages 46–48

NO. OR # WITH FIGURES

465   If the term *number* precedes a figure, express it as an abbreviation (sin-gular: *No.;* plural: *Nos.*). At the beginning of a sentence, however, spell out *Number* to prevent misreading.

> Our check covers the following invoices: *Nos.* 592, 653, and 654.
> *Number* 82175 has been assigned to your new policy.

a. If an identifying noun precedes the figure (such as *Invoice, Check, Room, Box,* or the like), the abbreviation *No.* is usually unnecessary.

> Our check covers *Invoices* 592, 653, and 654.

> **EXCEPTIONS:** License No. HLM 744; Social Security No. 169-35-8142; Patent No. 953,461

b. The symbol # may be used on business forms (such as invoices) and in technical matter.

▶   See ¶ 350 for the capitalization of nouns preceding figures.

ROMAN NUMERALS

466   Roman numerals are used chiefly for the important divisions of literary and legislative material, for main topics in outlines, and in dates on public buildings. (For methods of forming roman numerals, consult the dic-tionary.)

Chapter X	Part II
Volume I	MCMLXXII (1972 in roman numerals)

NOTE: Pages in the front section of a book (such as the preface and table of contents) are usually numbered in small roman numerals: *iii, iv, v,* etc. Other pages are numbered in arabic numerals: *1, 2, 3,* etc.

▶   Commas in figures: see ¶¶ 173–175.
Plurals of numbers: see ¶ 624.
Hyphenation of spelled-out numbers: see ¶¶ 830–833.
Division at end of a line: see ¶ 917.
House, street, and ZIP Code numbers: see ¶¶ 1418–1419, 1424, 1426*d*.

Section 5
ABBREVIATIONS

ABBREVIATIONS VERSUS CONTRACTIONS

501   An abbreviation is a shortened form of a word or a phrase used primarily to save space. Many abbreviations call for periods; others do not. (See ¶¶ 531–535.)

a. Abbreviations occur most frequently in technical writing, statistical data, and footnotes. In business letters and more formal writing, only a few kinds of abbreviations are regularly used. (**EXAMPLES:** *Mr., Mrs., Jr., Sr., Ph.D., a.m., p.m.*)

b. Some abbreviations have become accepted as words and are written without periods. (**EXAMPLE:** *ad* for *advertisement.*)

502   A contraction also is a shortened form of a word or a phrase; however, an apostrophe is inserted at the exact point where letters are omitted, and no period follows the contraction (unless the form falls at the end of a sentence). (**EXAMPLES:** *nat'l* for *national; doesn't* for *does not.*)

a. As a rule, contractions are used only in informal writing or in tabular matter where space is limited. However, contractions of verb phrases (such as *can't* and *shouldn't*) are commonly used in business letters where the writer is striving for an easy, colloquial tone. In formal writing, contractions are not used (except for *o'clock,* which is a more formal way to express time than *a.m.* or *p.m.*).

b. Whenever you have a choice between using an abbreviation or a contraction, choose the abbreviation. It not only looks better but is easier to type.

> cont. (**RATHER THAN:** cont'd)   secy. (**RATHER THAN:** sec'y)
> dept. (**RATHER THAN:** dep't)   mfg. (**RATHER THAN:** m'f'g)

c. Some words formerly written with the apostrophe are now recognized as complete words. (**EXAMPLE:** *phone.*)

BASIC RULES

503   Use abbreviations and contractions sparingly.

504   Be consistent within the same letter, report, or manuscript. Do not abbreviate a term in some sentences and spell it out in other sentences.

505   When you do abbreviate, use the generally accepted forms. A number of abbreviations have alternative forms, with differences in spelling, capitalization, and punctuation. Again, be consistent: having selected one particular style for an abbreviation (say, *a.m.*), do not use a different style (*A.M.*) elsewhere in the same material.

TITLES WITH SURNAMES

506 In sentences, when only the surname is used, spell out all titles except *Mr., Mrs., Messrs.,* and *Dr.*

> *Mr.* Ames will be the guest of *Professor* and *Mrs.* King.
>
> *Dr.* McConnell has announced that *Governor* Helstad will speak at the commencement.

NOTE: In formal writing, *Dr.* may be spelled out when used with only the surname.

▶ See ¶¶ 1408–1412 for the treatment of titles when a person's *full name* is used.

ACADEMIC DEGREES

507 Abbreviations of academic degrees require a period after each *element* in the abbreviation but no internal space.

B.A.	Ph.D.	LL.B.	B.Ch.E.	M.D.
M.S.	Ed.D.	Litt.D.	B.Arch.	D.D.S.

EXCEPTION: CPA (the style preferred by the American Institute of Certified Public Accountants)

▶ See also ¶¶ 1408, 1410, 1412.

NAMES OF ORGANIZATIONS

508 Names of well-known business organizations, labor unions, societies, and associations (trade, professional, charitable, and fraternal) often appear in abbreviated form, except in the most formal writing. When these abbreviations consist of all-capital initials, they are typed without periods or spaces.

IBM	International Business Machines
AT&T	American Telephone & Telegraph
AFL-CIO	American Federation of Labor and Congress of Industrial Organizations
ILGWU	International Ladies' Garment Workers' Union
AMS	Administrative Management Society
ASCAP	American Society of Composers, Authors, and Publishers
NAM	National Association of Manufacturers
CED	Committee for Economic Development
YMCA	Young Men's Christian Association
IOOF	Independent Order of Odd Fellows

NAMES OF BROADCASTING STATIONS AND SYSTEMS

509 The names of radio and television broadcasting stations and the abbreviated names of broadcasting systems are written in capitals without periods and without spaces.

Station KFRC   Station WPIX-Channel 11
Station WQXR-FM   Station WCBS-TV
ABC reporters   CBS officials

NAMES OF GOVERNMENT AND INTERNATIONAL AGENCIES

510 The names of well-known government and international agencies are often abbreviated. They are written without periods or spaces.

FCC Federal Communications   SEC Securities and Exchange
       Commission   Commission
UN   United Nations   ITO International Trade Organization

511 The name *United States* is often abbreviated when it is part of the name of a government agency. In all other uses, however, it should be spelled out.

U.S. Office of Education   **OR** USOE
U.S. Department of Agriculture **OR** USDA
U.S. Air Force   **OR** USAF

BUT: throughout the United States (**NOT:** throughout the U.S.)
     the United States government

GEOGRAPHICAL NAMES

512 Geographical abbreviations made up of single initials require a period after each initial but *no* space after each internal period.

U.S.A.   U.S.S.R.   S.A.   B.W.I.

NOTE: The U.S. Postal Service has introduced a new set of two-letter abbreviations for all state names. These abbreviations are typed in all capitals, without periods or internal space. (See ¶ 1426.)

513 If the geographical abbreviation contains more than single initials, space once after each internal period.

N. Mex.   N. Dak.   W. Va.   W. Aust.

▶ See ¶¶ 1420–1423, 1425–1426, 1428–1429 for the abbreviation or the spelling out of names of streets, cities, states, and countries.

COMPASS POINTS

514 Spell out compass points when they are used as ordinary nouns and adjectives.

He has large landholdings in the *Southwest.*

We purchased a lot at the *southwest* corner of Green and Union Streets.

▶ See ¶ 333 for the capitalization of compass points.

515 Spell out compass points included in street names; for example, *East 123d Street.* (See also ¶ 1420.) However, abbreviate compass points (with periods but no internal space) when they are used *following* a street name to indicate the section of the city.

1895 North 179th Street, N.W.

516 In technical work (real estate, legal, nautical), abbreviate compass points but omit the periods.

S   south   SW   southwest   SSW   south-southwest

DAYS, MONTHS, AND YEAR DATES

517 Do not abbreviate names of days of the week and months of the year except in tables or lists where space is limited. In such cases the following abbreviations may be used:

Sun.	Thurs., Thu.	Jan.	May	Sept.,Sep.
Mon.	Fri.	Feb.	June, Jun.	Oct.
Tues., Tue.	Sat.	Mar.	July, Jul.	Nov.
Wed.		Apr	Aug.	Dec.

TIME AND TIME ZONES

518 Use the abbreviations *a.m.* and *p.m.* in expressions of time. Small letters are preferred for these abbreviations. (See also ¶¶ 453, 502a.)

519 The standard time zones are abbreviated as follows: EST, CST, MST, and PST. When daylight saving prevails, the following forms are used:

DST (daylight saving time)   **OR**   EDT (Eastern daylight time)
CDT (Central daylight time)
MDT (Mountain daylight time)
PDT (Pacific daylight time)

MEASUREMENTS: WEIGHT, LENGTH, CAPACITY, AREA, VOLUME, TEMPERATURE

520 Abbreviate units of measure when they occur frequently, as in technical and scientific work, on invoices and other business forms, and in tabulated material.

a room 10 ft. 6 in. x 19 ft. 10 in.   **OR**   10′ 6″ x 19′ 10″ (see ¶ 432)

35° to 45° F.   **OR**   35°–45° F.   5½ x 8 in. (see ¶ 459)

NOTE: In technical matter, units of measure are often abbreviated without periods except where confusion might result.

rpm **(RATHER THAN:** r.p.m.)   **BUT:** in. **(RATHER THAN:** in)
ft   **(RATHER THAN:** ft.)

521 | 532

521 In nontechnical writing, spell out units of measure.

a 20-gallon container	a 20-degree drop in temperature
a 150-acre estate	8½ by 11 inches
14 yards of cotton	an 8½- by 11-inch book (see ¶ 812)

CHEMICAL AND MATHEMATICAL SYMBOLS
AND ABBREVIATIONS

522 Do not use a period after the symbols that represent chemical elements and formulas.

    K (potassium) H_2O (water)   NaCl (sodium chloride—table salt)

523 Do not use a period after such mathematical abbreviations as *log* (for *logarithm*) and *tan* (for *tangent*).

BUSINESS TERMS

524 The following terms are commonly abbreviated in business writing. Although some of the terms have several possible forms, only the form most frequently used is listed below.

FICA	Federal Insurance Contributions Act
FIFO	first in, first out
FUTA	Federal Unemployment Tax Act
FYI	for your information
GNP	gross national product
LCL	less-than-carload lot
LIFO	last in, first out
n/30	net amount due in 30 days
PERT	program evaluation and review technique
PR	public relations
R&D	research and development

525 A few common business abbreviations are often typed in small letters (with periods) when they occur within sentences but are typed in all-capital letters (without periods) when they appear on invoices or other business forms.

c.i.f. **OR** CIF	cost, insurance, and freight	e.o.m. **OR** EOM end of month
c.o.d. **OR** COD	cash on delivery	f.o.b. **OR** FOB free on board

FOREIGN EXPRESSIONS

526 Many foreign expressions contain short words, some of which are abbreviations and some of which are not. Use periods only with abbreviations.

ad hoc	(meaning "for a particular purpose")
e.g.	(*exempli gratia*, meaning "for example")
et al.	(*et alii*, meaning "and other people")
etc.	(*et cetera*, meaning "and other things," "and so forth")
ibid.	(*ibidem*, meaning "in the same place")
idem	(meaning "the same")
i.e.	(*id est*, meaning "that is")
loc. cit.	(*loco citato*, meaning "in the place cited")
N.B.	(*nota bene*, meaning "note well")
op. cit.	(*opere citato*, meaning "in the work cited")
re **OR** in re	(meaning "in the matter of," "concerning")
R.S.V.P.	(*répondez s'il vous plait*, meaning "please reply")

MISCELLANEOUS EXPRESSIONS

527   Do not use periods with capitalized letters that are not abbreviations.

IOU   Brand X   SOS   Customer A

BUT: Mr. A. (when *A* is an actual abbreviation of the man's last name).

528   The abbreviation *OK* is now commonly written without periods. In sentences, the forms *okay, okayed,* and *okaying* look better than *OK, OK'd,* and *OK'ing,* but the latter forms can be used.

529   The dictionary recognizes *x* as a verb; however, *cross out, crossed out,* and *crossing out* look better than *x out, x-ed out,* and *x-ing out.*

CAPITALIZATION AND HYPHENATION

530   Abbreviations usually follow the capitalization and hyphenation of the full words for which they stand.

| Mon. | Monday | a.m. | ante meridiem |
| ft.-lb. | foot-pound | D.C. | District of Columbia |

EXCEPTIONS: PTA   Parent-Teachers' Association   A.D.   anno Domini

▶   See also ¶ 525.

PUNCTUATION AND SPACING WITH ABBREVIATIONS

531   The abbreviation of a single word requires a period at the end.

| Mr. | Jr. | Dr. | cont. | Nos. |
| Mon. | Inc. | Co. | mfg. | pp. |

▶   See ¶ 520, note, for exceptions.

532   Small-letter abbreviations made up of single initials require a period after each initial but no space after each internal period.

a.m.   p.m.   f.o.b.   **BUT:** r.p.m.   **OR**   rpm

▶   See ¶ 520, note, for exceptions such as *rpm.*

533 All-capital abbreviations made up of single initials normally require *no periods* and *no internal space.*

RCA	ASME	FBI	CBS	IQ
UAW	BPOE	AID	WABC	FM

EXCEPTIONS: Retain the periods in abbreviations of geographical names (such as *U.S.A., U.S.S.R.*), academic degrees (such as *B.A., M.S.*), and a few miscellaneous expressions (such as *A.D., B.C.*).

534 If an abbreviation contains more than single initials, space once after each internal period.

sq. ft.	cu. in.	fl. oz.	gr. wt.	op. cit.

EXCEPTIONS: Ph.D., Ed.D., LL.B., Litt.D., and similar academic abbreviations

535 Initials in a person's name (or in a company name) should each be followed by a period and one space.

John T. Noonan   Mr. L. B. Anders
J. T. Noonan & Co.   L. B. Anders, Inc.

When personal initials stand alone, periods and internal space may be omitted.

JTN   OR   J.T.N.

536 *One space* should follow an abbreviation within a sentence unless another mark of punctuation must follow immediately.

Dr. Wilkins works in Washington, D.C., but his home is in Bethesda.
Please call tomorrow afternoon (before 5:30 p.m.).
Get JTN's approval before you send the letter. (See ¶¶ 640–641 for possessive forms of abbreviations.)

537 *Two spaces* should follow an abbreviation at the end of a statement.

The vase dates back to 400 B.C. (The period that marks the end of the abbreviation also marks the end of the sentence.)

538 *No space* should follow an abbreviation at the end of a question or an exclamation.

Can you see me tomorrow at 10:30 a.m.?

▶ Plurals of abbreviations: see ¶¶ 619–623.
Possessives of abbreviations: see ¶¶ 640–641.

Section 6
PLURALS AND POSSESSIVES

FORMING PLURALS

When you are uncertain about the plural form of a word, consult the dictionary. If no plural is shown, form the plural according to the rules in ¶¶ 601–605.

BASIC RULE

601 Plurals are regularly formed by adding *s* to the singular form.

    park   parks   employee   employees

NOUNS ENDING IN <u>S</u>, <u>X</u>, <u>CH</u>, <u>SH</u>, OR <u>Z</u>

602 When the singular form ends in *s, x, ch, sh,* or *z,* the plural is formed by adding *es* to the singular.

gas	gases	church	churches
business	businesses	sash	sashes
annex	annexes	quartz	quartzes

603 Singular nouns ending in silent *s* do not change their forms in the plural.

    one corps   two corps   one chassis   two chassis

NOUNS ENDING IN <u>Y</u>

604 When a singular noun ends in *y* preceded by a *consonant,* the plural is formed by changing the *y* to *i* and adding *es* to the singular.

company	companies	category	categories
vacancy	vacancies	authority	authorities

605 When a singular noun ends in *y* preceded by a *vowel,* the plural is formed by adding *s* to the singular.

    attorney   attorneys   EXCEPTION: soliloquy   soliloquies

NOUNS ENDING IN <u>O</u>

606 Singular nouns ending in *o* preceded by a *vowel* form their plurals by adding *s* to the singular.

    studio   studios   duo   duos

607   Singular nouns ending in *o* preceded by a *consonant* form their plurals differently.

a. Most nouns in this category simply add *s*.

piano   pianos   dynamo   dynamos

b. Some nouns in this category add *es*.

potato   potatoes   hero   heroes

c. Some of these nouns have two plural forms. (The preferred form is given first.)

cargo   cargoes, cargos   zero   zeros, zeroes

NOUNS ENDING IN F, FE, OR FF

608   **a.** Most singular nouns that end in *f, fe,* or *ff* form their plurals by adding *s*.

brief   briefs   safe   safes
proof   proofs   tariff   tariffs

b. Some commonly used nouns in this category form their plurals by changing the *f* or *fe* to *ve* and adding *s*.

half   halves   shelf   shelves
wife   wives   knife   knives
leaf   leaves   life   lives

c. A few of these nouns have two plural forms. (The preferred form is given first.)

scarf   scarves, scarfs   dwarf   dwarfs, dwarves

NOUNS WITH IRREGULAR PLURALS

609   The plurals of some nouns are formed by a change of letters within.

woman   women   foot   feet
mouse   mice   goose   geese

NOTE: The following nouns take regular plurals:

ottoman   ottomans   mongoose   mongooses

610   A few plurals end in *en*.

ox   oxen   child   children
brother   brethren (*an alternative plural to* brothers)

COMPOUND NOUNS

611   When a compound noun is a solid word, pluralize the final element in the compound as if it stood alone.

court*house*	court*houses*	fore*foot*	fore*feet*
hat*box*	hat*boxes*	tooth*brush*	tooth*brushes*
book*shelf*	book*shelves*	mouse*trap*	mouse*traps*
step*child*	step*children*		

EXCEPTION: *passerby*   *passersby*

612   The plurals of hyphenated or spaced compounds are formed by adding the plural sign to the chief element of the compound.

brother-in-law	*brothers*-in-law	*bill* of lading	*bills* of lading
senator-elect	*senators*-elect	*editor* in chief	*editors* in chief
looker-on	*lookers*-on	*runner*-up	*runners*-up

a. When a hyphenated compound does not contain a noun as one of its elements, simply pluralize the final element.

go-*between*	go-*betweens*	tie-*in*	tie-*ins*
write-*up*	write-*ups*	hand-me-*down*	hand-me-*downs*

b. Some of these compounds have two recognized plural forms. (The first plural is the preferred form.)

court-martial	*courts*-martial, court-*martials*
notary public	*notaries* public, notary *publics*
attorney general	*attorneys* general, attorney *generals*

PLURALS OF FOREIGN NOUNS

613   Many nouns of foreign origin retain their foreign plurals; others have been given English plurals; and still others have two plurals—an English and a foreign. When two plural forms exist, one may be preferred to the other or there may be differences in meaning that govern the use of each. Consult your dictionary to be sure of the plural forms and the meanings attached to them.

▶   See ¶ 1017 for agreement of foreign-plural subjects with verbs.

WORDS ENDING IN US

Singular	English Plural	Foreign Plural
alumnus		alumni
campus	campuses	
census	censuses	
nucleus	nucleuses	nuclei*
prospectus	prospectuses	
radius	radiuses	radii*
status	statuses	
stimulus		stimuli
stylus	styluses	styli*
syllabus	syllabuses	syllabi*

*Preferred form.

[Continued on page 98.]

WORDS ENDING IN A

Singular	English Plural	Foreign Plural
agenda	agendas	
alumna		alumnae
antenna	antennas (of radios)	antennae (of insects)
formula	formulas*	formulae

WORDS ENDING IN UM

Singular	English Plural	Foreign Plural
addendum		addenda
bacterium		bacteria
curriculum	curriculums	curricula*
datum	datums	data* (see ¶ 1017)
erratum		errata
medium	mediums	media (for advertising and communication)
memorandum	memorandums*	memoranda
millennium	millenniums	millennia*

WORDS ENDING IN IX OR EX

Singular	English Plural	Foreign Plural
appendix	appendixes*	appendices
executrix	executrixes	executrices*
index	indexes (of books)	indices (math symbols)

WORDS ENDING IN IS

Singular	English Plural	Foreign Plural
analysis		analyses
axis		axes
basis		bases
crisis		crises
diagnosis		diagnoses
hypothesis		hypotheses
parenthesis		parentheses
synopsis		synopses
synthesis		syntheses
thesis		theses

WORDS ENDING IN ON

Singular	English Plural	Foreign Plural
criterion	criterions	criteria*
phenomenon	phenomenons	phenomena*

WORDS ENDING IN EAU

Singular	English Plural	Foreign Plural
bureau	bureaus*	bureaux
plateau	plateaus*	plateaux
trousseau	trousseaus	trousseaux*

NOTE: The x ending for these foreign plurals is pronounced as s.

*Preferred form.

PROPER NAMES

614   **a.** Most *surnames* are pluralized by the addition of *s.*

Mr. and Mrs. Brinton	the Brintons
Mr. and Mrs. Van Allen	the Van Allens

b. When a surname ends in *s, x, ch, sh,* or *z,* add *es* to form the plural.

Mr. and Mrs. Banks	the Bankses
Mr. and Mrs. Van Ness	the Van Nesses
Mr. and Mrs. Maddox	the Maddoxes
Mr. and Mrs. March	the Marches
Mr. and Mrs. Welsh	the Welshes
Mr. and Mrs. Katz	the Katzes

NOTE: Add *es* to form the plural, even though the singular form already ends in *es*

the Joneses	the Barneses
the Jameses	the Gaineses

c. Never change the original spelling of a surname when forming the plural. Simply add *s* or *es,* according to *a* and *b* above.

Mr. and Mrs. McCarthy	the McCarthys (**NOT:** McCarthies)
Mr. and Mrs. Wolf	the Wolfs (**NOT:** Wolves)
Mr. and Mrs. Martino	the Martinos (**NOT:** Martinoes)
Mr. and Mrs. Goodman	the Goodmans (**NOT:** Goodmen)

615   To form the plurals of *first names,* add *s* or *es* but do not change the original spellings.

Marie	Maries	Mary	Marys
Thomas	Thomases	Max	Maxes
Charles	Charleses	Otto	Ottos

616   To form the plurals of *place names,* add *s* or *es.* Do not change the original spelling.

the Dakotas	the two Kansas Citys (**NOT:** Cities)

EXCEPTIONS:

the Alleghenies (for Allegheny Mountains)	the Rockies (for Rocky Mountains)

PERSONAL TITLES

617   The plural of *Mr.* is *Messrs.;* the plural of *Mrs.* or *Mme.* is *Mmes.;* the plural of *Miss* is *Misses* (no period follows).

Messrs. Walton and Finch have been appointed to the Finance Committee.

Mmes. Hopkins and Brown will handle all the arrangements for the luncheon.

Misses Eleanor Harris and Frances Cole will arrange for transportation.

NOTE: If the use of plural titles seems too formal or stilted for the situation, simply retain the singular form and repeat it with each name.

Miss Eleanor Harris and *Miss* Frances Cole will arrange for transportation.

618 When personal titles apply to two or more people with the same surname, the plural may be formed in two ways: (a) pluralize only the title (formal style); (b) pluralize only the surname (informal style).

Formal	**Informal**
the Messrs. Thomas	the Mr. Thomases
the Mmes. (or Mesdames) Bergeret	the Mrs. Bergerets
the Misses Corby	the Miss Corbys

ABBREVIATIONS, LETTERS, NUMBERS, AND WORDS

619 The plurals of most abbreviations are formed by adding *s* to the singular.

dept. depts.   yr. yrs.   No. Nos.   mo. mos.

620 The abbreviations of many units of weight and measure, however, are the same in both the singular and plural.

oz.   (for ounce and ounces)   ft.   (for foot and feet)
deg. (for degree and degrees)   in.   (for inch and inches)

NOTE: For a number of these abbreviations, two plural forms are widely used: for example, *lb.* or *lbs.* (meaning "pounds"), *yd.* or *yds.* (meaning "yards"), *qt.* or *qts.* (meaning "quarts").

621 The plurals of a few single-letter abbreviations (such as *p.* for *page* and *f.* for the *following page*) consist of the same letter doubled.

p. 39 (page 39)
pp. 39–43 (pages 39 through 43)

pp. 12 f. (page 12 and the following page)
pp. 12 ff. (page 12 and the following pages)

622 Capital letters and abbreviations ending with capital letters are pluralized by adding *s* alone.

four Cs   PTAs   M.D.s   three Rs   YWCAs   Ph.D.s

NOTE: Some authorities still sanction the use of an apostrophe before the *s* (for example, *four C's, PTA's*). However, the apostrophe is functionally unnecessary except where confusion might otherwise result.

623 For the sake of clarity, uncapitalized letters and uncapitalized abbreviations with internal periods are pluralized by adding an apostrophe plus *s*.

dotting the *i*'s   counting the c.o.d.'s

624 Numbers expressed in figures are pluralized by the addition of *s* alone. (See, however, ¶ 622, note.)

in the 1970s   temperature in the 80s

Numbers expressed in words are pluralized by the addition of *s* or *es*.

ones   twos   sixes   twenties   twenty-fives •

625 When words taken from other parts of speech are used as nouns, they are usually pluralized by the addition of *s* or *es*.

ands, ifs, and buts	pros and cons
dos and don'ts	whys and wherefores
yeses and noes	yeas and nays
the haves and the have-nots	the ins and outs

If the pluralized form is unfamiliar or is likely to be misread, use an apostrophe plus s to form the plural.

which's and that's	or's and nor's

If the singular form already contains an apostrophe, simply add s to form the plural.

ain'ts	doesn'ts	don'ts

NOUNS ALWAYS SINGULAR

626 Some nouns are always singular.

courage	arithmetic	news	music

NOUNS ALWAYS PLURAL

627 Each of the following nouns is plural in form and takes a plural verb when used as a subject, even though it refers collectively to a single thing.

auspices	pants	riches	thanks
credentials	pliers	savings	trousers
goods	proceeds	scissors	winnings
grounds	remains	shears	works (mechanism)

NOUNS HAVING THE SAME SINGULAR AND PLURAL FORM

628 Some nouns have the same form for both the singular and the plural. (See ¶ 1015 for agreement of verbs with these words as subjects.)

deer	sheep	moose	series

FORMING POSSESSIVES

POSSESSION VERSUS DESCRIPTION

629 An s-ending noun that is followed immediately by another noun is usually in the possessive form.

the employee's record (meaning the record of the employee)

Saunders' merchandise (meaning the merchandise of the Saunders store)

Thackeray's novels (meaning novels written by Thackeray)

To be sure that the possessive form should be used, try substituting an *of* phrase or a *by* phrase as in the examples above. If the substitution works, the possessive form is correct.

630   Do not mistake a descriptive form ending in *s* for a possessive form.

> sales effort (*sales* describes the kind of effort; the meaning is not "the effort of sales")
>
> savings account (*savings* describes the kind of account)

▶   See ¶ 1414e for descriptive and possessive forms in organizational names.

631   In a number of cases, only a slight difference in wording distinguishes a descriptive phrase from a possessive phrase. Compare the following examples:

Descriptive	Possessive
a two-week vacation	a two weeks' vacation
the New Jersey sales tax	New Jersey's sales tax
the Hess estate	Hess's estate
the Wilson house	the Wilsons' house

SINGULAR NOUNS

632   To form the possessive of a singular noun *not* ending in *s* or in an *s* sound, add an apostrophe plus *s* to the noun.

a man's self-respect	Mr. and Mrs. Fenton's claim
the company's assets	Sylvia's promotion

633   To form the possessive of a singular noun that ends in *s* or an *s* sound, be guided by the way the word is pronounced.

a. If a new syllable is formed in the pronunciation of the possessive, add an apostrophe plus *s*.

my boss's desk	Harris's letter
the witness's testimony	Mr. Jones's book

b. If the addition of an extra syllable would make an *s*-ending word hard to pronounce, add the apostrophe only.

Mr. Hawkins' order	Mr. Phillips' pen
for goodness' sake	Simmons' factory

CAUTION: In forming the possessive of any noun ending in *s*, always place the apostrophe at the end of the original word, never within it.

> Mr. Hodges' message (NOT: Mr. Hodge's message)

PLURAL NOUNS

634   To form the possessive of a *regular* plural noun, add only an apostrophe. (See ¶ 1414e for the use of the apostrophe in organizational names.)

students' marks	attorneys' offices
the witnesses' testimonies	the Joneses' contributions
a sellers' market	ladies' day

NOTE: Since the singular and plural possessives for the same word usually sound exactly alike, pay particularly close attention to the meaning in order to determine whether the noun in question is singular or plural.

A student's marks may not give a full picture of his abilities.

BUT: Students' marks must be submitted by Friday.

We have been invited to Mr. and Mrs. Jones's home.

BUT: We have been invited to the Joneses' home.

635 To form the possessive of an *irregular* plural noun, add an apostrophe plus *s*.

men's suits   children's shoes

IMPORTANT NOTE: To avoid mistakes in forming the possessive of plural nouns, form the plural first; then apply the rule in ¶ 634 or 635, whichever fits.

Singular	Plural	Plural Possessive
boy	boys	boys'
boss	bosses	bosses'
child	children	children's
alumnus	alumni	alumni's

COMPOUND NOUNS

636 To form the *singular* possessive of a compound noun (whether solid, spaced, or hyphenated), add an apostrophe plus *s* to the last element of the compound.

my mother-in-law's will   a businessman's investment
the secretary-treasurer's report   the attorney general's power

637 To form the *plural* possessive of a compound noun, first form the plural.

a. If the plural form ends in *s*, add only an apostrophe.

Singular	Plural	Plural Possessive
stockholder	stockholders	stockholders'
district attorney	district attorneys	district attorneys'
vice president	vice presidents	vice presidents'

b. If the plural form does not end in *s*, add an apostrophe plus *s*.

Singular	Plural	Plural Possessive
saleswoman	saleswomen	saleswomen's
editor in chief	editors in chief	editors in chief's
brother-in-law	brothers-in-law	brothers-in-law's

NOTE: To avoid the awkwardness of a plural possessive such as *editors in chief's* or *brothers-in-law's,* rephrase the sentence.

AWKWARD: Anderson's statement agrees with both *attorneys general's* views.

BETTER: Anderson's statement agrees with the views of both *attorneys general.*

PRONOUNS

638 The possessive forms of *personal pronouns* and of the relative pronoun *who* do not require the apostrophe. Each pronoun has its own special possessive form.

I: my, mine	she: her, hers	they: their, theirs
you: your, yours	it: its	who: whose
he: his	we: our, ours	

CAUTION: Do not confuse personal possessive pronouns with similarly spelled contractions. (See ¶ 1048*d* for examples.)

639 Some *indefinite pronouns* have regular possessive forms.

one's choice	the other's claim	anybody's guess
anyone else's job	the others' claim	no one's responsibility

For those indefinite pronouns that do not have possessive forms, use an *of* phrase.

Although children in this group seem very much alike, the needs *of each* are different. (**NOT:** each's needs.)

ABBREVIATIONS

640 To form the singular possessive of an abbreviation, add an apostrophe plus *s*. To form the plural possessive, add an *s* plus an apostrophe to the singular form. (See also ¶ 641.)

Mr. C.'s opinion	the M.D.s' diagnoses	the CPA's audit
the FCC's ruling	the Ph.D.s' theses	the CPAs' meeting

PERSONAL AND ORGANIZATIONAL NAMES

641 To form the possessive of a personal or organizational name that ends with an abbreviation or a number, add an apostrophe plus *s* at the end of the complete name.

George Thompson, Inc.'s stationery	Mr. John Smith, Jr.'s new house
the A. & V. Co.'s ad	Henry Ford II's announcement

NOTE: The comma is omitted after *Inc.'s* and *Jr.'s* and similar abbreviations in order to bring the possessive element as near as possible to the noun it modifies.

▶ See ¶ 1414e for the names of organizations that contain possessive forms.

NOUNS IN APPOSITION

642 Sometimes a noun that ordinarily would be in the possessive is followed by an explanatory word. In such cases add the sign of the possessive to the explanatory word only.

That is Miss Case, the *file clerk's,* responsibility.

NOTE: This kind of construction is usually awkward; whenever possible, use an *of* phrase instead.

That is the responsibility *of Miss Case,* the file clerk.

SEPARATE AND JOINT POSSESSION

643 To indicate separate possession, add the sign of the possessive to the name of each individual.

the buyer's and the seller's signatures   the Joneses' and the Browns' houses

NOTE: The repetition of *the* with each noun further indicates that separate ownership is intended.

644 To indicate joint (or common) ownership, add the sign of the possessive to the *final* noun alone.

Bruce & Hall's Department Store   Tom and Ed's boat

POSSESSIVES STANDING ALONE

645 Sometimes the noun that the possessive modifies is merely understood.

Please call for my order at the *grocer's* (store).
Mary's (transcript) was the best transcript handed in.
This month's sales figures are better than last *month's* (sales figures).

INANIMATE POSSESSIVES

646 As a rule, nouns referring to inanimate things should not be in the possessive. Use an *of* phrase instead.

the hood of the car (**NOT:** the car's hood)
the terms of the contract (**NOT:** the contract's terms)
the format of the letter (**NOT:** the letter's format)

647 In many common expressions that refer to time and measurements, however, and in phrases implying personification, the possessive form has come to be accepted usage. (See also ¶ 812*b*.)

one day's notice	a dollar's worth	a stone's throw
an hour's work	several dollars' worth	for heaven's sake
two years' progress	at arm's length	for conscience' sake
the company's assets	New Year's resolutions	(see ¶ 633*b*)
the sun's rays	this morning's news	the earth's atmosphere

POSSESSIVES PRECEDING VERBAL NOUNS

648 When a noun or a pronoun modifies a gerund (the *ing* form of a verb used as a noun), the noun or pronoun should be in the possessive form.

[Continued on page 106.]

I am opposed to *your* entering that school.

Was there a report of the *salesman's* being recalled?

The *dog's* barking awakened us.

POSSESSIVES IN OF PHRASES

649 The object of the preposition *of* should not be in the possessive form since the *of* phrase as a whole expresses possession. However, possessives are used in a few idiomatic expressions.

He is a friend of *Tom's*. (**NOT**: of Tom.)

He is a neighbor of *mine*. (**NOT**: of me.)

POSSESSIVES MODIFYING POSSESSIVES

650 Avoid attaching a possessive form to another possessive. Change the wording if possible.

AWKWARD: I have not yet seen the *utility company's lawyer's* petition.

BETTER: I have not yet seen the petition of the *utility company's* lawyer.

Section 7
SPELLING

In matters of spelling, the most important rule is this: *When in doubt, consult the dictionary*. The next most important rule: *Try to master the principles of spelling so as to avoid frequent trips to the dictionary*.

Section 7 offers two kinds of assistance to the puzzled speller. ¶¶ 701–714 present the basic guidelines for correct spelling. ¶ 715 provides a 12-page list of look-alike and sound-alike words for review and fast reference.

NOTE: *Webster's Seventh New Collegiate Dictionary* (published by the G. & C. Merriam Company) is the authority for the spelling in this manual. Whenever two spellings are allowable, only the first form is usually given here.

SPELLING GUIDES

WHEN A FINAL CONSONANT IS DOUBLED

701 When a word of one syllable ends in a single consonant (ba<u>g</u>) preceded by a single vowel (b<u>a</u>g), double the final consonant before a suffix beginning with a vowel (bagg<u>age</u>) or before the suffix y (bagg<u>y</u>).

drop	dropped	swim	swimming	ship	shipper
slip	slippage	glad	gladden	bet	bettor
clan	clannish	skin	skinny	chum	chummy

EXCEPTION: gas   gaseous

▶   Compare ¶ 703.

702   When a word of more than one syllable ends in a single consonant (defe*r*) preceded by a single vowel (def*e*r) and the accent falls on the last syllable of the root word (de*fer*), double the final consonant before a suffix beginning with a vowel (deferr*ed*).

begin	beginning	transfer	transferred (**BUT:** transferable)
concur	concurrent	control	controller

NOTE: If the accent *shifts* to the first syllable of a word when a suffix beginning with a vowel is added, the final consonant is not doubled.

defer	deferred	**BUT:** deference	prefer	preferred	**BUT:** preferable

▶   Compare ¶ 704.

WHEN A FINAL CONSONANT IS NOT DOUBLED

703   When a word of one syllable ends in a single consonant (ba*d*) preceded by a single vowel (b*a*d), *do not* double the final consonant before a suffix beginning with a *consonant* (bad*ly*).

ship	ship*ment*	glad	glad*ness*	drop	drop*let*

704   When a word of more than one syllable ends in a single consonant (benefi*t*) preceded by a single vowel (benef*i*t) and the accent *does not* fall on the last syllable of the root word (*ben*efit), *do not* double the final consonant before a suffix beginning with a vowel (benefit*ed*).

profit	profited, profiting	parallel	paralleled, paralleling
differ	differed, differing	cancel	canceled, canceling
credit	credited, creditor		(**BUT:** cancellation)

EXCEPTIONS:

program	programmed, programming	kidnap	kidnapped, kidnapping

705   When a word of one or more syllables ends in a single consonant (clou*d*, repea*t*) preceded by more than one vowel (cl*ou*d, rep*ea*t), do not double the final consonant before any suffix, whether it begins with a consonant or a vowel (cloud*less*, repeat*ing*).

eat	eaten	deceit	deceitful
look	looking	chief	chiefly
groan	groaned	wood	woody

706   When a word of one or more syllables ends with more than one consonant (wo*rk*, deta*ch*), do not double the final consonant before any suffix (work*man*, detach*ed*).

confirm	confirming	hand	handful
return	returned	warm	warmly

[Continued on page 108.]

NOTE: Words ending in *ll* usually retain both consonants before a suffix. However, when adding the suffix *ly,* drop one *l* from the root word; when adding the suffixes *less* or *like,* insert a hyphen between the root and the suffix.

| skill | skillful | full | fully | hull | hull-less |
| install | installment | dull | dully | shell | shell-like |

FINAL SILENT E

707 Words ending in silent e usually *drop* the e before a suffix beginning with a vowel.

use	us*age*	judge	judg*ing*
force	for*cible*	desire	desir*ous*
separate	separat*ing*	arrive	arriva*l*

EXCEPTIONS:

notice	noticeable	manage	manageable
advantage	advantageous	mile	mileage
Europe	European	dye	dyeing
service	serviceable	outrage	outrageous

708 Words ending in silent e usually *retain* the e before a suffix beginning with a consonant.

| manage | management (**BUT:** managing) | excite | excitement (**BUT:** excitable) |
| like | likeness (**BUT:** likable) | agree | agreement (**ALSO:** agreeing) |

EXCEPTIONS:

judge	judgment	acknowledge	acknowledgment
whole	wholly	argue	argument
nine	ninth	true	truly
gentle	gently	due	duly

WHEN FINAL Y IS CHANGED TO I

709 Words ending in y preceded by a consonant change the y to i before any suffix except one beginning with i.

ordinary	ordinari*ly*	heavy	heavi*est*	**BUT:** bury	bury*ing*
happy	happi*ness*	defy	defi*ant*	thirty	thirty*ish*
likely	likeli*hood*	modify	modifi*er*	copy	copy*ist*

710 Words ending in y preceded by a vowel usually retain the y before any suffix.

| delay | delayed | annoy | annoyance |
| obey | obeying | betray | betrayal |

EXCEPTIONS:

| pay | paid | day | daily |
| lay | laid | say | said |

EI AND IE WORDS

711   Put *i* before *e*   Or when sounded like *a*
      Except after *c*   As in *neighbor* and *weigh*.

I before e   **After c**
chief   field   niece   piece   deceive   ceiling
brief   yield   variety fierce   receipt   receive

Sounded like a   EXCEPTIONS:
freight   their   eight   seize   weird   forfeit
weight   heir   vein   height   ancient   financier

WORDS ENDING IN ABLE AND IBLE

712   The more usual ending is *able*. However, some of the most commonly used words end with *ible*.

advis*able*   prob*able*   receiv*able*   sal*able*   valu*able*
collect*ible*   divis*ible*   flex*ible*   permiss*ible* suscept*ible*

WORDS ENDING IN CEDE, CEED, AND SEDE

713   **a.** Only *one* word ends in *sede: supersede.*

b. Only *three* words end in *ceed: exceed, proceed, succeed.* (Note, however, that derivatives of these three words are spelled with only one *e*: *excess, procedure, success.*)

c. All other words ending with the syllable pronounced "seed" are spelled *cede: precede, secede, recede, concede.*

WORDS ENDING IN ISE, IZE, AND YZE

714   The most usual ending is *ize*. However, some of the most commonly used words end with *ise*. Only a few words end with *yze*.

apolog*ize*   author*ize*   critic*ize*   real*ize*   summar*ize*
advert*ise*   comprom*ise*   exerc*ise*   merchand*ise* superv*ise*
analyze   paralyze

WORDS THAT SOUND ALIKE OR LOOK ALIKE

715   The following list contains two types of words: (a) words that are pronounced *exactly alike*, though spelled differently, and for which the shorthand outlines are therefore identical; and (b) words that look and sound *somewhat alike*, and for which the shorthand outlines may be very nearly the same.

NOTE: A small triangle is used to mark the start of each group of similar words.

▸accede	to comply with
exceed	to surpass
▸accent	stress in speech or writing
ascent	act of rising
assent	consent
▸accept	to take; to receive
except	(v.) to exclude; (prep.) excluding
▸access	admittance
excess	surplus
▸ ad	short for *advertisement*
add	to join
▸adapt	to adjust
adept	proficient
adopt	to choose
▸addenda	(see *agenda*)
▸addition	something added
edition	one version of a printed work
▸adherence	attachment
adherents	followers
▸adverse	opposing
averse	disinclined
▸advice	(n.) information; recommendation
advise	(v.) to recommend; to give counsel
▸affect	to influence; to change; to assume (always a verb)
effect	(n.) result; outcome; (v.) to fulfill; to bring about
▸agenda	list of things to be done
addenda	additional items
▸air	atmosphere
heir	one who inherits
▸aisle	(see *isle*)
▸allowed	permitted
aloud	audibly
▸allusion	an indirect reference
illusion	an unreal vision
delusion	a false belief
elusion	adroit escape
▸almost	nearly (see ¶ 1101)
all most	all very much

▸already	previously (see ¶1101)
all ready	all prepared
▸altar	part of a church
alter	to change
▸alternate	(n.) substitute; (v.) to take turns
alternative	(n.) one of several things from which to choose
▸altogether	entirely (see ¶ 1101)
all together	everyone in a group
▸always	at all times (see ¶ 1101)
all ways	all means or methods
▸annual	yearly
annul	to cancel
▸ante-	a prefix meaning "before"
anti-	a prefix meaning "against"
▸antecedence	priority
antecedents	preceding things; ancestors
▸anyone	anybody (see ¶ 1101)
any one	any one person in a group
▸anyway	in any case (see ¶ 1101)
any way	any method
▸apportion	(see *portion*)
▸appraise	to set a value on
apprise	to inform
▸area	surface; extent
aria	a melody
arrears	that which is due but unpaid
▸arrange	to put in order
arraign	to call into court
▸ascent	(see *accent*)
▸assay	to test, as an ore or a chemical
essay	(n.) a treatise; (v.) to attempt
▸assent	(see *accent*)
▸assistance	help
assistants	those who help
▸assure	(see *ensure*)
▸attain	to gain; to achieve
attend	to be present at

▸**attendance** — presence
attendants — escorts; followers; companions; associates
▸**aught** — anything (incorrect for *naught,* meaning "cipher")
ought — should
▸**averse** — (see *adverse*)
▸**awhile** — (adv.) for a short time
a while — (phrase) a short period of time (see ¶ 1101)
▸**bail** — (n.) security; the handle of a pail; (v.) to dip water
bale — a bundle
▸**bare** — naked; exposed; empty
bear — (n.) an animal; (v.) to carry; to endure; to produce
▸**base** — (n.) foundation; (adj.) mean
bass — lower notes in music; a fish
▸**bases** — plural of *base* and of *basis*
basis — foundation
▸**beat** — (n.) throb; tempo; (v.) to strike
beet — a vegetable
▸**berry** — a fruit
bury — to submerge; to cover over
▸**berth** — a bed
birth — being born
▸**beside** — by the side of; separate from
besides — in addition to; also
▸**biannual** — occurring twice a year
biennial — occurring once in two years
▸**bibliography** — list of writings pertaining to a given subject or author
biography — written history of a person's life
▸**billed** — charged
build — to construct

▸**board** — a piece of wood; an organized group; meals
bored — penetrated; wearied
▸**boarder** — one who pays for his meals and often his lodging as well
border — edge
▸**bolder** — more daring
boulder — a large rock
▸**born** — brought into life
borne — carried; endured
▸**boy** — a male child
buoy — a float
▸**brake** — (n.) a retarding device; (v.) to retard
break — (n.) an opening; a fracture; (v.) to shatter; to divide
▸**bread** — food
bred — brought up
▸**breath** — respiration
breathe — (v.) to inhale and exhale
breadth — width
▸**broach** — to open; to introduce
brooch — ornamental clasp
▸**build** — (see *billed*)
▸**bullion** — uncoined gold or silver
bouillon — broth
▸**bury** — (see *berry*)
▸**calendar** — a record of time
calender — a machine used in finishing paper and cloth
colander — a strainer
▸**callous** — (adj.) hardened
callus — (n.) a hardened surface
▸**cannot** — usual form
can not — two words in the phrase *can not only*
▸**canvas** — (n.) a coarse cloth
canvass — (v.) to solicit
▸**capital** — (n.) a seat of government; a principal sum of money; a large-sized letter; (adj.) chief; foremost

capitol	the building in which a state legislative body meets
Capitol	the building in which the U.S. Congress meets
►carton	a pasteboard box
cartoon	a caricature
►casual	incidental
causal	pertaining to a cause
►cease	to stop
seize	to grasp
►cede	to grant; to give up
seed	that from which anything is grown
►ceiling	top of a room; any overhanging area
sealing	closing
►cell	(see sell)
►cellar	(see seller)
►census	statistics of population
senses	mental faculties
►cent	(see scent)
►cereal	any grain food
serial	arranged in a series
►cession	a yielding up
session	the sitting of a court or other body
►choose	to select
chose	did choose (past tense of choose)
chews	masticates
►chord	combination of musical tones
cord	string or rope
►chute	(see shoot)
►cite	(v.) to quote; to summon
sight	a view; vision
site	a place
►clothes	garments
cloths	fabrics
close	(n.) the end; (v.) to shut
►coarse	rough; common
course	direction; action; a way; part of a meal
►colander	(see calendar)
►collision	a clashing
collusion	a scheme to defraud
►coma	an unconscious state
comma	a mark of punctuation
►command	(n.) an order; (v.) to order
commend	to praise; to entrust
►commence	(v.) to begin
comments	(n.) remarks
►complement	that which completes
compliment	(n.) a flattering speech; (v.) to praise
►comprehensible	understandable
comprehensive	extensive
►confidant	a friend; an adviser (feminine form: confidante)
confident	sure; positive
►confidently	certainly; positively
confidentially	privately
►conscience	(n.) the sense of right and wrong
conscious	(adj.) cognizant; sensible; aware
►conservation	preservation
conversation	a talk
►continual	occurring in rapid and steady succession or at intervals
continuous	uninterrupted; unbroken
►cooperation	the art of working together
corporation	a form of business organization
►cord	(see chord)
►correspondence	letters
correspondents	those who write letters
corespondents	parties in divorce suits
►costume	dress
custom	habit
►council	an assembly
counsel	(n.) an attorney; advice; (v.) to give advice
consul	a foreign representative
►course	(see coarse)

▶courtesy	a favor; politeness	▶device	(n.) a contrivance
curtesy	a husband's life in-terest in the lands of his deceased wife	devise	(v.) to plan; to convey real estate by will
curtsy	a gesture of respect	▶die	(n.) a tool; (v.) to cease living
▶credible	believable		
creditable	meritorious; de-serving of praise	dye	(n.) that which changes the color of; (v.) to change the color of
▶cue	a hint		
queue	a line of people	▶disapprove	to withhold ap-proval
▶currant	a berry		
current	(adj.) belonging to the present; (n.) a flow of water or electricity	disprove	to prove the falsity of
		▶disassemble	to take apart
		dissemble	to disguise; to feign
▶dairy	source of milk products	▶disburse	to pay out
		disperse	to scatter
diary	daily record	▶discreet	prudent
▶deceased	dead	discrete	distinct; separate
diseased	sick	▶disinterested	unbiased; im-partial
▶decent	proper; right		
descent	going down	uninterested	bored; uncon-cerned
dissent	disagreement		
▶decree	a law	▶dissent	(see decent)
degree	a grade; a step	▶divers	various or sundry; plural of diver
▶deduce	to infer		
deduct	to subtract	diverse	different
▶defer	to put off	▶do	to perform
differ	to disagree	due	owing
▶deference	respect; regard for another's wishes	dew	moisture
		▶done	finished
difference	dissimilarity; con-troversy	dun	a demand for pay-ment
▶delusion	(see allusion)	▶dose	a measured quan-tity
▶deposition	a formal written statement		
		doze	to sleep lightly
disposition	temper; disposal	▶dual	double
▶depraved	morally debased	duel	a combat
deprived	taken away from	▶dying	near death
▶deprecate	to disapprove	dyeing	changing the color of
depreciate	to lessen in esti-mated value		
		▶edition	(see addition)
▶desert	(n.) barren land; a deserved reward; (v.) to abandon	▶effect	(see affect)
		▶elapse	(see lapse)
		▶elicit	to draw forth
dessert	the last course of a meal	illicit	unlawful
		▶eligible	fitted; qualified
▶desolate	lonely; sad	illegible	unreadable
dissolute	loose in morals	▶elusion	(see allusion)
▶detract	to take from	▶elusive	baffling; hard to catch
distract	to divert the at-tention of		
		illusive	misleading; unreal

►emerge	to rise out of	►facet	aspect
immerge	to plunge into	faucet	a tap
►emigrate	to go away from a country	►facetious	witty
		factitious	artificial
immigrate	to come into a country	fictitious	imaginary
		►facilitate	to make easy
►eminent	well-known; prominent	felicitate	to congratulate
		►facility	ease
imminent	threatening; impending	felicity	joy
		►fair	(adj.) favorable; just; (n.) an exhibit
emanate	to originate from; to come out of	fare	(n.) cost of travel; food; (v.) to go forth
►en route	(see *root*)		
►ensure	to make certain	►farther	at a greater distance (refers to space)
insure	to protect against loss		
		further	moreover; in addition (refers to time, quantity, or degree)
assure	to give confidence to someone		
►envelop	(v.) to cover; to wrap		
		►faze	to disturb
envelope	(n.) a wrapper for a letter	phase	a stage in development
►equable	even; tranquil	►feet	plural of *foot*
equitable	just; right	feat	an act of skill or strength
►erasable	capable of being erased		
		►fictitious	(see *facetious*)
irascible	quick-tempered	►finale	the end
►especially	to an exceptional degree	finally	at the end
		finely	in a fine manner
specially	particularly, as opposed to generally	►fineness	delicacy
		finesse	tact
		►fir	a tree
►essay	(see *assay*)	fur	skin of an animal
►everyday	daily (see ¶ 1101)	►fiscal	(see *physical*)
every day	each day	►flair	aptitude
►everyone	each one (see ¶ 1101)	flare	a light; a signal
		►flew	did fly
every one	each one in a group	flue	a chimney
►exceed	(see *accede*)	flu	short for *influenza*
►except	(see *accept*)	►flour	ground meal
►excess	(see *access*)	flower	blossom
►expand	to increase in size	►for	a preposition
expend	to spend	fore	first; preceding; the front
►expansive	capable of being extended		
		four	numeral
expensive	costly	►forbear	to bear with
►expatiate	to enlarge on	forebear	an ancestor
expiate	to atone for	►forgo	to relinquish; to let pass
►explicit	easily understood		
implicit	unquestioning	forego	to go before
►extant	still existing		
extent	measure		

►formally	in a formal manner
formerly	before
►fort	a fortified place
forte	(n.) area where one excels
forte	(adj.) loud (musical direction)
►forth	away; forward
fourth	next after third
►forward	ahead
foreword	preface
►foul	unfavorable; unclean
fowl	a bird
►fur	(see *fir*)
►further	(see *farther*)
►genius	talent
genus	a classification in botany or zoology
►gibe	(n.) a sarcastic remark; (v.) to scoff at
jibe	to agree
►grate	(n.) a frame of bars (as in a fireplace); (v.) to scrape; to irritate
great	large; magnificent
►guessed	past tense of *guess*
guest	visitor
►hall	a corridor
haul	to drag
►heal	to cure
heel	part of the foot or a shoe
►healthful	promoting health (e.g., a *healthful* food)
healthy	being in good health (e.g., a *healthy* person)
►hear	to perceive by ear
here	in this place
►heard	past tense of *hear*
herd	a group of animals
►heir	(see *air*)
►holy	sacred
holey	full of holes
wholly	entirely
holly	a tree

►human	pertaining to mankind
humane	kindly
►hypercritical	overcritical
hypocritical	pretending virtue
►ideal	a standard of perfection
idle	unoccupied; without worth
idol	object of worship
idyll	a description of rural life
►illegible	(see *eligible*)
►illicit	(see *elicit*)
►illusion	(see *allusion*)
►illusive	(see *elusive*)
►imitate	to resemble; to mimic
intimate	(adj.) innermost; familiar; (v.) to hint; to make known
►immerge	(see *emerge*)
►immigrate	(see *emigrate*)
►imminent	(see *eminent*)
►implicit	(see *explicit*)
►imply	to suggest (see ¶ 1101)
infer	to deduce
►inane	senseless
insane	of unsound mind
►incidence	range of occurrence
incidents	accidental happenings
►incinerate	to burn
insinuate	to imply
►incite	(v.) to arouse
insight	(n.) understanding
►indict	to consider guilty
indite	to compose and write
►indifferent	without interest
in different	in other (see ¶ 1101)
►indigenous	native
indigent	needy
indignant	angry
►indirect	not direct
in direct	*in* (preposition) + *direct* (adjective) (see ¶ 1101)
►ingenious	clever
ingenuous	naive

▸insoluble	incapable of being dissolved
insolvable	not explainable
insolvent	pertaining to a person unable to pay his debts
▸instants	short periods of time
instance	an example
▸insure	(see *ensure*)
▸intelligent	possessed of understanding
intelligible	understandable
▸intense	acute; strong
intents	aims
▸interstate	between states
intrastate	within one state
▸intimate	(see *imitate*)
▸into, in to	(see ¶ 1101)
▸irascible	(see *erasable*)
▸isle	island
aisle	passage between rows
▸its	possessive form of *it*
it's	contraction of *it is* (see ¶ 1048*d*)
▸jibe	(see *gibe*)
▸lapse	to become void
elapse	to pass
relapse	to slip back into former condition
▸last	final
latest	most recent
▸later	more recent; after a time
latter	second in a series of two
▸lath	a strip of wood
lathe	a wood-turning machine
▸lay	to place (see ¶ 1101)
lie	(n.) a falsehood; (v.) to recline; to tell an untruth
lye	a strong alkaline solution
▸lead	(n.) heavy metal; (v.) to guide
led	guided (past tense of *to lead*)

▸lean	(adj.) thin; (v.) to incline
lien	a legal claim
▸leased	rented
least	smallest
▸legislator	a lawmaker
legislature	a body of lawmakers
▸lend	to allow the use of temporarily
loan	(n.) something lent; (v.) to lend
lone	solitary
▸lessee	a tenant
lesser	smaller
lessor	one who gives a lease
▸lessen	(v.) to make smaller
lesson	(n.) an exercise assigned for study
▸levee	embankment of a river
levy	(n.) an amount collected by levying; (v.) to raise a collection of money
▸liable	responsible
libel	defamatory statement
▸lie	(see *lay*)
▸lightening	making lighter
lightning	accompaniment of thunder
lighting	illumination
▸loan, lone	(see *lend*)
▸loath	(adj.) reluctant
loathe	(v.) to detest
▸local	pertaining to a particular place
locale	a particular place
▸loose	(adj.) free; not bound; (v.) to release
lose	(v.) to suffer the loss of; to part with unintentionally
loss	something lost
▸lye	(see *lay*)
▸made	constructed
maid	a servant

▶**magnificent**	having splendor
munificent	unusually generous
▶**mail**	correspondence
male	masculine
▶**main**	(adj.) chief; (n.) a conduit
mane	long hair on the neck of certain animals
▶**manner**	a way of acting
manor	an estate
▶**marital**	pertaining to marriage
martial	military
marshal	(n.) an official; (v.) to arrange
▶**maybe**	perhaps
may be	*two words* (see ¶ 1101)
▶**mean**	(adj.) unpleasant; (n.) the midpoint; (v.) to intend
mien	appearance
▶**meat**	flesh of animals
meet	to join
mete	to measure
▶**medal**	a badge of honor
meddle	to interfere
metal	a mineral
mettle	courage; spirit
▶**miner**	a worker in a mine
minor	(adj.) lesser, as in size, extent, or importance; (n.) a person who is under legal age
▶**mist**	haze
missed	failed to do
▶**mite**	a tiny particle
might	(n.) force; (v.) past tense of *may*
▶**mood**	disposition
mode	fashion; method
▶**moral**	virtuous
morale	spirit
▶**morality**	virtue
mortality	death rate
▶**morning**	before noon
mourning	grief
▶**munificent**	(see *magnificent*)
▶**naught**	a cipher; zero
nought	nothing

▶**nobody**	no one
no body	no group (see ¶ 1101)
▶**none**	not one
no one	nobody (see ¶ 1101)
▶**oculist**	one who treats eyes
optician	one who makes eyeglasses
optometrist	one who measures vision
▶**official**	authorized
officious	overbold in offering services
▶**one**	a single thing
won	did win
▶**ordinance**	a local law
ordnance	arms; munitions
▶**ought**	(see *aught*)
▶**overdo**	to do too much
overdue	past due
▶**packed**	crowded
pact	an agreement
▶**pail**	a bucket
pale	(adj.) light-colored; (n.) an enclosure
▶**pain**	suffering
pane	window glass
▶**pair**	two of a kind
pare	to peel
pear	a fruit
▶**parameter**	a quantity with an assigned value; a constant
perimeter	the outer boundary
▶**partition**	division
petition	prayer; a formal written request
▶**partly**	in part
partially	to some degree
▶**past**	(n.) time gone by; (adj., adv., or prep.) gone by
passed	moved along; transferred (past tense of *pass*)
▶**patience**	composure; endurance
patients	sick persons
▶**peace**	calmness
piece	a portion

▶peak	the top	▶pole	a long, slender
peek	to look slyly at		piece of wood or
pique	(n.) resentment;		metal
	(v.) to offend; to	poll	(n.) the casting of
	arouse		votes for a body of
piqué	cotton fabric		persons; (v.) to reg-
▶peal	to ring out		ister the votes of
peel	to strip off	▶poor	(adj.) inadequate;
▶pear	(see *pair*)		(n.) needy
▶pedal	(adj.) pertaining to	pore	to study; to gaze
	the foot; (n.) a		intently
	treadle	pour	to flow
peddle	to hawk; to sell	▶populace	the common
▶peer	(n.) one of equal		people; the masses
	rank; a nobleman;	populous	thickly settled
	(v.) to look steadily	▶portion	a part
pier	a wharf	proportion	a ratio of parts
▶perfect	without fault	apportion	to allot
prefect	an official	▶practicable	workable
▶perpetrate	to be guilty of	practical	useful
perpetuate	to make perpetual	▶pray	to beseech
▶perquisite	privilege	prey	a captured victim
prerequisite	a preliminary re-	▶precede	to go before
	quirement	proceed	to advance
▶persecute	to oppress	▶precedence	priority
prosecute	to sue	precedents	established rules
▶personal	private	▶preposition	a part of speech
personnel	the staff	proposition	an offer
▶perspective	a view in correct	▶prescribe	to designate
	proportion	proscribe	to outlaw
prospective	anticipated	▶presence	bearing; being
▶peruse	to read		present
pursue	to chase	presents	gifts
▶petition	(see *partition*)	▶presentiment	a foreboding
▶phase	(see *faze*)	presentment	a proposal
▶physic	a medicine	▶pretend	to make believe
physique	bodily structure	portend	to foreshadow
psychic	pertaining to the	▶principal	(adj.) chief; leading;
	mind or spirit		(n.) a capital sum
▶physical	relating to the body		of money that
fiscal	pertaining to		draws interest;
	finances		chief official of a
psychical	mental		school
▶piece	(see *peace*)	principle	a general truth; a
▶plain	(adj.) undecorated;		rule
	(n.) prairie land	▶profit	gain
plane	(n.) a level surface;	prophet	one who forecasts
	(v.) to make level	▶prophecy	a prediction
▶plaintiff	party in a lawsuit	prophesy	to foretell
plaintive	mournful	▶propose	to suggest
▶pleas	plural of *plea*	purpose	intention
please	to be agreeable	▶prosecute	(see *persecute*)

▶prospective   (see *perspective*)
▶psychic   (see *physic*)
▶psychical   (see *physical*)
▶purpose   (see *propose*)
▶pursue   (see *peruse*)
▶queue   (see *cue*)
▶quiet   calm; not noisy
quite   entirely; wholly
quit   to stop
▶rain   falling water
rein   part of a bridle; a curb
reign   (n.) the term of a ruler's power; (v.) to rule
▶raise   to lift something
raze   to destroy
rays   beams
▶rap   to knock
wrap   (n.) a garment; (v.) to enclose
▶read   to perform the act of reading
reed   a plant; a musical instrument
red   a color
▶real   actual
reel   (n.) a spool; a dance; (v.) to whirl
▶reality   actuality
realty   real estate
▶receipt   an acknowledgment of a thing received
recipe   a formula for mixing ingredients
▶recent   late
resent   (v.) to be indignant
▶reference   that which refers to something
reverence   profound respect
▶relapse   (see *lapse*)
▶residence   a house
residents   persons who reside in a place
▶respectably   in a manner worthy of respect
respectfully   in a courteous manner
respectively   in order indicated

▶right   (adj.) correct; (n.) a privilege
rite   a ceremony
wright   a workman (chiefly as a combining form, as in *playwright*)
write   to inscribe
▶role   a part in a play
roll   (n.) a list; a type of bread; (v.) to revolve
▶root   (n.) underground part of a plant; (v.) to implant firmly
route   (n.) an established course of travel; (v.) to send by a certain route
en route   on or along the way
rout   (n.) confused flight; (v.) to defeat utterly
▶rote   repetition
wrote   did write
▶sail   (n.) part of a ship's rigging; (v.) to travel by water
sale   the act of selling
▶scene   a setting; an exhibition of strong feeling
seen   past participle of *to see*
▶scent   odor
sent   did send
cent   penny
sense   meaning
▶sealing   (see *ceiling*)
▶seam   a line of junction
seem   to appear
▶seed   (see *cede*)
▶seize   (see *cease*)
▶sell   to transfer for a price
cell   a small compartment
▶seller   one who sells
cellar   an underground room
▶senses   (see *census*)

▸serge — a kind of cloth
surge — (n.) a billow; (v.) to rise in surges
▸serial — (see *cereal*)
▸session — (see *cession*)
▸shear — to cut; to trim
sheer — transparent; unqualified
▸shoot — to fire
chute — a slide
▸shown — displayed; revealed; past participle of *show*
shone — gave off light; did shine
▸sight, site — (see *cite*)
▸sleight — dexterity, as in sleight of hand
slight — (adj.) slender; scanty; (v.) to make light of
▸so — therefore
sew — to stitch
sow — to scatter seed
▸soar — (see *sore*)
▸soared — did fly
sword — weapon
▸sole — one and only
soul — the immortal spirit
▸some — a part of
sum — a total
▸someone — somebody (see ¶ 1101)
some one — some person in a group
▸sometime — at some unspecified time (see ¶ 1101)
some time — a period of time
sometimes — now and then
▸son — male child
sun — the earth's source of light and heat
▸sore — painful
soar — to fly
▸spacious — having ample room
specious — outwardly correct but inwardly false
▸specially — (see *especially*)
▸staid — grave; sedate
stayed — past tense and past participle of *to stay*

▸stair — a step
stare — to look at
▸stake — (n.) a pointed stick; a hazard; (v.) to wager
steak — a slice of meat or fish
▸stationary — fixed
stationery — writing materials
▸statue — a carved or molded figure
stature — height
statute — a law
▸steal — to take unlawfully
steel — a form of iron
▸straight — not crooked; directly
strait — a water passageway; (plural) a distressing situation
▸suit — (n.) a legal action; clothing; (v.) to please
suite — a group of things forming a unit; a retinue
sweet — having an agreeable taste; pleasing
▸sum — (see *some*)
▸sun — (see *son*)
▸superintendence — management
superintendents — supervisors
▸surge — (see *serge*)
▸sword — (see *soared*)
▸tare — allowance for weight
tear — (n.) a rent; (v.) to rip
tear — a drop of secretion from the eye
tier — a row or layer
▸taught — did teach
taut — tight; tense
▸team — a group
teem — to abound
▸tenant — one who rents property
tenet — a principle
▸than — conjunction of comparison
then — (adv.) at that time

►their — belonging to them
there — in that place
they're — contraction of *they are*
►theirs — possessive form of *they,* used without a following noun
there's — contraction of *there is* or *there has*
►therefor — for that thing
therefore — consequently
►through — by means of; from beginning to end; because of
threw — did throw
thorough — carried through to completion
►to — (prep.) toward
too — (adv.) more than enough; also
two — one plus one
►track — a trail
tract — a treatise
►trial — examination; an experiment; hardship
trail — a path
►undo — to open; to render ineffective
undue — improper; excessive
►uninterested — (see *disinterested*)
►urban — pertaining to the city
urbane — polished; suave
►vain — proud; conceited
vane — a weathercock
vein — a blood vessel; a bed of mineral materials
►vendee — purchaser
vendor — seller
►veracious — truthful
voracious — greedy
►veracity — truthfulness
voracity — ravenousness; greediness
►vice — wickedness; a prefix used with nouns to designate title of office
vise — a clamp

►waist — part of the body; a garment
waste — (n.) needless destruction; useless consumption; (v.) to expend uselessly
►wait — to stay
weight — quantity of heaviness
►waive — (v.) to give up
wave — (n.) a bellow; a gesture; (v.) to swing back and forth
►waiver — the giving up of a claim
waver — to hesitate
►want — (n.) a need; (v.) to lack; to desire
wont — a custom
won't — contraction of *will not*
►ware — goods
wear — to have on
were — form of *to be*
where — at the place in which
►way — direction; distance; manner
weigh — to find the weight of
►weak — not strong
week — period of seven days
►weather — (n.) state of the atmosphere; (v.) to come through safely
whether — if (see ¶ 1101)
►whoever — anyone who
who ever — *two words* (see ¶ 1101)
►wholly — (see *holy*)
►whose — possessive of *who*
who's — contraction of *who is*
►won — (see *one*)
►wrap — (see *rap*)
►wright, write — (see *right*)
►wrote — (see *rote*)
►your — pronoun
you're — contraction of *you are*

Section 8
COMPOUND WORDS

Some compound words are written as solid words, some are written as separate words, and some are hyphenated. As in other areas of style, authorities do not agree on the rules. Moreover, style is continually changing: many words that used to be hyphenated are now written solid or as separate words. The only complete guide is an up-to-date dictionary. However, a careful reading of the following rules could save you many a trip to the dictionary.

COMPOUND NOUNS

801 Compound nouns follow no regular pattern. Some are written solid, some are spaced, and some are hyphenated.

checkbook	check mark	check-in	airmail	air express
courtroom	court reporter	court-martial	bankbook	bank draft
crossroad	cross section	cross-reference	brainstorm	brain trust
eyewitness	eye shadow	eye-opener	bylaw	by-line
footstep	foot brake	foot-pound	daylight	day coach
goodwill	good sense	good-bye	handshake	hand truck
halfback	half step	half-truth	homeowner	home rule
lighthouse	light meter	light-year	masterpiece	master plan
nightclub	night letter	night-light	paperweight	paper clip
timetable	time zone	time-saver	salesclerk	sales slip
trademark	trade name	trade-in	schoolteacher	school board

NOTE: To be sure of the spelling of a compound noun, check a dictionary. If the noun is not listed, treat the components as separate words. For the spelling of compounds in company names, check letterheads for possible variations. (Compare, for example, *American Airlines* with *United Air Lines*.)

802 Some solid and hyphenated compound nouns closely resemble verb phrases. Be sure, however, to treat the elements in a verb phrase as separate words.

Nouns	**Verb Phrases**
a *breakdown* in communications	when communications *break down*
a thorough *follow-up* of the report	to *follow up* the report thoroughly
operate a *drive-in*	*drive in* to your dealer's
a high school *dropout*	don't *drop out* of high school
at the time of *takeoff*	planes cannot *take off* or land

Nouns	Verb Phrases
come to a *standstill*	we can't *stand still*
let's have a *run-through*	let's *run through* the plan
plan a *get-together*	plan to *get together*
they have the *know-how*	they *know how* to handle it

803   Always hyphenate two nouns when they signify that one person or one thing has two functions.

| secretary-treasurer | dinner-dance |
| clerk-typist | receptionist-switchboard operator |

804   Do not hyphenate civil, military, and naval titles of two or more words.

| Chief of Police Murphy | Attorney General Bradford |
| General Manager Henderson | Rear Admiral Byrd |

a. Hyphenate compound titles containing *ex* and *elect*. (See also ¶¶ 315, 352.)

ex-President Johnson   Governor-elect Smith

Also use a hyphen when *ex* is attached to a noun (for example, *ex-wife*, *ex-convict*), but omit the hyphen in Latin phrases (for example, *ex officio*, *ex cathedra*).

b. The hyphen is being dropped from titles containing *vice*. It is still customary in *vice-chairman,* but it is rapidly disappearing from *vice president* and it is gone from *vice admiral.*

Vice-Chairman Andrews   Vice President Agnew   Vice Admiral Kenny

▶   Capitalization of hyphenated compound nouns: see ¶ 352.
Plurals of compound nouns: see ¶¶ 611–612.
Possessives of compound nouns: see ¶¶ 636–637.

COMPOUND VERBS

805   Compound verbs are usually hyphenated or solid.

to air-condition	to dry-clean	to backstop	to pinpoint
to blue-pencil	to quick-freeze	to downgrade	to proofread
to cross-examine	to spot-check	to handpick	to sidetrack
to double-space	to tape-record	to highlight	to waterproof

NOTE: Do not hyphenate verb-adverb combinations such as *make up, slow down, tie in.* (See also ¶ 802.)

806   If the infinitive form of a compound verb contains a hyphen, retain the hyphen in all the other forms of the verb. (See ¶ 807 for one exception.)

Would you like to *air-condition* your entire house?

The theater was not *air-conditioned.*

You need an *air-conditioning* expert to advise you.

[Continued on page 124.]

Please *double-space* this letter.

This material should not be *double-spaced.*

BUT: Leave a *double space* between paragraphs. (No hyphen in *double space* as a compound noun.)

807 The gerund derived from a hyphenated compound verb requires no hyphen unless it is followed by an object.

Dry cleaning is the best way to clean this garment.

BUT: *Dry-cleaning* this *sweater* will not remove the spot.

Air conditioning is no longer as expensive as it used to be.

BUT: In *air-conditioning* an *office,* you must take more than space into account.

Spot checking is all we have time for.

BUT: In *spot-checking* Ferguson's *data,* I have found some disturbing discrepancies.

COMPOUND ADJECTIVES

No aspect of style causes greater difficulty than compound adjectives. When a compound adjective is shown hyphenated in the dictionary, you can safely assume only that the expression is hyphenated when it occurs directly *before* a noun. When the same combination of words falls elsewhere in the sentence, the use or omission of hyphens depends on how the words are used.

¶¶ 808–810 give the basic rules. For detailed comments on specific kinds of compound adjectives and similar modifiers, see the following paragraphs:

▶ Adjective + noun (as in *short-term* note): see ¶ 811.
Number + noun (as in *40-hour* week): see ¶ 812.
Compound noun (as in *high school* graduate): see ¶ 813.
Proper name (as in *Madison Avenue* agencies): see ¶ 814.
Noun + adjective (as in *tax-free* imports): see ¶ 815.
Noun + participle (as in *time-consuming* details): see ¶ 816.
Adjective + participle (as in *nice-looking* receptionist): see ¶ 817.
Adjective + noun + ed (as in *quick-witted* girl): see ¶ 818.
Adverb + participle (as in *privately owned* stock): see ¶ 819a.
Adverb + participle (as in *well-known* facts): see ¶ 819b.
Adverb + adjective (as in *very exciting* job): see ¶ 820.
Adjective + adjective (as in *black leather* notebook): see ¶ 821.
Phrasal compound (as in *up-to-date* accounts): see ¶ 822.

BASIC RULES

808   A compound adjective consists of two or more words that function as a unit and express a single thought. These one-thought modifiers are derived from (and take the place of) adjective phrases and clauses. In the following examples the left column shows the original phrase or clause; the right column shows the compound adjective.

Adjective Phrase or Clause	Compound Adjective
imports *that are free of duty*	*duty-free* imports
a man *who speaks quietly*	a *quiet-spoken* man
an actor *who is well known*	a *well-known* actor
a conference *held at a high level*	a *high-level* conference
a building *ten stories high*	a *ten-story* building
a report *that is up to date*	an *up-to-date* report

NOTE: In the process of becoming compound adjectives, the adjective phrases and clauses are usually reduced to a few essential words. In addition, these words frequently undergo a change in form (for example, *ten stories high* becomes *ten-story*); sometimes they are put in inverted order (for example, *free of duty* becomes *duty-free*); sometimes they are simply extracted from the phrase or clause without any change in form (for example, *well-known, high-level*).

809   Hyphenate the elements of a compound adjective that occurs *before* a noun. (Reason: The words that make up the compound adjective are not in their normal order or a normal form and require hyphens to hold them together.)

> an *old-fashioned* dress (a dress *of an old fashion*)
> a *$10,000-a-year* salary (a salary *of $10,000 a year*)
> *long-range* plans (plans *projected over a long range of time*)

EXCEPTIONS: A number of compounds like *real estate* and *high school* do not need hyphens when used as adjectives before a noun. See ¶ 813.

810   **a.** When these expressions occur *elsewhere in the sentence,* drop the hyphen if the individual words occur in a normal order and in a normal form. (In such cases the expression no longer functions as a compound adjective.)

Before the Noun	Elsewhere in Sentence
an *X-ray* treatment	The intern studied the *X ray*. (Object of verb.)
an *up-to-date* report	The report is *up to date*. (Prepositional phrase.)
a *high-level* decision	A decision must be made at a *high level*. (Object of preposition.)
a *never-to-be forgotten* book	That book is *never to be forgotten*. (Adverb + infinitive phrase.)
an *off-the-record* comment	This comment is *off the record*. (Prepositional phrase.)

[Continued on page 126.]

b. If these expressions exhibit an inverted word order or an altered form when used elsewhere in the sentence, retain the hyphen.

Before the Noun	Elsewhere in Sentence
a *tax-exempt* purchase	The purchase was *tax-exempt*.
	BUT: The purchase was *exempt from taxes*.
government-owned lands	These lands are *government-owned*.
	BUT: These lands are *owned by the government*.
a *friendly-looking* salesman	That salesman is *friendly-looking*.
	BUT: That salesman *looks friendly*.
high-priced goods	These goods are *high-priced*.
	BUT: These goods carry a *high price*.

NOTE: The following kinds of compound adjectives are always hyphenated:

▶ Noun + adjective (for example, *tax-exempt*): see ¶ 815.
Noun + participle (for example, *government-owned*): see ¶ 816.
Adjective + participle (for example, *friendly-looking*): see ¶ 817.
Adjective + noun + *ed* (for example, *high-priced*): see ¶ 818.

ADJECTIVE + NOUN (see also ¶¶ 812–814)

811 **a.** Hyphenate this combination of elements *before* a noun. Do not hyphenate these elements when they play a normal function *elsewhere in the sentence* (for example, as the object of a preposition or of a verb). However, if the expression continues to function as a compound adjective, retain the hyphen.

Before the Noun	Elsewhere in Sentence
a *short-term* loan	This loan runs only for a *short term*. (Object of preposition.)
low-risk investments	These investments carry a *low risk*. (Object of verb.)
high-grade ore	This ore is of a *high grade*. (Object of preposition.)
	BUT: This ore is *high-grade*. (Compound adjective.)

b. Combinations involving comparative or superlative adjectives plus nouns follow the same pattern.

Before the Noun	Elsewhere in Sentence
a *larger-size* shirt	He wears a *larger size*. (Object of verb.)
the *finest-quality* goods	These goods are of the *finest quality*. (Object of preposition.)

NUMBER + NOUN

812 **a.** When a number and a noun form a one-thought modifier *before* a noun (as in *four-story* building), make the noun singular and hyphenate the expression. When the expression has a normal form and a normal function *elsewhere in the sentence,* do not hyphenate it.

Before the Noun	Elsewhere in Sentence
a *50-cent* fee	a fee of *50 cents*
a *two-year* contract	a contract for *two years*
twentieth-century painting	painting of the *twentieth century*
an *8-foot* ceiling	a ceiling *8 feet* high
a *50-mile-an-hour* speed limit	a speed limit of *50 miles an hour*
an *8½- by 11-inch* sheet of paper (see ¶ 823)	a sheet of paper *8½ by 11 inches*

EXCEPTIONS: a *20 percent* increase, *$12 million* profit

b. A hyphenated compound adjective and an unhyphenated possessive expression often provide *alternative* ways of expressing the same thought. Do not use both styles together.

a *three-week* vacation   **OR**   a *three weeks'* vacation

(**BUT NOT:** a three-weeks' vacation)

COMPOUND NOUN

813   A number of adjective-noun combinations (such as *life insurance* and *real estate*) are actually well-established compound nouns serving as adjectives. Unlike *short-term, low-risk,* and the other examples in ¶ 811, these expressions refer to well-known concepts or institutions. Because they are easily grasped as a unit, such combinations *do not* require a hyphen.

civil service examination	*income tax* return	*real estate* agent
data processing procedures	*life insurance* policy	*safe deposit* box
mass production techniques	*high school* diploma	*social security* tax

NOTE: When dictionaries and style manuals do not provide guidance on a specific adjective-noun combination, consider whether the expression resembles a well-known compound like *social security* or whether it is more like *short-term.* Then space the combination or hyphenate it accordingly.

PROPER NAME

814   **a.** Do not hyphenate the elements in a proper name used as an adjective.

a *Supreme Court* decision   a *Western Union* telegram
a *South American* industrialist   a *Park Avenue* address

b. When two or more distinct proper names are specially combined as a one-thought modifier, use a hyphen to connect the elements.

a *German-American* restaurant   the cuisine is *German-American*

the *New York-Chicago-Los Angeles* flight (no hyphens within *New York* or *Los Angeles*)   **BUT:** the flight to New York, Chicago, and Los Angeles

NOUN + ADJECTIVE

815   **a.** When a compound adjective consists of a noun plus an adjective, hyphenate this combination both *before* and *after* the noun. (See ¶ 810*b*.)

duty-free	stone-deaf	tax-exempt
fire-resistant	top-heavy	water-repellent

The income from these bonds is *tax-exempt.*

We import these *water-repellent* fabrics *duty-free.*

b. Through usage a few compound adjectives in this category are now written solid (for example, *carefree, praiseworthy, waterproof*). Moreover, compound adjectives ending in *wide* are now usually written solid (*worldwide, nationwide, statewide, storewide*) unless the first element ends in *y* (*city-wide, country-wide, industry-wide*).

NOUN + PARTICIPLE

816   **a.** When a compound adjective consists of a noun plus a participle, hyphenate this combination both *before* and *after* the noun. (See ¶ 810*b*.)

air-cooled	interest-bearing	time-consuming
awe-inspiring	power-driven	tongue-tied
government-owned	tailor-made	weather-beaten

The old procedures were all too *time-consuming.*

A number of *city-owned* properties will be auctioned off next week.

b. A few words in this category are now written solid—for example, *handmade, handwoven, handwritten, timesaving, timeworn.*

ADJECTIVE + PARTICIPLE

817   **a.** When a compound adjective consists of an adjective plus a participle, hyphenate this combination both *before* and *after* the noun. (See ¶ 810*b*.)

smooth-talking	odd-sounding	high-ranking
soft-spoken	sweet-smelling	friendly-looking (see ¶ 819a)

He is a *smooth-talking* operator, who never delivers what he promises.

Lloyd was anything but *soft-spoken* in arguing against the new procedures.

b. Retain the hyphen even when a comparative or superlative adjective is combined with a participle—for example, *nicer-looking, oddest-sounding, better-tasting, best-looking.*

As the *highest-ranking* official present, Mr. Sisco took charge of the meeting.

Your new secretary is *nicer-looking* than the one who used to work for you.

ADJECTIVE + NOUN + ED

818   **a.** When a compound adjective consists of an adjective plus a noun plus *ed,* hyphenate this combination both *before* and *after* the noun. (See ¶ 810*b*.)

able-bodied	left-handed	short-lived
blue-eyed	light-headed	(pronounced *līvd*)
double-spaced (see ¶ 806)	middle-aged	small-sized
good-natured	old-fashioned	tough-minded
high-priced	quick-witted	two-fisted

Our success was *short-lived:* the business folded after six months.

These symptoms commonly occur in *middle-aged* executives.

b. Retain the hyphen when a comparative or superlative adjective is combined with a noun plus *ed*—for example, *smaller-sized, highest-priced, best-natured.*

Our *higher-priced* articles sold well this year.

These goods are *higher-priced* than the samples you showed me.

c. A few compound adjectives in this category are now written solid—for example, *hardheaded, lighthearted, shortsighted.*

ADVERB + PARTICIPLE (see also ¶ 820)

819   **a.** Do not hyphenate an adverb-participle combination if the adverb ends in *ly.*

a *poorly constructed* house   a *privately owned* corporation
a *highly valued* employee   a *newly created* staff

NOTE: Hyphenate adjectives ending in *ly* when they are used with participles. (See ¶ 817.)

a *friendly-sounding* voice   a *motherly-looking* woman

b. Other adverb-participle compounds are hyphenated *before* the noun. When these same combinations occur in the predicate, drop the hyphen if the participle is part of the verb.

Before the Noun	Elsewhere in Sentence
a *well-known* consultant	This consultant *is* well *known*.
much-needed reforms	These reforms *were* much *needed*.
the *above-mentioned* facts	These facts *were mentioned* above.
the *ever-changing* tides	The tides *are* ever *changing*.
a *long-remembered* tribute	Today's tribute *will be* long *remembered*.

However, if the participle does not become part of the verb and continues to function with the adverb as a one-thought modifier in the predicate, retain the hyphen.

Before the Noun	Elsewhere in Sentence
a *well-behaved* child	The child is *well-behaved*.
a decision with *far-reaching* implications	The implications are *far-reaching*.

[Continued on page 130.]

Before the Noun	Elsewhere in Sentence
a *clear-cut* position	His position was *clear-cut.*
a *fast-moving* narrative	The narrative is *fast-moving.*
	BUT: The narrative <u>*is*</u> fast <u>*moving*</u> toward a climax.

c. Hyphenated adverb-participle combinations like those in *b* retain the hyphen even when the adverb is in the comparative or superlative.

a *better-known* brand	the *hardest-working* secretary
the *best-behaved* child	a *faster-moving* stock clerk

ADVERB + ADJECTIVE

820 **a.** A number of adverb-adjective combinations closely resemble the adverb-participle combinations described in ¶ 819. However, since an adverb normally modifies an adjective, do not use a hyphen to connect these words.

a *not too interesting* report	a *very moving* story
a *rather irritating* delay	feeling *quite tired*

b. Do not hyphenate comparative or superlative forms, where the adverbs *more, most, less,* or *least* are combined with an adjective.

a *more determined* person	a *less complicated* transaction
the *most exciting* event	the *least interesting* lecture

ADJECTIVE + ADJECTIVE

821 **a.** Do not hyphenate independent adjectives preceding a noun.

a *distinguished public* orator (*public* modifies *orator; distinguished* modifies *public orator*)

a *long* and *tiring* trip (*long* and *tiring* each modify *trip*)

a *warm, enthusiastic* reception (*warm* and *enthusiastic* each modify *reception;* a comma marks the omission of *and*)

b. In a few special cases, two adjectives joined by *and* are hyphenated because they function as one-thought modifiers. These, however, are rare exceptions to the rule stated in *a.*

a *hard-and-fast* rule	a *cut-and-dried* proposal

Henry views the matter in *black-and-white* terms. (A one-thought modifier.)
BUT: She wore a *black and white* dress to the party. (Two independent adjectives.)

c. Hyphenate expressions such as *blue-black, green-grey,* and *red-hot* before and after a noun. However, do not hyphenate expressions such as *bluish green, dark grey,* or *bright red* (where the first word clearly modifies the second).

Always use *blue-black* ink in this office.

The dress she wore was *bluish green.*

PHRASAL COMPOUND

822 **a.** Hyphenate phrases used as compound adjectives *before* a noun. Do not hyphenate such phrases when they occur normally elsewhere in the sentence.

Before the Noun	Elsewhere in Sentence
an *up-to-date* report	The report is *up to date.*
a *change-of-address* notice	This notice shows his *change of address.*
an *out-of-town* visitor	The visitor is from *out of town.*
a *question-and-answer* period	Leave time for *questions and answers.*
a *life-and-death* matter	It is a matter of *life and death.*
a *hit-and-miss* approach	His approach *hits and misses* the mark. **BUT:** His approach is *hit-and-miss.*
a *twelve-year-old* girl	The girl is only *twelve years old.*
a *$100-a-week* job	The job pays *$100 a week.*
a *straight-from-the-shoulder* talk	He spoke *straight from the shoulder.*
a *would-be* authority	He thought he *would be* an authority.
a *pay-as-you-go* plan	This plan lets you *pay as you go.*
unheard-of prices	These prices are *unheard of.*

b. Do not hyphenate foreign phrases used as adjectives before a noun. (See also ¶ 287.)

an ad hoc ruling	an a la carte menu
a bona fide offer	a prima facie case

SUSPENDING HYPHEN

823 **a.** When a series of hyphenated adjectives has a common basic element and this element is shown only with the last term, a "suspending" hyphen follows each adjective.

long- and short-term securities	10- and 20-year bonds
8½- by 11-inch paper	hard- and soft-coal dealers

b. Space once after each suspending hyphen unless a comma is required at that point.

a six- to eight-week delay	3-, 5-, and 8-gallon buckets

PREFIXES AND SUFFIXES

824 In general, when the first part of a word is a prefix or the last part is a suffix, no hyphen is used.

[Continued on page 132.]

*after*thought	*post*script	king*dom*
*ante*date	*pre*requisite	thought*ful*
*anti*climax	*re*organize	neighbor*hood*
*bi*annual	*semi*annual	accoun*ting*
*by*laws (**BUT:** by-product)	*step*mother	forty*ish*
*extra*legal	*sub*division	heart*less**
*fore*most	*super*abundant	child*like**
*hyper*critical	*trans*action	excite*ment*
*inter*office	*ultra*critical	costli*ness*
*mono*syllable	*under*current	leader*ship*
*non*essential	*un*related	lone*some*
*over*confident	*up*take	back*ward*

*If, in the addition of these suffixes, three *l*'s occur in succession, use a hyphen; for example, *bell-like, shell-less.*

825   When the prefix ends with *a* or *i* and the base word begins with the same letter, use a hyphen after the prefix to prevent misreading.

    ultra-active   anti-intellectual
    intra-abdominal   semi-independent

826   When the prefix ends with *e* or *o* and the base word begins with the same letter, the hyphen is almost always omitted.

    coordinate   reeducate   reemphasize   preempt
    cooperative (**BUT:** co-op)   reemploy   (**BUT:** de-emphasize)   preexamine

827   Use a hyphen after *self* when it serves as a prefix.

    self-confidence   self-addressed   self-evident

When *self* serves as the base word and is followed by a suffix, *do not* use a hyphen.

    selfish   selfsame   selfless

828   As a rule, the prefix *re* (meaning "again") should not be followed by a hyphen. A few words require the hyphen so that they can be distinguished from other words with the same spelling but a different meaning.

    to re-mark the ticket   as he remarked to me
    to re-form the class   to reform a sinner
    to re-cover a chair   to recover from an illness
    to re-collect the slips   to recollect the mistake

829   When a prefix is added to a word that begins with a capital, use a hyphen after the prefix.

    anti-American   mid-January   pre-Revolutionary War days
    non-Asiatic   trans-Canadian   post-World War II period

    BUT: transatlantic, transpacific, the Midwest

COMPOUND NUMBERS

830 Hyphenate spelled-out numbers between 21 and 99 (or 21st and 99th), whether they stand alone or as part of a number over 100.

> twenty-five   one hundred and twenty-fifth   twenty-five hundred
> five thousand seven hundred and twenty-five

Do not hyphenate other elements of a spelled-out number over 100.

> six hundred   three thousand   four million   twenty billion
> six hundredth   three thousandth   four millionth   twenty billionth

831 When a spelled-out number consists of more than two words, the word *and* may be omitted between hundreds and tens.

> one hundred and fifty **OR** one hundred fifty

a. When spelling out the year in dates, retain the *and*.

> nineteen hundred and sixty-nine **OR** one thousand nine hundred and sixty-nine

b. When spelling out amounts of money, omit the *and* between hundreds and tens of dollars if *and* is used before the fraction representing "cents."

> Three Thousand One Hundred and no/100 Dollars
>
> Six Hundred Thirty-two and 75/100 Dollars
>
> **BUT:** Six Hundred and Thirty-two Dollars **OR** Six Hundred Thirty-two Dollars. (See also ¶ 428.)

832 When a fraction is spelled out, the numerator and the denominator should be separated by a hyphen unless either element already contains a hyphen.

> seven-twelfths   five thirty-seconds
> nine-sixteenths   twenty-five thirty-seconds

a. Do not hyphenate fractions in constructions like this:

> *One half* of the shipment was damaged beyond use; the *other half* was partially salvageable.

b. When spelling out mixed numbers, always retain the word *and* between the whole number and the fraction, as in *two and two-thirds*.

833 Distinguish between large spelled-out fractions (which are hyphenated) and large spelled-out ordinals (which are not).

> The specifications permit a tolerance of *one-hundredth* of an inch. (Hyphenated fraction.)
>
> **BUT:** This year the company will be celebrating the *one hundredth* anniversary of its founding. (Unhyphenated ordinal.)

▶ Hyphens in numbers representing a continuous sequence: see ¶ 463. Numbers in compound adjectives: see ¶ 812.

SOMETIMES ONE WORD, SOMETIMES TWO WORDS

834 A number of common words may be written either as one solid word or as two separate words, depending on the meaning. See individual entries listed alphabetically in ¶ 1101 for the following words:

Almost–all most	Indirect–in direct
Already–all ready	Into–in to (see *In*)
Altogether–all together	Maybe–may be
Always–all ways	Nobody–no body
Anyone–any one	None–no one
Anyway–any way	Onto–on to (see *On*)
Awhile–a while	Someone–some one
Everyday–every day	Sometime–sometimes–some time
Everyone–every one	Upon–up on (see *On*)
Indifferent–in different	Whoever–who ever

Section 9
WORD DIVISION

Whenever possible, avoid dividing a word at the end of a line. Word divisions are unattractive, and they often slow down or even confuse the reader. When word division is unavoidable, try to divide at a point that will least disrupt the reader's grasp of the word.

The rules that follow are intended for typists. (Printers may take greater liberties.) The rules fall into two categories: (1) those that a typist must never violate (see ¶¶ 901–906) and (2) those that a typist should follow whenever space permits a choice (see ¶¶ 907–920).

BASIC RULES

901 Words may be divided only between syllables. Whenever you are unsure of the syllabication of a word, consult a dictionary. See also ¶¶ 921–922 for some guides to correct syllabication.

902 Do not divide one-syllable words. Even when *ed* is added to some words, they still remain one-syllable words and cannot be divided.

weight	thought	strength	scheme
passed	trimmed	weighed	shipped

903   Do not set off a one-letter syllable at the beginning or the end of a word.

> amount (**NOT:** a- mount)   bacteria (**NOT:** bacteri- a)
> ideal   (**NOT:** i- deal)   piano   (**NOT:** pian- o)

NOTE: So as to discourage word division at the beginning or end of a word, some dictionaries no longer mark one-letter syllables at these points.

904   Do not divide a word unless you can leave a syllable of at least three characters (the last of which is the hyphen) on the upper line and you can carry a syllable of at least three characters (the last may be a punctuation mark) to the next line.

> *ad-* joining   *de-* tract   *un-* important   *im-* possible
> bluff- *ing*   bet- *ter*   check- *up,*   there- *of.*

NOTE: This rule represents the extreme limits at which word division can take place. In almost every case it should be possible to avoid dividing any word with fewer than six letters.

905   Do not divide abbreviations.

> ILGWU   UNESCO   SEATO   ASCAP
> Ph.D.   admin.   f.o.b.   unasgd.

NOTE: An abbreviation such as *AFL-CIO* could be divided after the hyphen.

906   Do not divide contractions.

> doesn't   couldn't   can't   o'clock

PREFERRED PRACTICES

While it is acceptable to divide a word at any syllable break shown in the dictionary, it is often better to divide at some points than at others in order to obtain a more intelligible grouping of syllables. The following rules indicate preferred practices whenever the typist has sufficient space left in the typed line to permit a choice.

907   Divide a solid compound word between the elements of the compound.

> business- man   time- table   home- owner   sales- woman

908   Divide a hyphenated compound word at the point of the hyphen.

> self- control   brother- in-law   get- together   baby- sitter

909   Divide a word *after* a prefix (rather than within the prefix).

Preferred	Acceptable
. . . . intro-	. . . . in-
duce . . . . . . inter-	troduce . . . . in-
national . . . super-	ternational . . . . su-
sonic . . . . . . circum-	personic . . . . . . cir-
stances . . . . ambi-	cumstances . . . am-
dextrous	bidextrous

[Continued on page 136.]

However, avoid divisions like the following, which can easily confuse a reader.

Confusing	Better
. . . . inter-	. . . . in-
pret . . . . . . super-	terpret . . . . su-
fluous . . . . circum-	perfluous . . . . . cir-
ference . . . ambi-	cumference . . . am-
tious	bitious

910   Divide a word *before* a suffix (rather than within the suffix).

practi- cable (**RATHER THAN:** practica- ble)
convert- ible (**RATHER THAN:** converti- ble)

911   When a word has both a prefix and a suffix, choose the division point that groups the syllables more intelligibly.

consign- ment (**RATHER THAN:** con- signment)

The same principle applies when a word contains a suffix added on to a suffix. Choose the division point that produces the more meaningful grouping.

careless- ness (**RATHER THAN:** care- lessness)

912   Whenever you have a choice, divide after a prefix or before a suffix (rather than within the root word).

pre- mature (**RATHER THAN:** prema- ture)   legal- ize (**RATHER THAN:** le- galize)

913   When a one-letter syllable occurs within the root of a word, divide *after* it (rather than before it).

criti- cal   sepa- rate   simi- lar   regu- late

914   When two separately sounded vowels come together in a word, divide between them (rather than immediately before or after them).

radi- ator   valu- able   cre- ative   retro- active
gradu- ation   propri- etary

915   Try to keep together certain kinds of word groups that need to be read together—for example, page and number, month and day, month and year, title and surname, surname and abbreviation, number and abbreviation, or number and unit of measure.

page 63	March, 1968	David Frank, M.D.	6:05 p.m.
January 16	Mr. Harris	Joseph Finley, Jr.	12 feet

916   When necessary, longer word groups may be divided according to the following rules:

a. *Dates* may be divided between the day and year.

. . . . September 21,   **NOT:** . . . . September
1971 . . . .   21, 1971 . . . .

b. *Street addresses* may be divided between the name of the street and *Street, Avenue,* etc.

.... 914 Glen   **NOT:** 914
Avenue ....   Glen Avenue ....

c. *Names of places* may be divided between the city and the state.

.... Cincinnati,
Ohio ....

d. *Names of persons* may be divided between the given name (including middle initial if given) and surname.

.... William E.   **NOT:** .... William
Roberts ....   E. Roberts ....

e. *Names preceded by very long titles* may be divided between the title and the name.

.... The Reverend
Henry S. Brewster ....

f. *A numbered or lettered list* may be divided before any number or letter.

.... these points: **NOT:** .... these points: (1)
(1) All cards should ....   All cards should ....

917 When absolutely necessary, an extremely long number can be divided after a comma; for example, *10,649,- 376,000.*

918 Do not allow more than two consecutive lines to end in hyphens.

919 Do not divide at the end of the first line or the last full line in a' paragraph.

920 Do not divide the last word on a page.

GUIDES TO CORRECT SYLLABICATION

921 Syllabication is generally based on pronunciation rather than on roots and derivations. Careful pronunciation will often aid you in determining the correct syllabication of a word.

knowl- edge (**NOT:** know- ledge)   prod- uct (**NOT:** pro- duct)
chil- dren (**NOT:** child- ren)   ser- vice (**NOT:** serv- ice)

Note how syllabication changes as pronunciation changes.

Verbs	**Nouns**
pre- sent (to make a gift)	pres- ent (a gift)
re- cord (to make an official copy)	rec- ord (an official copy)
pro- ject (to throw forward)	proj- ect (an undertaking)

922 The following paragraphs offer some guides to syllabication. You are not obliged to divide a word at the points named, but you can safely do so without checking a dictionary.

[Continued on page 138.]

a. If a word ends in double consonants *before* a suffix is added, you can safely divide *after* the double consonants (so long·as the suffix creates an extra syllable).

> sell- ers   full- est   staff- ing   buzz- ers
>
> **BUT:** filled, distressed

b. If a final consonant is doubled *because* a suffix is added, you can safely divide *between* the double consonants (so long as the suffix creates an extra syllable).

> ship- ping   omit- ted   begin- ner   refer- ral
>
> **BUT:** shipped, referred

c. When double consonants appear elsewhere *within* the base word (but not as the final consonants), you can safely divide between them.

> neces- sary   ter- rible   mil- lion   recom- mend
> con- nect   suc- cess   dif- fer   sup- pose

d. When a single consonant comes between two single vowels (as in ba*l*ance and pro*duc*t), keep the consonant with the first syllable if the first vowel is *short* and *accented* (as in *bal- ance* and *prod- uct*). Keep the consonant with the second syllable if the first vowel is *long* (as in *se-dan* and *pro- duction*).

Section 10
GRAMMAR

SUBJECT AND VERB

1001 A verb must agree with its subject in number and person.

> *She is* ready to leave the office. (Third person singular subject *she* with third person singular verb *is*.)
>
> The *men are* ready to move the safe. (Third person plural subject *men* with third person plural verb *are*.)
>
> *I am* interested in applying for the job. (First person singular subject *I* with first person singular verb *am*.)

a. A plural verb is always required after *you*, even when *you* is singular, referring to only one person.

> *You were* very kind to me during my illness.

b. Although *s* added to a *noun* indicates the plural form, *s* added to a verb indicates the third person singular.

> He *favors* the move.　　　　They *favor* the expansion.

SUBJECTS JOINED BY <u>AND</u>

1002 If the subject consists of *two singular words* connected by *and* or by *both . . . and,* the subject is plural and requires a plural verb.

> Mr. *Johnson* and Mr. *Bruce* have received promotions.
>
> Both the *collection* and the *delivery* of mail *are* to be curtailed. (The repetition of *the* with the second subject makes it doubly clear that two different items are meant.)

EXCEPTIONS:

a. If a subject consisting of two singular nouns connected by *and* refers to the same person or thing, a singular verb is used. (See also ¶ 1027, third example.)

> The *secretary and treasurer* (one officer) *has* already read the minutes.
>
> *Corned beef and cabbage is* our Monday special.

b. When two subjects connected by *and* are preceded by *each, every, many a,* or *many an,* a singular verb is used. (See also ¶ 1009b.)

> *Each* man and boy *is* expected to meet his obligation.
>
> *Every* hat, suit, and topcoat *is* marked for reduction.
>
> *Many an* office boy and clerk *has* become an executive in his company.

SUBJECTS JOINED BY <u>OR</u> OR SIMILAR CONNECTIVES

1003 If the subject consists of *two singular* words connected by *or, either . . . or, neither . . . nor,* or *not only . . . but also,* the subject is singular and requires a singular verb.

> *Tom* or *John has* the stapler.
>
> Either *July* or *August is* a good vacation month.
>
> Neither the *Credit Department* nor the *Accounting Department has* a record of the transaction.
>
> Not only a *typewriter* but also a *stand is* needed.

1004 When the subject consists of *two plural* words connected by *or, either . . . or, neither . . . nor,* or *not only . . . but also,* the subject is plural and requires a plural verb.

> Neither the regional *managers* nor the *salesmen have* access to the data you want.

1005 If the subject is made up of both singular and plural words connected by *or, either . . . or, neither . . . nor,* or *not only . . . but also,* the verb agrees with the nearer part of the subject. Since sentences with singular and plural subjects usually sound better with plural verbs, try to locate the plural subject closer to the verb whenever this can be done without sacrificing the emphasis desired.

Either *Mr. Hertig* or his *assistants have* the data. (The verb *have* agrees with the nearer subject, *assistants.*)

Neither the *salesmen* nor the *buyer is* in favor of the system. (The verb *is* agrees with the nearer subject, *buyer.*)

BETTER: Neither the *buyer* nor the *salesmen are* in favor of the system. (The sentence reads better with the plural verb *are.* The subjects *buyer* and *salesmen* have been rearranged without changing the emphasis.)

Not only the *teachers* but also the *superintendent is* in favor of the plan. (The verb *is* agrees with the nearer subject, *superintendent.* Note that with the use of *not only . . . but also* the emphasis falls on the subject following *but also.*)

Not only the *superintendent* but also the *teachers are* in favor of the plan. (When the sentence is rearranged, the nearer subject *teachers* requires the plural verb *are.* Note, however, that the emphasis of the sentence has now changed.)

Not only my *colleagues* but *I am* in favor of the plan. (The first-person verb *am* agrees with the nearer subject *I.* Rearranging this sentence will change the emphasis.)

▶ See the last four examples in ¶ 1027 for *neither . . . nor* constructions following *there is* or *there are;* see also ¶ 1045c for examples of subject-verb-pronoun agreement in these constructions.

INTERVENING PHRASES AND CLAUSES

1006 When establishing agreement between subject and verb, disregard intervening phrases and clauses. (See ¶¶ 1012, 1024 for exceptions.)

The lost *box* of new letterheads *has* not been found. (Disregard *of new letter-heads. Box* is the subject and takes a singular verb *has.*)

The *prices* of the new model *vary* with the dealer.

One of the items ordered *has* been delivered. (See also ¶ 1008a.)

Her *experience* as adviser to boys and girls *gives* her excellent qualifications for the position.

1007 The insertion of phrases introduced by *with, together with, along with, as well as, plus, in addition to, besides, including, accompanied by, followed by, rather than,* etc., between subject and verb does not affect the number of the verb. If the subject is singular, use a singular verb; if the subject is plural, use a plural verb.

Mrs. Smith, together with her son and daughter, *is* going to the theater this evening.

This *study,* as well as many earlier reports, *shows* that the disease can be arrested if detected in time.

The sales *reports,* including the summary, *were* sent to Mr. Giles.

No one, not even the company officers, *has* been told.

ONE OF . . .

1008 **a.** Use a singular verb after a phrase beginning with *one of* or *one of the;* the singular verb agrees with the subject *one.* (Disregard any plural that follows *of* or *of the.*)

> *One* of the books *has* been lost.
>
> *One* of the reasons for his resignation *is* poor health.
>
> *One* of us *has* to take the responsibility.
>
> *One* of you *is* to be nominated for the office.

b. The phrases *one of those who* and *one of the things that,* however, are followed by plural verbs because the verbs refer to *those* or *things* (rather than to *one*).

> He is one of *those* who *favor* increasing the staff. (In other words, of *those* who *favor* increasing the staff, he is one. *Favor* is plural to agree with *those*.)
>
> She is one of our *employees* who *are* never late. (Of our *employees* who *are* never late, she is one.)
>
> I ordered one of the *skirts* that *were* advertised. (Of the *skirts* that *were* advertised, I ordered one.)
>
> John is only one of the *men* who *are* going with me. (Of the *men* who *are* going with me, John is only one.)

EXCEPTION: When the words *the only* precede such phrases, however, the meaning is singular and a singular verb is required. Note that both words, *the* and *only,* are required to produce a singular meaning.

> John is *the only one* of our men who *is* going with me. (Of our men, John is *the only one* who *is* going. Here, the singular verb *is* is required to agree with *one.*)

INDEFINITE PRONOUNS ALWAYS SINGULAR

1009 **a.** The words *each, every, either, neither, one,* and *another* are always singular. When they are used as subjects or as adjectives modifying subjects, a singular verb is required.

> *Each is* eating his lunch.
>
> *Each* employee *is* responsible for closing his window in the evening.
>
> *Every* child *sits* quietly.
>
> *Neither* of the women *is* eligible.
>
> *Neither* woman *is* eligible.
>
> *One* shipment *has* already gone out; *another is* to leave the warehouse tomorrow. (See also ¶ 1008 for the use of *one.*)

▶ See ¶¶ 1003-1005 for the use of *either . . . or* and *neither . . . nor.*

b. When *each, every, many a,* or *many an* precedes two subjects joined by *and,* the verb should be singular. (See ¶ 1002*b.*)

[Continued on page 142.]

EXCEPTION: When the word *each* follows a plural subject, keep the verb plural. In that position, *each* has no effect on the number of the verb. To test the correctness of such sentences, mentally omit *each*.

> The *members* each *feel* their responsibility.
> *They* each *have* high expectations.
> *Twelve* each of these items *are* required.

1010 The following compound pronouns are always singular and require a singular verb:

anybody	everybody	nobody	somebody
anything	everything	nothing	something
anyone	everyone	no one	someone
OR any one	**OR** every one		**OR** some one

> *Everyone is* required to register in order to vote.
> *Something tells* me I'm wrong.

NOTE: A singular verb is still required when two such subjects are joined by *and*.

> *Anyone* and *everyone is* entitled to a fair hearing.

INDEFINITE PRONOUNS ALWAYS PLURAL

1011 The words *both, few, many, others,* and *several* are always plural. When they are used as subjects or as adjectives modifying subjects, a plural verb is required.

> *Several* members *were* invited, while *others were* overlooked.
> *Both* books *are* out of print.
> *Many were* asked, but *few were* able to answer.

INDEFINITE PRONOUNS SINGULAR OR PLURAL

1012 *All, none, any, some, more,* and *most* may be singular or plural, depending on the noun they refer to. (The noun often occurs in an *of* phrase immediately following.)

> *All* the manuscript *has* been finished.
> *All* the reports *have* been handed in.
>
> *Some was* acceptable. (Meaning some of the manuscript.)
> *Some were* acceptable. (Meaning some of the reports.)
>
> *Is* there any (ice cream) left? *Are* there any (cookies) left?
>
> *Do any* of you *know* John Ferguson well? (*Any* is plural because it refers to the plural *you;* hence the plural verb *do know.*)
> *Does any* one of you *know* John Ferguson well? (*Any* is singular because it refers to the singular *one;* hence the singular verb *does know.*)

More than one customer *has complained* about that item. (*More* refers to the singular noun *customer;* hence the singular verb *has complained.*)

More than five customers *have complained* . . . (*More* refers to the plural noun *customers;* hence the plural verb *have complained.*)

Most of the stock *has* been sold, but *more* of these suits *are* due.

Some of the food *seems* too high-priced.

Some of the items *seem* too high-priced.

None of the bond paper *was* used.

None of the packages *were* well wrapped.

None were injured. (Meaning none of the passengers.)

NOTE: In formal usage, *none* is still considered a singular pronoun. In general usage, however, *none* is considered singular or plural, depending on the number of the noun to which it refers. *No one* or *not one* is often used in place of *none* to stress the singular idea.

NOUNS ALWAYS SINGULAR

1013 Some nouns are always singular in meaning (see ¶ 626). When used as subjects, these nouns require singular verbs.

The *news* from abroad *is* very discouraging.

NOUNS ALWAYS PLURAL

1014 Some nouns are always plural in meaning, even though they refer to a single thing (see ¶ 627). When used as subjects, these nouns require plural verbs.

The *proceeds* of the concert *are* to be given to charity.

The *goods are* being shipped today.

The *scissors are* in the second drawer on the left.

NOUNS SINGULAR OR PLURAL

1015 Some nouns have the same form in the plural as in the singular (see ¶ 628). When used as subjects, these nouns take singular or plural verbs according to the meaning.

The *series* of concerts planned for the spring *looks* very enticing. (One series.)

Three *series* of tickets *are* going to be issued. (Three series.)

1016 Many nouns ending in *ics* (*economics, ethics, politics, statistics,* etc.) take singular or plural verbs, depending on how they are used. When they refer to a body of knowledge or a course of study, they are *singular.* When they refer to qualities or activities, they are *plural.*

Economics (a course of study) *is* a prerequisite for advanced business courses.

The *economics* (the economic aspects) of his plan *are* not very sound.

NOUNS WITH FOREIGN PLURALS

1017 Be alert to recognize nouns with foreign-plural endings (see ¶ 613). Such plural nouns, when used as subjects, require plural verbs.

> No *criteria have* been established. (**BUT:** No *criterion has* been established.)
>
> *Parentheses are* required around such references. (**BUT:** The closing *parenthesis was* omitted.)
>
> The *media* through which we reach our clients *are* quality magazines and radio broadcasts. (**BUT:** The *medium* we find most effective *is* television.)

NOTE: The noun *data* (which is plural in form) is now commonly followed by a singular verb.

> The *data* obtained after two months of experimentation *is* now being analyzed.
>
> **BUT:** The *data* assembled by six researchers *are* now being compared. (When the term *data* implies several distinct sets of information, use a plural verb.)

COLLECTIVE NOUNS

1018 The following rules govern the form of verb to be used when a collective noun is the subject. (A *collective noun* is a word that is singular in form but represents a group of persons, animals, or things; for example, *army, audience, board, cabinet, class, committee, company, corporation, council, department, firm, faculty, group, jury, majority, minority, public, society, school.*)

a. If the group is thought of as acting as a unit, the verb should be singular.

> The *Board of Directors meets* Friday.
>
> The *committee has* agreed to submit *its* report on Monday. (The pronoun *its* is also singular to agree with *committee.*)
>
> The *firm is* one of the oldest in the field.

b. If the members of the group are thought of as acting separately, the verb should be plural.

> The *committee are* not in agreement on the action *they* should take. (The pronoun *they* is plural here to agree with the plural *committee.*)

NOTE: The use of a collective noun with a plural verb often produces an awkward sentence. Whenever possible, recast the sentence by inserting a phrase like *the members of* before the collective noun.

> The *members* of the committee *are* not in agreement on the action *they* should take.

PROPER NAMES

1019 Proper names that are plural in form are treated as *singular* if they refer to only one thing.

The *United States has* undertaken a new foreign aid program.

BUT: These *United States are* bound together by a common heritage of political and religious liberty.

COMPANY NAMES

1020 Company names may be either singular or plural according to the meaning. The plural form emphasizes the individual personnel making up the company. If a company is referred to as *they,* a plural verb is required. If a company is referred to as *it,* a singular verb is used.

> Morris & Company *have* the reputation of going to any length to retain the goodwill of a customer. As a result, *they* seldom *lose* a customer.
>
> The Rice Company *has* lost *its* lease.
>
> Brooks & Sons *is* opening another store.

TITLES OF PUBLICATIONS

1021 The title of a book or magazine is considered singular, even though it is plural in form.

> *Changing Times* is published every month by Kiplinger.
>
> *U.S. News & World Report* comes out once a week.

THE NUMBER; A NUMBER

1022 The expression *the number* has a singular meaning and requires a singular verb; *a number* has a plural meaning and requires a plural verb.

> *The number* of orders still to be filled *is* estimated at nearly a hundred.
>
> *A number* of our staff *are* going on vacation today.

EXPRESSIONS OF TIME, MONEY, AND QUANTITIES

1023 When nouns expressing periods of time, amounts of money, or quantities represent a total amount, singular verbs are used. When these nouns represent a number of individual units, plural verbs are used.

> *Three months is* too long a time to wait.
>
> **BUT:** *Three months have* passed since our last exchange of letters.
>
> That *$10,000 was* an inheritance from my uncle.
>
> **BUT:** *Thousands* of dollars *have* already been spent on the project.
>
> *Ten acres is* considered a small piece of property in this area.
>
> **BUT:** *Ten acres were* plowed last spring.

FRACTIONAL EXPRESSIONS

1024 After such expressions as *one-half of, two-thirds of, a part of,* and *a majority of:*

a. Use a *singular verb* if a *singular noun* follows the *of.*

> *Three-fourths* of the mailing list *has* been checked.
>
> A *part* of the building *is* closed.
>
> A *majority* of 2,000 *indicates* his popularity. (The noun *2,000* is considered singular because it is a total amount. See ¶ 1023.)

b. Use a *plural verb* when a *plural noun* follows the *of.*

> *Two-thirds* of our customers *live* in the suburbs.
>
> *Part* of the walls *are* to be papered.
>
> The *majority* of our students *live* at home.

PHRASES AND CLAUSES AS SUBJECTS

1025 When a phrase or clause serves as the subject, the verb should be singular.

> *Watching the stock market takes* all his time these days.
>
> *Whether the decision was right or not is* no longer important.
>
> *That they will accept the offer is* far from certain.
>
> *Whomever you support is* likely to be elected.

NOTE: Clauses beginning with *what* may be singular or plural according to the meaning.

> *What we need is* a new statement of policy.
>
> *What we need are* some guidelines.

SUBJECTS IN INVERTED SENTENCES

1026 In sentences in which the verb precedes the subject, make sure that the subject and verb agree.

> On the results of this survey *depend* the *extent* and the *type* of campaign we shall wage.
>
> Attached *are* two carbon *copies.*
>
> What *are* his *reasons* for resigning?
>
> What *is* the *likelihood* of persuading him to stay?

1027 In a sentence beginning with *there is, there are, here is,* or *here are,* the real subject follows the verb. Use *is* when the real subject is singular, *are* when it is plural.

> *There is* a vast *difference* between the two plans. (Subject is *difference.*)
>
> *There are* a great many *angles* to this problem. (Subject is *angles.*)
>
> *Here is* an old *friend* and former *partner* of mine. (The subject, *friend and partner,* is singular because only one person is referred to. See ¶ 1002a.)
>
> *Here are* a *catalog* and an *order blank.* (The subject is *catalog* and *order blank.*)
>
> *There is* more than one *way* to solve the problem. (See also ¶ 1012.)
>
> *There are* more than five *candidates* for the job.

There are a number of problems to be resolved. (See also ¶ 1022.)

Here is the number of orders received since Monday.

Here is ten dollars as a contribution. (See also ¶ 1023.)

Here are ten silver *dollars* for your collection.

There is neither a *student* nor a *teacher* who can solve that problem. (See ¶ 1003 for two singular subjects joined by *neither . . . nor.*)

There are neither *staples* nor *paper clips* in the supplies cabinet. (See ¶ 1004 for two plural subjects joined by *neither . . . nor.*)

There are neither *carbon ribbons* nor *cleaning fluid* left in stock. (*Are* agrees with the nearer subject. See also ¶ 1005 for singular and plural subjects joined by *neither . . . nor.*)

There is neither *ink eradicator* nor *ink erasers* on hand. (*Is* agrees with the nearer subject, *ink eradicator.* See also ¶ 1005.)

SUBJECTS AND PREDICATE COMPLEMENTS

1028 Sentences containing a linking verb (such as *become* or some form of *to be*) sometimes have a singular subject and a plural complement. In such cases make sure that the verb agrees with the *subject* (and not with the complement).

One of the things you should keep track of *is* entertainment expenses. (Use *is* to agree with *one,* the subject.)

It is they who are at fault. (Use *is* to agree with *it,* the subject.)

NOTE: Do not confuse these examples with the *inverted* sentences shown in ¶ 1027. In a sentence beginning with *here is* or *there is,* the subject follows the linking verb. In a sentence beginning with *it is* or *one . . . is,* the subject precedes the linking verb.

VERB PROBLEMS

In addition to the problem of making verbs agree with their subjects, which was discussed in ¶¶ 1001–1028, there are a number of other verb problems that are frequently encountered.

PRINCIPAL PARTS

1029 The principal parts of a verb are the four simple forms upon which all tenses and other modifications of the verb are based.

a. In most verbs, the past and the past participle are formed simply by adding *d* or *ed* to the present form; the present participle is formed by adding *ing* to the present.

Present	Past	Past Participle	Present Participle
fill	filled	filled	filling
need	needed	needed	needing

[*Continued on page 148.*]

b. In many frequently used verbs, however, the principal parts are irregularly formed.

Present	Past	Past Participle	Present Participle
choose	chose	chosen	choosing
do	did	done	doing
forget	forgot	forgotten **OR** forgot	forgetting
see	saw	seen	seeing
sing	sang	sung	singing
write	wrote	written	writing

The dictionary shows the principal parts for all irregular verbs. If you are in doubt about any form, consult the dictionary.

c. The past participle and the present participle, if used as a part of a verb phrase, must *always* be used with one or more helping (or auxiliary) verbs. The most common helping verbs are:

is	was	can	do	had	have	might	shall	will
are	were	could	did	has	may	must	should	would

1030 The first principal part of the verb (the *present*) is used:

a. To express *present time.*

> We *fill* all orders promptly.   They *do* what is expected of them.

b. To make a statement that is *true at all times.*

> Water *seeks* its own level.

c. Combined with *shall* or *will,* to express *future time.*

> We *will order* (**OR** *shall order*) our spring goods next week. (For the use of these auxiliary verbs in the future tense, see the entry for *shall-will* in ¶ 1101.)

▶ See also ¶ 1034 for the third person singular form of the present tense.

1031 The second principal part of the verb (the *past*) is used to express *past time.* (No helping verb is used with this form.)

> We *filled* the order yesterday.
> They *did* what was expected of them.

NOTE: Do not use a past participle form to express the past tense.

> He *drank* his coffee. (**NOT:** He *drunk* it.)
> I *saw* it. (**NOT:** I *seen* it.)
> They *sang* it together. (**NOT:** They *sung* it.)
> He was the one who *did* it. (**NOT:** . . . the one who *done* it.)

1032 The third principal part of the verb (the *past participle*) is used:

a. To form the *present perfect tense.* This tense indicates action that has been completed at some *indefinite time before the present.* It is made up of the helping verb *have* or *has* combined with the past participle.

> We *have filled* the orders. (**NOT:** We *have filled* the orders *yesterday.*)
> She *has done* what was expected of her.

b. To form the *past perfect tense*. This tense indicates action that was completed *before another past action*. It is made up of the helping verb *had* combined with the past participle.

>We *had filled* the orders before we saw your letter.
>They *had done* the job before we arrived.

c. To form the *future perfect tense*. This tense indicates action that will be completed *before a certain time in the future*. It is made up of the helping verb *shall have* or *will have* combined with the past participle.

>We *shall have filled* the orders by that time.
>They *will have done* the job by that time.

NOTE: Be careful not to use a past tense form (the second principal part) in place of a past participle.

>I have *broken* the racket. (NOT: I have *broke* the racket.)
>The dress has *shrunk*. (NOT: The dress has *shrank*.)
>Prices have *risen* again. (NOT: Prices have *rose* again.)
>He has *worn* his shoes out. (NOT: He has *wore* his shoes out.)

1033 The fourth principal part of the verb (the *present participle*) is used:

a. To form the *present progressive tense*. This tense indicates action still in progress. It is made up of the helping verb *am, is,* or *are* combined with the present participle.

>We *are filling* all orders as fast as we can.
>They *are doing* all that can be expected of them.

b. To form the *past progressive tense*. This tense indicates action in progress sometime in the past. It is made up of the helping verb *was* or *were* combined with the present participle.

>We *were waiting* for new stock at the time your order came in.
>They *were doing* a good job when I last checked on them.

c. To form the *future progressive tense*. This tense indicates action that will be in progress in the future. It is made up of the helping verb *shall be* or *will be* combined with the present participle.

>We *shall be working* overtime for the next two weeks.
>They *will be receiving* additional stock throughout the next two weeks.

d. To form the *present perfect progressive*, the *past perfect progressive*, and the *future perfect progressive tenses*. These tenses are exactly like the simple perfect tenses (see ¶ 1032) except that the progressive element suggests continuous action. These tenses are made up of the helping verbs *has been, have been, had been, shall have been,* and *will have been* combined with the present participle. Compare the following examples with those in ¶ 1032.

>We *have been filling* these orders with Model 212A instead of 212. (Present perfect progressive.)

[Continued on page 150.]

We *had been filling* these orders with Model 212A until we saw your directive. (Past perfect progressive.)

By next Friday we *shall have been working* overtime for two straight weeks. (Future perfect progressive.)

1034 The first principal part of the verb undergoes a change in form to express the third person singular in the present tense.

a. Most verbs simply add *s* in the third person singular.

I (you, we, they) type   he (she, it) types

b. Verbs ending in *s, x, z, sh, ch,* or *o* add *es.*

he misses	he wishes
she fixes	she watches
it buzzes	it goes

c. The verb *to be* is irregular since *be,* the first principal part, is not used in the present tense.

I am	we are
you are	you are
he, she, it is	they are

d. A few verbs remain unchanged in the third person singular.

he may	she can	it will
he might	she could	it would

VERBS FOLLOWING CLAUSES OF NECESSITY, DEMAND, ETC.

1035 Sentences that express *necessity, demand, strong request, urging,* or *resolution* in the main clause require a subjunctive verb in the dependent clause that follows.

a. If the verb in the dependent clause requires the use of the verb *to be,* use the form *be* with all three persons (not *am, is,* or *are*).

NECESSITY: It is necessary (or important or essential) that these questions *be* answered at once. (**NOT:** are answered.)

DEMAND: I demand that I *be* given a hearing on this matter. (**NOT:** am given.)

REQUEST: They have asked that you *be* notified at once. (**NOT:** are notified.)

URGING: We urge (or suggest) that he *be* given a second chance. (**NOT:** is given.)

RESOLUTION: The committee has resolved (or decided or ruled) that the decision *be* deferred until the next meeting. (**NOT:** is deferred.)

b. If the verb in the dependent clause is a verb other than *be,* use the ordinary *present tense* form for all three persons. However, do not add *s* for the third person singular.

NECESSITY: It is essential that he *arrive* on time. (**NOT:** arrives.)

DEMAND: They insist that she *do* the work over. (**NOT:** does.)

REQUEST: They have asked that he *remain* on the committee awhile longer. (**NOT:** remains.)

URGING: We suggest that she *type* the material triple-spaced on the first draft. (**NOT:** types.)

RESOLUTION: They have resolved that Fred *represent* them at the grievance hearing. (**NOT:** represents.)

VERBS FOLLOWING WISH CLAUSES

1036   Sentences that start with *I wish, he wishes,* etc., require a subjunctive verb in the dependent clause that follows.

a. To express *present* time in the dependent clause, put the verb in the *past tense.*

> I wish I *knew* how to proceed.
> I wish I *could attend.*

NOTE: If the verb is *to be,* use *were* (not *was*) for all persons.

> I wish I *were going* to the reception.
> I wish he *were going* with me.

b. To express *past* time in the dependent clause, put the verb in the *past perfect tense.*

> I wish that she *had invited* me.
> I wish that I *had been* there.
> I wish that I *could have attended.*

c. To express *future* time in the dependent clause, use the auxiliary verb *would* instead of *will.*

> I wish he *would arrive* on time.

VERBS IN IF CLAUSES

1037   When an *if* clause states a condition that is *highly improbable, doubtful,* or *contrary to fact,* the verb in the *if* clause requires special treatment, like that described in ¶ 1036: *to express present time, use the past tense; to express past time, use the past perfect tense.* (In the following examples note the relationship of tenses between the dependent clause and the main clause.)

> If I *knew* the answer (but I don't), I *would* not *ask* you.
> If I *had known* the answer (but I didn't), I *would* not *have asked* you.
>
> If I *were* you (but I am not), I *would take* the job.
> If I *had been* in your shoes (but I wasn't), I *would have taken* the job.
>
> If he *were invited* (but he isn't), he *would be* glad to go.
> If he *had been invited* (but he wasn't), he *would have been* glad to go.

1038   When an *if* clause states a condition that is *possible* or *likely,* the verb in the *if* clause requires no special treatment. *To express present time, use the present tense; to express past time, use the past tense.* Compare the following pairs of examples. Those labeled "Probable" reflect the verb forms described here in ¶ 1038. Those labeled "Improbable" reflect the verb forms described in ¶ 1037.

> **PROBABLE:** If I *leave* this job (and I may do so), I *will take* a teaching position.
>
> **IMPROBABLE:** If I *left* this job (but I probably won't), I *would take* a teaching position.
>
> **PROBABLE:** If he *goes* to San Francisco (and he may), he *will want* you to go with him.
>
> **IMPROBABLE:** If he *were going* to San Francisco (but he probably won't), he *would want* you to go with him.
>
> **PROBABLE:** If he *was* in the office yesterday (and he may have been), I *did* not *see* him.
>
> **IMPROBABLE:** If he *had been* in the office yesterday (but he wasn't), I *would have seen* him.

VERBS IN AS IF OR AS THOUGH CLAUSES

1039 When an *as if* or *as though* clause expresses a condition *contrary to fact*, the verb in the clause requires special treatment, like that described in ¶ 1037.

> She acts as if she *were* the only person who mattered. (But she isn't.)
>
> He talks as if he *knew* the facts of the situation. (But he doesn't.)
>
> She acts as if she *hadn't* a care in the world. (But she has.)

1040 *As if* or *as though* clauses are now often used to express a condition that is *highly probable*. In such cases do not give the verb special treatment. *Use the present tense to express present time and the past tense to express past time.*

> It looks as if it *will* rain. (**OR:** It looks as if it *is* going to rain.)
>
> She acts as if she *plans* to look for another job.

INFINITIVES

1041 An infinitive is the form of the verb preceded by *to* (for example, *to write, to do, to be*). When two or more infinitives are used in a parallel construction, the word *to* may be omitted after the first infinitive unless special emphasis is desired.

> Ask Mr. Paulsen *to sign* both copies of the contracts, *return* the original to us, and *keep* the carbon copy for his own files. (*Return* and *keep* are infinitives without *to*.)
>
> I would like you *to explain* the job to Harry, *to give* him help if he needs it, and *to see* that the job is done properly. (For emphasis, *to* is used with all three infinitives—*explain, give,* and *see*.)

NOTE: The word *to* is usually dropped when the infinitive follows such verbs as *see, hear, feel, let, help,* and *need.*

> Will you please help me *prepare* the report. (**RATHER THAN:** help me *to prepare* the report.)
>
> You need not *return* the clipping. (**OR:** You do not need *to return* the clipping.)

1042 Infinitives have two main tense forms: the present and the perfect.

a. The perfect infinitive is used to express action that has been completed before the time of the main verb.

> I *am* sorry *to have caused* you so much trouble last week. (The act of causing trouble was completed before the act of expressing regret; therefore, the perfect infinitive is used.)

b. The present infinitive is used in all other cases.

> I planned *to leave* early. (**NOT:** to have left. The act of leaving could not have been completed before the act of planning; therefore, the present infinitive is used.)

1043 *Splitting an infinitive* (that is, inserting an adverb between *to* and the verb) should be avoided because (*a*) it typically produces an awkward construction and (*b*) the adverb usually functions more effectively in another location.

> **WEAK:** It was impossible to *even* see a foot ahead.
> **BETTER:** It was impossible to see *even* a foot ahead.
>
> **WEAK:** He always tries to *carefully* do the work.
> **BETTER:** He always tries to do the work *carefully*.

However, split the infinitive when alternative locations of the adverb produce an awkward or weakly constructed sentence.

a. Before splitting an infinitive, first try to place the adverb *after the object* of the infinitive. In many instances the adverb functions most effectively in that location.

> You ought *to review* these plans *thoroughly*. (**MUCH BETTER THAN:** You ought to thoroughly review these plans.)
> I need *to make* the decision *quickly*. (**MUCH BETTER THAN:** I need to quickly make the decision.)

b. If step *a* does not produce an effective sentence, try to locate the adverb directly *before* or directly *after* the infinitive. In some cases the adverb functions effectively in this position; in other cases the resulting sentence is awkward.

> **CONFUSING:** I want you *to supervise* the work that is to be done *personally*. (When the object of the infinitive is long or involved, it is difficult to place the adverb after the object without creating confusion. Here *personally* seems to modify *to be done* when in fact it should modify *to supervise*.)
> **GOOD:** I want you *personally* to supervise the work that is to be done.
> **AWKWARD:** I want you to supervise *personally* the work that is to be done.

c. If steps *a* and *b* fail to produce an effective sentence, try splitting the infinitive. If a good sentence results, keep it; if not, try rewording the sentence.

> **CONFUSING:** I want you *to consider* Jenkins' proposal to handle all our deliveries *carefully*. (When *carefully* is located after the complete object, it no longer clearly refers to *to consider*.)

[Continued on page 154.]

AWKWARD: I want you *carefully* to consider Jenkins' proposal to handle all our deliveries.

AWKWARD: I want you to consider *carefully* Jenkins' proposal to handle all our deliveries.

GOOD: I want you to *carefully* consider Jenkins' proposal to handle all our deliveries.

d. When an infinitive consists of *to be* plus a past participle of another verb, inserting an adverb before the past participle is not considered splitting an infinitive.

These plans need to be *thoroughly* reviewed.

Time appears to be *fast* running out.

NOTE: Nevertheless, in many such sentences the adverb may be located to better advantage elsewhere in the sentence.

▶ See also ¶ 1074*b* for dangling infinitive phrases.

SEQUENCE OF TENSES

1044 When the verb in the main clause is in the past tense, the verb in a subordinate *that* clause should also express past time. Compare the following pairs of examples:

He *says* (present) that he *is* still waiting (present).
He *said* (past) that he *was* still waiting (past).

He *says* (present) that he *has seen* (present perfect) your résumé.
He *said* (past) that he *had seen* (past perfect) your résumé.

He *says* (present) that he *will see* (future) you tomorrow.
He *said* (past) that he *would see* (past form of *will see*) you tomorrow.

EXCEPTION: The verb in the subordinate clause should remain in the present tense if it expresses a general truth.

Our legal adviser *pointed out* (past) that all persons under 21 *are* (present) legally considered minors. (General truth.)

TROUBLESOME VERBS

▶ See individual entries listed alphabetically in ¶ 1101 for the following verbs:

Bring–take	Leave–let
Come–go	May–can
Done, Don't	Raise–rise
Have got	Set–sit
Imply–infer	Shall–will
Lay–lie	Should–would
Learn–teach	Would have

PRONOUNS

AGREEMENT OF PRONOUNS WITH ANTECEDENTS

1045 a. A pronoun must agree with its *antecedent* (the word for which the pronoun stands) in number, gender, and person.

> *Frank* said that *he* could do the job alone.
>
> *Alice* wants to know whether *her* wallet has been turned in.
>
> The *company* has not decided whether or not to change *its* policy on vacations. (See ¶ 1020.)
>
> The company's *managers* are holding *their* monthly meeting tomorrow.
>
> The *Jergensons* are giving a party at *their* house.
>
> The *grand jury* has completed *its* investigation. (See ¶ 1018 for collective nouns.)
>
> Why not have *each witness* write *his* version of the accident? (See ¶ 1045e–h for indefinite pronouns as antecedents.)
>
> It is *I* who *am* at fault. (*Who* agrees in person and number with its antecedent *I;* the verb *am* also agrees with *I.*)
>
> It is *you* who *are* to blame. (*Who* refers to *you;* hence the verb *are* also agrees with *you.*)
>
> **BUT:** You are the *person* who *is* to blame. (*Who* refers to *person;* hence the verb *is* also agrees with *person.*)
>
> It is *they* who *are* behind schedule.

b. Use a plural pronoun when the antecedent consists of two nouns joined by *and.*

> *Harry* and *I* think *we* can handle the assignment.
>
> Can *Mary* and *you* give us *your* decision by Monday?
>
> *George* and *Dave* say *they* will attend.
>
> The *Maxwells* and the *Weavers* have sent *their* regrets.

c. Use a singular pronoun when the antecedent consists of two *singular* nouns joined by *or* or *nor.* Use a plural pronoun when the antecedent consists of two *plural* nouns joined by *or* or *nor.* (See also ¶¶ 1003–1005.)

> Either *Will* or *Ed* will have to give up *his* office. (**NOT:** their.)
>
> Neither *Joan* nor *Helen* wants to do *her* share. (**NOT:** their.)
>
> Either the *Wilsons* or the *Henleys* will bring *their* phonograph.

NOTE: When *or* or *nor* joins a singular noun and a plural noun, a pronoun that refers to this construction should agree in number with the nearer noun. However, a strict application of this rule can lead to problems in sentence structure and meaning. Therefore, always try to make this kind of construction plural.

> Neither Mr. Baker nor his *employees have* reached *their* goal. (The plural pronoun *their* is used to agree with the nearer noun, *employees;* the verb *have* is also in the plural.)
>
> **NOT:** Neither the employees nor Mr. *Baker has* reached *his* goal. (The sentence follows the rule—*his* agrees with *Mr. Baker,* the nearer noun—but the meaning of the sentence has been distorted.)

[Continued on page 156.]

d. When the antecedent applies to either sex or to both, a masculine pronoun is used.

> A *parent* is responsible for the conduct of *his* children.
> *Each* person should hold *his* own ticket.
> *Each boy and girl* should hold *his* own ticket.
> **OR:** *Each boy and girl* must hold *his* or *her* own ticket. (For exactness, *his* or *her* may be substituted for *his.*)

e. Use a singular pronoun when the antecedent is a singular indefinite pronoun. The following indefinite pronouns are always singular:

anyone	everyone	someone	no one
anybody	everybody	somebody	nobody
anything	everything	something	nothing
each	every	either	one
each one	many a	neither	another

> *Everyone* has submitted *his* expense account today. (**NOT:** their.)
> *Nobody* could have helped *himself* in a situation like that. (**NOT:** themselves.)
> If *anyone* should ask for me, tell *him* that I won't return until Monday. (**NOT:** them.)
> *Every* company has *its* own vacation policy. (**NOT:** their.)
> While the conference is in session, does *every* secretary know how *she* is to handle *her* boss's correspondence?
> *Many a* saleswoman has had *her* problems with that customer.
> *Neither* of the clerks has *his* records up to date. (*His* agrees in number with *neither,* not with *clerks.*)
> Has *either* of the receptionists had *her* lunch? (*Her* agrees in number with *either; her* agrees with *receptionists* only in gender.)

▶ See also ¶¶ 1009–1010 for agreement of these indefinite pronouns with verbs.

f. Use a plural pronoun when the antecedent is a plural indefinite pronoun. The following indefinite pronouns are always plural:

many	few	several	others	both

> *Many* customers prefer to help *themselves; others* like someone to wait on *them.*
> A *few* of the secretaries have not yet taken *their* vacations.
> *Several* salesmen have made *their* annual goals in nine months.

▶ See also ¶ 1011 for agreement of these indefinite pronouns with verbs.

g. The following indefinite pronouns may be singular or plural, depending on the noun they refer to.

all	none	any	some	more	most

When these words are used as antecedents, carefully determine whether they are singular or plural. Then make the pronouns that refer to these antecedents agree in number.

Some employees have not yet had *their* annual physical checkup. (*Some* refers to *employees* and is plural; *some* is the antecedent of *their*.)

Some of the manuscript has been typed, but *it* has not been proofread. (*Some* refers to *manuscript* and is singular; *some* is the antecedent of *it* in the second clause.)

▶ See also ¶ 1012 for agreement of these indefinite pronouns with verbs.

h. Since indefinite pronouns express the third person, pronouns referring to these antecedents should also be in the third person (*he, she, it, they*).

> If *anyone* wants a salary advance, *he* should apply for it in writing.
>
> (**NOT:** If *anyone* wants a salary advance, *you* should apply for it in writing.)

If the indefinite pronoun is modified so that it strongly expresses the first or second person, the personal pronoun must also agree in number. Compare the following examples:

> *Most* parents want *their* children to go to college. (Third person.)
> *Most* of us want *our* children to go to college. (First person.)
>
> A *few* have missed *their* deadlines. (Third person.)
> A *few* of you have missed *your* deadlines. (Second person.)
>
> *Each* employee knows how much *he* ought to contribute. (Third person.)
> **BUT:** *Each* of us knows how much *he* ought to contribute. (Third person. In this sentence, *of us* does not shift the meaning to the first person; the emphasis is on what the individual contributes, not on what *we* contribute.)

▶ **IMPORTANT NOTE:** Pronouns take different forms, not only to indicate a difference in person (*I, you, he*), number (*he, they*), and gender (*he, she*), but also to indicate a difference in *case* (nominative, possessive, objective). Although a pronoun must agree with its antecedent in person, number, and gender, it *does not* necessarily agree with its antecedent in *case*. The case of a pronoun depends on its own relation to the other words in the sentence. The rules in ¶¶ 1046–1056 indicate how to choose the right case for pronouns.

PERSONAL PRONOUNS

1046 Use the *nominative* forms of personal pronouns (*I, we, you, he, she, it, they*):

a. When the pronoun is the subject of a verb.

> *I* wrote to Miss McIntyre, but *she* hasn't answered.
> Are *they* planning to follow up?
> Jack and *I* can handle the job ourselves. (**NOT:** Jack and me.)
> Either *he* or *I* can work late tonight. (**NOT:** him or me.)

NOTE: In sentences like the last two above, try each subject alone with the verb. You would not say "Me can handle the job" or "Him can work late tonight." Therefore, *I* and *he* must be used.

[*Continued on page 158.*]

b. When the pronoun appears in the predicate after some form of the verb *to be* (*am, is, are, was, were*) or after a verb phrase containing some form of *to be* (see the list below). Pronouns that follow these verb forms should be in the nominative.

shall (**OR** will) be	have (**OR** has) been
should (**OR** would) be	had been
shall (**OR** will) have been	may (**OR** might) be
should (**OR** would) have been	may (**OR** might) have been
can (**OR** could) be	must (**OR** ought to) be
could have been	must have (**OR** ought to have) been

It might have been *I.*	Was it *he* or *she* who phoned?
It could have been *they.*	The "culprit" was *she.*
It is *I.*	This is *she.*

NOTE: Sentences like "It is me" and "This is her" are acceptable in colloquial speech but should not be used in writing.

▶ See ¶ 1056 for special rules governing pronouns with the infinitive *to be*.

1047 Use the *objective* forms of personal pronouns (*me, us, you, him, her, it, them*):

a. When the pronoun is the direct or indirect object of a verb.

Frank gave Maris and *us* tickets for the opening.
They invited my wife and *me* for the weekend.

NOTE: When *my wife and* is mentally omitted, the objective form *me* is clearly the correct pronoun.

They invited *me* for the weekend.

b. When the pronoun is the object of a preposition.

This is for *you* and *me.*
No one knows except *us.*
Between *you* and *me,* that decision is unfair.

EXCEPTION: He is a friend of *mine* (*yours, his, hers, ours, theirs*). (See also ¶ 649.)

c. When the pronoun is the subject or the object of an infinitive. (See also ¶ 1056.)

The department head asked *him* to resign. (*Him* is the subject of *to resign.*)
Did you ask Jim to call *me?* (*Me* is the object of *to call.*)

1048 Most personal pronouns have two *possessive* forms.

a. Use *my, your, his, her, its, our,* or *their* when the possessive pronoun immediately precedes the noun it modifies.

That is *my* book.   It was *their* choice.

b. Use *mine, yours, his, hers, its, ours,* or *theirs* when the possessive pronoun stands apart from the noun it refers to.

That book is *mine*.   The choice was *theirs.*

He is a client of *ours*.   George is a neighbor of *hers.*

c. A pronoun that modifies a *gerund* (a verbal noun ending in *ing*) should be in the possessive. (See also ¶ 648.)

I appreciate *your* shipping the order so promptly.

d. Do not confuse certain possessive pronouns with contractions that sound like the possessive pronouns.

its (possessive)   it's (it is **OR** it has)
their (possessive)   they're (they are)
theirs (possessive)   there's (there is **OR** there has)
your (possessive)   you're (you are)

As a test for the correct form, try to substitute *it is* (or *they are, it has, there has, there is,* or *you are,* whichever is appropriate). If the substitution does not make sense, use the corresponding possessive form.

The nation should protect *its* resources. ("Protect it is resources" makes no sense.)

BUT: *It's* time to take stock of our achievements.

Their investing in high-risk stocks was a bad idea.

BUT: *They're* investing in high-risk stocks.

Theirs no longer works; that's why they borrow ours.

BUT: *There's* no use expecting him to change.

Your thinking is sound, but we lack the funds to underwrite your proposal.

BUT: *You're* thinking of applying for a transfer, I understand.

▶ See also ¶¶ 638–639 for other possessive pronouns.

1049 When a pronoun follows *than* or *as* in a comparison, determine the correct form of the pronoun by mentally supplying the words that are implied.

She types better than *I*. (*Than I do.*)

I like you better than *him*. (*Than I like him.*)

You are not as healthy as *he*. (*As healthy as he is.*)

1050 When a pronoun is used to identify a noun or another pronoun, it is either nominative or objective, depending on whether the antecedent is nominative or objective.

Mr. Clark called *us*, Ruth and *me*, into his office. (Since *us* is objective, the identifying pronoun *me* is also objective.)

The explanation was for the *newcomers,* Marie and *me*. (Was for *me*.)

The exceptions were the *newcomers,* Marie and *I*. (Exception was *I*.)

Let's *you* and *me* go to the picnic. (*Let's* is a contraction for *let us.* Since *us* is the objective form, the explanatory pronouns *you* and *me* are also objective.)

Mr. Hoyt wants *us* employees to work on Saturdays.

We employees need to confer.

[*Continued on page 160.*]

NOTE: In sentences like those preceding, mentally omit the noun (*employees*) to determine the correct form.

> Mr. Hoyt wants *us* to work on Saturday.
> *We* need to confer.

1051 Dictators often use *we* instead of *I* to avoid any seeming overemphasis on themselves. By current standards, however, it is preferable to use *we* only when you are speaking on behalf of an organization you represent and to use *I* when speaking for yourself alone.

> *We* shall prepare the necessary forms as soon as you send *us* a signed release. (This writer is speaking on behalf of his firm.)

> It is *my* opinion that this patient may be discharged at once. (This writer is speaking only for himself. Under these circumstances it would sound pompous to say, "It is *our* opinion.")

COMPOUND PERSONAL PRONOUNS

1052 The *self-* or *selves*-ending pronouns (*myself, yourself, himself, herself, itself, ourselves, yourselves, themselves*) should be used:

a. To direct the action expressed by the verb back to the subject.

> *He* found *himself* the only one in favor of the move.
> *We* have satisfied *ourselves* as to the wisdom of the action.
> We think that *they* have insured *themselves* against a possible loss.

b. To emphasize or to intensify a noun or pronoun already expressed.

> The *director himself* arranged the program.
> *I myself* am bewildered.
> *I* will write him *myself.*

NOTE: Do not use a compound personal pronoun unless the noun or pronoun to which it refers is expressed in the same sentence.

> The tickets are for Miss Barnet and *me.* (**NOT:** myself.)
> Henry and *I* can distribute all the mail. (**NOT:** Henry and myself.)

INTERROGATIVE AND RELATIVE PRONOUNS

1053 *Who* and *whom; whoever* and *whomever*

a. These pronouns are both *interrogative* pronouns (used in asking questions) and *relative* pronouns (used to refer to a noun in the main clause of a sentence).

> *Who* is going? (Interrogative.)
> Mr. Sears is the man *who* is going. (Relative, referring to *man.*)
> To *whom* shall I deliver the message? (Interrogative.)
> Miss Brown, *whom* I have never met, is in charge today. (Relative, referring to *Miss Brown.*)

b. These pronouns may be either singular or plural in meaning.

> *Who* is talking? (Singular.)
> *Who* are to be selected? (Plural.)
> *Whom* do you prefer for this job? (Singular.)
> *Whom* do you prefer for these jobs? (Plural.)

c. *Who* (or *whoever*) is the nominative form. Use it whenever *he* (or *she, they, I, we*) could be substituted in the *who* clause. (If in doubt, mentally rearrange the clause as is done in parentheses after each of the following examples.)

> *Who* is at the door? (*He* is at the door.)
> *Who* sang the duet with you? (*He* sang.)
> *Who* shall we say referred us? (We shall say *he* referred us.)
> *Who* did they say was chosen? (They did say *he* was chosen.)
> *Who* could it have been? (It could have been *he*.)
> The matter of *who should pay* was not decided. (*He* should pay.)
> We want to know *who you think should be appointed*. (You think *he* should be appointed.)
> *Whoever wins the primary* will win the election. (*He* wins the primary.)
> I will hire *whoever meets our minimum qualifications*. (*He* meets our minimum qualifications.)
> I will speak to *whoever answers the phone*. (*He* answers the phone.)
> Please write at once to *whoever you think can supply the information desired*. (You think *he* can supply the information desired.)
> Frank is the one *who can best do the job*. (*He* can best do the job.)
> James is the boy *who we expect will win*. (We expect *he* will win.)
> Please vote for the member *who you believe has done the most for the class*. (You believe *he* has done the most for the class.)
> We have referred your claim to our attorney, *who we are sure will reply soon*. (We are sure *he* will reply soon.)
> We have sent this order blank to all *who we have reason to believe are interested in our book*. (We have reason to believe *they* are interested in our book.)

d. *Whom* (or *whomever*) is the objective form. Use it whenever *him* (or *her, them, me, us*) could be substituted as the object of the verb or as the object of a preposition in the *whom* clause.

> *Whom* did you see today? (You did see *him* today.)
> To *whom* were you talking? (You were talking to *him*.)
> *Whom* were you talking about? (You were talking about *him*.)
> *Whom* did you say you wanted to see? (You did say you wanted to see *him*.)
> It depends on *whom they mean*. (They mean *him*.)
> The question of *whom we should charge* must be resolved. (We should charge *him*.)
> *Whomever you designate* will get the promotion. (You designate *him*.)
> I will hire *whomever I can find*. (I can find *him*.)

[Continued on page 162.]

I will speak to _whomever you suggest_. (You suggest _him_.)

I will give the job to _whomever you think you can safely recommend_. (You think you can safely recommend _him_.)

BUT: I will give the job to _whoever you think can be safely recommended_. (You think _he_ can be safely recommended.)

I need a cashier _whom I can trust_. (I can trust _him_.)

The man _to whom I was referring_ is Ed Dugan. (I was referring to _him_.)

The executive _whom I was thinking of_ doesn't have all those qualifications. (I was thinking of _him_.)

The person _whom we invited to address the committee_ cannot attend. (We invited _him_ to address the committee.)

John Ellsworth is the nominee _whom they plan to support_. (They plan to support _him_.)

Parsons is the person _whom we all thought the committee would nominate_. (We all thought the committee would nominate _him_.)

Frank Haley, _whom I considered to be their most promising representative_, resigned this month. (I considered _him_ to be their most promising representative.)

1054 _Who, which,_ and _that_

a. _Who_ and _that_ are used when referring to persons, _who_ being used when the individual person or the individuality of a group is meant and _that_ when a class, species, or type is meant. For example:

She is the girl _who_ understands French.

He is the kind of student _that_ we want.

b. _Which_ and _that_ are used when referring to places, objects, and animals. _Which_ is always used to introduce nonessential clauses, and _that_ is ordinarily used to introduce essential clauses.

Frank's report on personnel benefits, _which_ I sent you last week, should be of some help. (_Which_ introducing a nonessential clause.)

The report _that_ I sent you last week should be of some help. (_That_ introducing an essential clause.)

NOTE: A number of writers now use either _which_ or _that_ to introduce an essential clause. Indeed, _which_ is to be preferred to _that_ (a) when there are two or more parallel essential clauses in the same sentence, (b) when _that_ has already been used in the sentence, or (c) when the essential clause is introduced by such expressions as _this . . . which, that . . . which, these . . . which,_ or _those . . . which._

He is taking courses _which_ will earn him a higher salary rating in his current job and _which_ will qualify him for a number of higher-level jobs.

That is a movie _which_ you must not miss.

We need to reinforce those ideas _which_ were presented in earlier units.

1055 Do not confuse _whose_ (the possessive form of _who_) with _who's_ (a contraction meaning _who is_ or _who has_).

Whose house is it? (It is _his_.)

Who's the owner of that house? (_He_ is.)

PRONOUNS WITH **TO BE**

1056   **a.** If a pronoun is the subject of *to be,* use the *objective* form.

> I want *him* to be successful.
> I expected *her* to be late.
> *Whom* do you consider to be the more expert draftsman? (You do consider *whom* to be the more expert draftsman?)

b. If *to be* has a subject and is followed by a pronoun, put that pronoun in the *objective* case.

> They believe the *visitors* to be *us.* (*Visitors,* the subject of *to be,* is in the objective; therefore, the predicate pronoun following *to be* is objective, *us.*)
> They took *her* to be *me.*
> *Whom* do you take *him* to be? (You do take *him* to be *whom*?)

c. If *to be* has *no* subject and is followed by a pronoun, put that pronoun in the *nominative* case.

> The *caller* was thought to be *I.* (*I* agrees with the subject of sentence, *caller.*)
> *They* were thought to be *we.*
> *Who* was he thought to be? (*He* was thought to be *who*?)

▶ See ¶¶ 1009–1012 for problems concerning indefinite pronouns.

ADJECTIVES AND ADVERBS

1057, Only an adverb can modify an adjective.

> Packard's will give you a *really* good buy. (**NOT:** real good.)

1058   When the word following a verb describes the *subject* of the sentence, make sure the word is an *adjective* (not an adverb). Verbs of the *senses* (*smell, sound, taste, feel, look*) and *linking* verbs (the various forms of *appear, be, become, seem*) in most cases are followed by adjectives. A few other verbs (such as *grow, prove, come, get*) are sometimes followed by adjectives. (See, however, ¶ 1059, note.)

He looked *well.*	The *tree* grew *tall.*
He looked *bad.*	*Sugar* tastes *sweet.*
He feels *bad.*	The *typing* looks *neat.*
He is *well.*	Her *voice* sounded *strong.*
He became *famous.*	*She* appeared (**OR** seemed) *shy.*

TEST: If *is, are, was,* or *were* can be substituted for the verb, choose the adjective.

> He *looks happy.*   He *is happy.*

1059   When the word following a verb refers to the *action of the verb,* use an adverb.

[*Continued on page 164.*]

He *reads slowly* but he *talks rapidly.*
She *entered* the room *timidly.*
We guarantee *to ship* the goods *promptly.*
She *was injured badly* in the accident.

TEST: If *in a . . . manner* can be substituted for the *ly*-ending word, choose the adverb.

Read the directions *carefully.* (In a careful manner.)

NOTE: In the following group of examples, verbs of the senses and linking verbs (¶ 1058) are used as verbs of action. Since the modifier refers to the action of the verb (and does not describe the subject), the modifier must be an adverb.

He *looked suspiciously* at the visitor in the reception room.
He *felt carefully* along the ledge for the key.
That tree *has grown quickly.*
I *tasted* her new dessert *cautiously.*
The sexton *sounds* the bell *punctually.*
He *appeared quietly* in the doorway.

1060 Several of the most frequently used adverbs have two forms.

close, closely	fair, fairly	loud, loudly	short, shortly
deep, deeply	hard, hardly	quick, quickly	slow, slowly
direct, directly	late, lately	right, rightly	wide, widely

a. In a number of cases the two forms have different meanings.

Ship the goods *direct.* (Meaning "straight," "without detour.")
He was *directly* responsible for the dissatisfaction. (Meaning "without any intervention.")

They arrived *late.*
I haven't seen her *lately.*

The truck stopped *short.*
You will hear from us *shortly.*

You're hitting the keys too *hard.*
I could *hardly* hear him.

Turn *right* at the first traffic light.
I don't *rightly* remember.

b. In some cases the choice is largely one of usage. Some verbs take the *ly* form; others take the short form.

dig deep	go slow	come close	play fair
wound deeply	proceed slowly	bind closely	treat fairly

c. In still other cases the choice is simply one of formality. The *ly* forms are more formal.

sell cheap   **OR**   sell cheaply   talk loud   **OR**   talk loudly

1061 Although the *ly* ending usually signifies an adverb, several adjectives also end in *ly*—for example, *costly, orderly, timely, motherly, fatherly, friendly, neighborly.*

Check the stock in an *orderly* fashion.

Her offer to help the new clerk was a *friendly* gesture.

1062 A few common *ly*-ending words are used both as adjectives and adverbs—for example, *cowardly, early, likely, only, daily, weekly, monthly.*

I always go to bed at an *early hour.* (Adjective.)

The explosion *occurred early* in the day. (Adverb.)

1063 Problems of comparison

a. The comparative degree of one-syllable adjectives and adverbs is formed by adding *er* to the positive form; the superlative degree, by adding *est*. (See *e* below for a few exceptions.)

thin: thinner, thinnest   soon: sooner, soonest

b. The comparative degree of two-syllable adjectives and adverbs may be formed either by adding *er* to the positive form or by inserting either *more* or *less* before the positive form; the superlative degree, by adding *est* in some cases or by inserting *most* or *least* before the positive form.

happy: happier, more happy   often: oftener, less often
likely: likeliest, most (least) likely   highly: highest, most (least) highly

c. The superlative degree of adjectives and adverbs containing three or more syllables is always formed by inserting either *most* or *least* before the positive degree.

acceptable: most acceptable   carefully: least carefully

d. Avoid double comparisons.

cheaper (**NOT:** more cheaper)   unkindest (**NOT:** most unkindest)

e. A few adjectives have irregular comparisons.

Positive	Comparative	Superlative
bad or ill	worse	worst
good or well	better	best
far	farther, further	farthest, furthest
late	later, latter	latest, last
little	littler, less, lesser	littlest, least
many, much	more	most
. . . .	inner	innermost, inmost
. . . .	outer	outermost, outmost

f. Some adjectives and adverbs, from their very meanings, do not logically admit comparison. (Examples: *square, round, unique, completely, universally, correct, perfect, always, never, dead.*) Nevertheless, a number of these words may be modified by *more, less, nearly, hardly,* and similar adverbs to suggest an approach to the absolute.

Next year we hope to do a *more complete* study.

He is looking for a *more universally* acceptable solution.

Craftsmanship of this caliber is *virtually unique* these days.

[Continued on page 166.]

g. When referring to *two* persons, places, or things, use the comparative form; when referring to *more than two*, use the superlative form.

> That is the *finer* piece of linen. (Only two pieces are involved; hence the comparative form.)

> This is the *finest* piece of linen I could find. (Many pieces are involved; hence the superlative form.)

> Of the two positions open, you have chosen the *more* promising.

> Of the three positions open, you have chosen the *most* promising.

> That is the *more* efficient of the two methods.

> This is the *most* efficient method that could be devised.

> I like Wagner's plan *better* than Harrison's or Bromley's. (Although three things are involved in this comparison, they are being compared two at a time. Therefore, the comparative is used.)

h. When comparing a person or a thing *within* the group to which it belongs, use the superlative. When comparing a person or a thing with individual members of the group, use the comparative and the words *other* or *else.*

> Frank is the *most* conscientious employee on the staff.

> Frank is *more* conscientious than any *other* employee on the staff. (Without the word *other,* the sentence would imply that Frank is not on the staff.)

> Los Angeles is the *largest* city in California.

> Los Angeles is *larger* than any *other* city in California. (Without *other,* the sentence would imply that Los Angeles is not in California.)

> Bert's proposal was the *best* of all that were presented to the committee.

> Bert's proposal was *better* than anyone *else's.* (NOT: anyone's.)

i. Be sure to compare like things. (See also ¶ 645.)

> This year's output is lower than last year's. (In other words, "This year's output is lower than last year's *output.*")

> NOT: This year's output is lower than last year. (Incorrectly compares *this year's output* with *last year.*)

1064 The adverbs *only, nearly, almost, ever, scarcely, merely, too,* and *also* should be placed as close to the word modified—usually before—as possible. Putting the adverb in the wrong position may change the entire meaning of the sentence.

> Our list of depositors now numbers *almost* 50,000. (NOT: almost numbers.)

> *Only* the Board of Directors can nominate the three new officers. (Cannot be nominated by anyone else.)

> The Board of Directors can *only* nominate the three officers. (They cannot elect.)

> The Board of Directors can nominate *only* the three officers. (They cannot nominate anyone else.)

> *Only* Robert liked her. (No one else liked her.)

> Robert *only* liked her. (Robert did not love her.)

> Robert liked *only* her. (Robert liked no one else.)

1065 Do not use an adverb to express a meaning already contained in the verb.

return back:	omit *back*
cooperate together:	omit *together*
repeat again:	omit *again*

TROUBLESOME ADJECTIVES AND ADVERBS

▶ See individual entries listed alphabetically in ¶ 1101 for the following adjectives and adverbs:

Bad–badly	Good–well	Real–really
Different–differently	Hardly	Scarcely
Fewer–less	Kindly	Sure–surely
Former, Latter	Only	Very

NEGATIVES

1066 To express a negative idea in a simple sentence, use only one negative expression in the sentence. (A *double negative*—two negative expressions in the same sentence—gives a *positive* meaning.)

> We can sit by and do *nothing.*
>
> We *cannot* sit by and do *nothing.* (The *not* and *nothing* create a double negative; the sentence now has a positive meaning: "We ought to do something.")
>
> Jim is *un*aware of the facts. (Here the negative expression is the prefix *un.*)
>
> Jim is *not un*aware of the facts. (With the double negative, the sentence means "Jim *is* aware of the facts.")

NOTE: A double negative is not wrong in itself. As the examples above indicate, a double negative may offer a more effective way of expressing a *positive thought* than a straightforward positive construction would. However, a double negative *is* wrong if the sentence is intended to have a negative meaning. (REMEMBER: Two negatives make a positive.)

1067 A negative expression gives a negative meaning to the *clause* in which it appears. In a simple sentence, where there is only one clause, the negative expression affects the entire sentence (see ¶ 1066). In a sentence where there are two or more clauses, a negative expression affects only the clause in which it appears. Therefore, each clause may safely contain one negative expression. A double negative results when there are two negative expressions within the *same* clause.

> If Mr. Parker can*not* lower his price, there is *no* point in continuing the negotiations. (The *if* clause contains the negative *not;* the main clause contains the negative *no.* Each clause has its own negative meaning.)
>
> I have *not* met Halliday, and I have *no* desire to meet him.
>
> OR: I have *not* met Halliday, *nor* do I have *any* desire to meet him. (When the negative conjunction *nor* replaces *and,* the adjective *no* changes to *any* to avoid a double negative.)

[Continued on page 168.]

We have *never* permitted, *nor* will we permit, any lowering of our standards. (Here the second clause interrupts the first clause. If written out in full, the sentence would read, "We have never permitted any lowering of our standards, *nor* will we permit any lowering of our standards.")

NOTE: A second negative expression may be used in a clause simply to repeat or intensify the first negative expression. This construction is not a double negative.

No, I did *not* make that statement.

I *never, never* said a thing like that.

1068 To preserve the *negative* meaning of a clause, follow these basic principles:

a. If the clause has a *negative verb* (a verb modified by *not* or *never*), do not use any additional negative expressions, such as *nor, neither . . . nor, no, none, no one,* or *nothing.* Use corresponding positive expressions instead, such as *or, either . . . or, any, anyone,* or *anything.*

I have *not* invited *anyone.* (**WRONG:** I have *not* invited *no one.*)

She does *not* want *any.* (**WRONG:** She does *not* want *none.*)

Mary did *not* have *anything* to do yesterday. (**WRONG:** Mary did not have *nothing* to do yesterday.)

I can*not* find *either* the letter *or* the envelope. (**WRONG:** I can*not* find *neither* the letter *nor* the envelope.)

He did *not* say whether he would mail the money to us *or* whether he would bring it himself. (**WRONG:** He did *not* say whether he would mail the money to us *nor* whether he would bring it himself.)

b. If a clause contains any one of the following expressions—*no, no one, none, nothing,* or *neither . . . nor* (this counts as one expression)—make sure that the verb and all other words are *positive.*

I see *nothing* wrong with *either* proposal. (**NOT:** neither proposal.)

Neither Paul *nor* Charlie *can* handle the meeting for me. (**NOT:** cannot.)

c. The word *nor* may be used alone as a conjunction (see the example at the top of this page) or together with *neither.* Do not use *nor* in the same clause with any other negative; use *or* instead.

There are *neither* pens *nor* pencils in the stockroom.
BUT: There are *no* pens *or* pencils in the stockroom. (**WRONG:** *no* pens *nor* pencils.)

There are *no* clear-cut rights *or* wrongs in the situation. (**WRONG:** *no . . .* rights *nor* wrongs.)

Francine has *not* called *or* written us for some time. (**WRONG:** *not* called *nor* written.)

Never try to argue *or* debate with Lawrence. (**WRONG:** *Never . . .* argue *nor* debate.)

▶ See individual entries in ¶ 1101 for *hardly, only,* and *scarcely,* which have a negative meaning.

PREPOSITIONS

WORDS REQUIRING CERTAIN PREPOSITIONS

1069 Usage requires that certain words be followed by certain prepositions. Some of the most frequently used combinations are listed below.

account for something or someone: I find it hard to *account for* his behavior.

account to someone: You will have to *account to* Miss Endicott for the loss of the key.

agree on or **upon** (reach an understanding): We cannot *agree on* the price.

agree to (accept another person's plan): Will you *agree to* their terms?

agree with (concur with a person or an idea): I *agree with* your objectives.

angry at or **about** something: He was *angry about* the total disorder of the office.

angry with someone: You have every right to be *angry with* me.

apply for a position: You ought to *apply for* Harry's job, now that he has left.

apply to someone or something: You must *apply* yourself *to* the job in order to master it. I am thinking of *applying to* the Field Engineering Company.

argue about something: We *argued about* the terms of the contract.

argue with a person: It doesn't pay to *argue with* Bremer.

compare to (assert a likeness): He *compared* my writing *to* E. B. White's. (He said I wrote like E. B. White.)

compare with (analyze for similarities and differences): When he *compared* my writing *with* E. B. White's, he said that I had a similar kind of humor but that my sentences lacked the clean and easy flow of White's material.

conform to (preferred to *with*): These blueprints do not *conform to* the original plans.

consists in (exists in): Happiness largely *consists in* knowing what it is that will make you happy.

consists of (is made up of): His new formula for a wage settlement *consists of* the same old terms expressed in different language.

convenient for (suitable): What time will be most *convenient for* you?

convenient to (near at hand): Our plant is *convenient to* all major transportation facilities.

correspond to or **with** (agree with): The shipment does not *correspond to* the sample.

correspond with (exchange letters): It may be better to see him in person than to *correspond with* him.

differ about (something): We *differed about* means but not about objectives.

differ from (something else): This job *differs* very little *from* the one that I used to have.

differ with (someone): I *differ with* you over the likely consequences of the discussion.

[Continued on page 170.]

different from: This soap powder is *different from* the one I normally use.

different than: I view the matter in a *different* way *than* you do. (Although *from* is normally preferred, *than* is acceptable in order to avoid sentences like "I view the matter in a different way from the way in which you do.")

identical with (not *to*): This $50 suit is *identical with* one advertised for $70 at other stores.

independent of (not *from*): He wants to be *independent of* his family's money.

interested in: We are *interested in* discussing the matter further with you.

retroactive to (not *from*): This salary adjustment is *retroactive to* May 1.

speak to (tell something to): You ought to *speak to* Brown about his absences.
speak with (discuss with): It was good to *speak with* you yesterday.

SUPERFLUOUS PREPOSITIONS

1070 Do not use prepositions that are not needed. In the following examples prepositions add nothing to the meaning. (See also the entry for *Up* in ¶ 1101.)

> Where is she (at)?
> Where did that paper go (to)?
> The new stenographer seems to be (of) about sixteen years of age.
> She could not help (from) crying.
> His house is opposite (to) hers.
> The chair is too near (to) the desk.
> Let us meet at about one o'clock. (Omit either *at* or *about*.)
> The papers fell off (of) the desk.

NECESSARY PREPOSITIONS

1071 Conversely, do not omit essential prepositions.

> I bought a couple *of* books. (**NOT:** I bought a couple books.)
> *Of* what use is this gadget? (**NOT:** What use is this gadget?)
> We don't sell that type of filter. (**NOT:** that type filter.)
> You seem to have a great interest *in,* as well as a deep respect *for,* fine antiques. (**NOT:** You seem to have a great interest, as well as a deep respect *for,* fine antiques.)
> He frequently appears in movies, *in* plays, and on television. (**NOT:** in movies, plays, and on television.)

PREPOSITIONS AT THE END OF SENTENCES

1072 A sentence may or may not end with a preposition, depending on the emphasis and effectiveness desired.

> **WEAK:** I wish I knew the magazine that his article appeared *in.*
> **STRONGER:** I wish I knew the magazine *in which* his article appeared.

STILTED: It is difficult to know *about* what he is thinking.

NATURAL: It is difficult to know what he is thinking *about*.

Short questions frequently end with prepositions.

How many can I count *on?*   What is this good *for?*

TROUBLESOME PREPOSITIONS

▶ See individual entries listed alphabetically in ¶ 1101 for the following prepositions:

Beside-besides	Except	Like-as, as if
Between-among	From-off	Off
Due to-because of-	In-into-in to	On-onto-on to
on account of	In regards to	On-upon-up on

SENTENCE STRUCTURE

PARALLEL STRUCTURE

1073 Express parallel ideas in parallel form.

a. Adjectives should be paralleled by adjectives, nouns by nouns, infinitives by infinitives, subordinate clauses by subordinate clauses, etc.

WRONG: Our new course is challenging and an inspiration. (Adjective and noun.)

RIGHT: Our new course is *challenging* and *inspiring*. (Two adjectives.)

WRONG: This machine is inexpensive, efficient, and it is easily operated. (Two adjectives and a clause.)

RIGHT: This machine is *inexpensive, efficient,* and *easily operated.* (Three adjectives.)

WRONG: The seniors have already started reviewing and to cram. (Participle and infinitive.)

RIGHT: The seniors have already started *reviewing* and *cramming.* (Two participles.)

RIGHT: The seniors have already started *to review* and *cram.* (Two infinitives.)

NOTE: Parallelism is especially important in displayed enumerations.

WRONG: The duties of the committee hostess are:
1. To greet guests.
2. Ordering refreshments.
3. Arrangement of flowers.

RIGHT: The duties of the committee hostess are:
1. To greet guests.
2. To order refreshments.
3. To arrange flowers.

b. Correlative conjunctions (*both . . . and, either . . . or, neither . . . nor, not only . . . but also, whether . . . or,* etc.) should be followed by elements in parallel form.

[Continued on page 172.]

WRONG: She is not only proficient in shorthand but also in typing.

RIGHT: She is proficient not only *in shorthand* but also *in typing.*

WRONG: I have sent a telegram both to Chicago and San Francisco.

RIGHT: I have sent a telegram to both *Chicago* and *San Francisco.*

RIGHT: I have sent a telegram both *to Chicago* and *to San Francisco.*

WRONG: He would neither apologize nor would he promise to reform.

RIGHT: He would neither *apologize* nor *promise to reform.*

RIGHT: He would not apologize, nor would he promise to reform.

DANGLING CONSTRUCTIONS

1074   When a sentence begins with a participial phrase, an infinitive phrase, a gerund phrase, or an elliptical clause (one in which essential words are missing), make sure that it logically agrees with the subject of the sentence; otherwise, the construction will "dangle." To correct a dangling construction, make the subject of the sentence the doer of the action expressed by the opening phrase or clause. If that is not feasible, use an entirely different construction.

a. Participial phrases

WRONG: Having studied your cost estimates, a few question occur to me.

RIGHT: Having studied your cost estimates, I would like to ask you a few questions.

WRONG: Putting the matter of costs aside, the matter of production delays remains to be discussed.

RIGHT: Putting the matter of costs aside, we must still discuss the matter of production delays.

b. Infinitive phrases

WRONG: To produce satisfactory carbon copies, unwrinkled carbon paper must be used.

RIGHT: To produce satisfactory carbon copies, the typist must use unwrinkled carbon paper.

WRONG: To obtain the free booklet, this coupon should be mailed at once.

RIGHT: To obtain the free booklet, mail this coupon at once.

c. Prepositional-gerund phrases

WRONG: In passing the store windows, many handsome displays caught my eye.

RIGHT: In passing the store windows, I noticed many handsome displays.

WRONG: In analyzing these specifications, several errors have been found.

RIGHT: In analyzing these specifications, I have found several errors.

d. Elliptical clauses

WRONG: If ordered before May 1, a 5 percent discount will be allowed.

RIGHT: If ordered before May 1, these goods will be sold at a 5 percent discount.

WRONG: When four years old, my family moved to Omaha.

RIGHT: When I was four years old, my family moved to Omaha.

NOTE: *Absolute phrases* (typically involving passive participles) are not considered to "dangle" even though they come at the beginning of a sentence and do not refer to the subject. Such constructions, though grammatically correct, are usually awkward and should be avoided.

WEAK: The speeches having been concluded, we proceeded to take a vote.

BETTER: After the speeches were concluded, we proceeded to take a vote.

1075 When verbal phrases and elliptical clauses fall elsewhere in the sentence, be alert for illogical or confusing relationships. Adjust the wording as necessary.

WRONG: I caught a glimpse of the astronauts, running to the window.

RIGHT: Running to the window, I caught a glimpse of the astronauts.

WRONG: The desk should be cleared of papers before going out to lunch.

RIGHT: You should clear your desk of papers before going out to lunch (OR before you go out to lunch).

Section 11
USAGE

1101 The following words and phrases are often used incorrectly.

A-an. The article *a* is used before all consonant sounds, including sounded *h*, long *u*, and *o* with the sound of *w* (as in *one*); for example, *a day, a week, a home, a house, a unit, a union, a uniform, a one-week seminar, a CPA, a 60-day note.*

An is used before all vowel sounds except long *u* and before words beginning with silent *h;* for example, *an evening, an army, an outlet, an umbrella, an umpire, an heir, an hour, an honor, an R* (pronounced "ar"), *an f.o.b. order* (pronounced "ef o b"), *an 8-hour day.*

A-per. (See *Per–a.*)

Accidently. No such word. Use *accidentally.*

A.D.-B.C. *A.D.* (abbreviation of *anno Domini,* Latin for "in the year of our Lord") and *B.C.* ("before Christ") are written in all capitals, with a period following each letter.

a. *B.C.* follows the year (*150 B.C.*).

b. *A.D.* ordinarily follows the year (*465 A.D.*), but in formal writing it precedes the year (*A.D. 465*).

NOTE: Do not use a comma to separate *B.C.* or *A.D.* from the year.

Age-aged-at the age of

I interviewed a man *aged 52* for the job. (**NOT:** a man age 52.)

You can collect these benefits *at the age of 62.* (Avoid the construction *at age 62* in nontechnical writing.)

All of. *Of* is not necessary after *all* unless the following word is a pronoun.

All the men belong to the softball team. (**ALSO:** All of the men . . .)

All of us belong to the softball team.

All right. Like *all wrong,* the expression *all right* should be spelled as two words. (Some dictionaries acknowledge the existence of the one-word form *alright,* but this spelling is not generally accepted as correct.)

Almost-all most. (See also *Most.*)

The plane was *almost* (nearly) three hours late.

We are *all most* pleased (all very much pleased) with the new schedule.

Already-all ready

The order had *already* (previously) been shipped.

The order is *all ready* (all prepared) to be shipped.

Altogether-all together

He is *altogether* (entirely) too lazy to be a success.

The papers are *all together* (all in a group) on Mr. Green's desk.

Always-all ways

She has *always* (at all times) done good work.

We have tried in *all ways* (by all methods) to keep our employees satisfied.

Among. (See *Between-among.*)

Amount-number. Use *amount* for things in bulk, as in "a large amount of lumber." Use *number* for individual items, as in "a large number of students."

And etc. Never use *and* with *etc.* (See *Etc.*)

And/or. This is a legalistic term and should be avoided in ordinary writing.

And which. Use only to introduce a clause that parallels a preceding clause introduced by *which.*

To meet our quota, we need several large orders, which we expect to receive next week *and which* will be credited to our department.

Anyone-any one

Anyone (anybody) could follow these directions.

Any one of us (any person of a group) could have made the same mistake.

NOTE: Spell *any one* as two words when it is followed by an *of* phrase or when it implies "one of a number of things."

Anyway-any way

> *Anyway* (in any case) we can't spare him now.
> If we can help in *any way* (by any method), please phone.

As. Do not use for *that* or *whether;* for example, "I do not know *whether* (**NOT** as) I can go." Prefer *because, since,* or *for* to *as* in clauses of reason; for example, "I cannot attend the meeting in Omaha, *because* (**NOT** as) I will be out on the Coast that day."

At about. Use either *at* or *about,* but not both words together. For example, "Plan to arrive *at* ten" **OR** "Plan to arrive *about* ten." (**BUT NOT:** Plan to arrive *at about* ten.)

Awhile-a while. One word as an adverb; two words as a noun.

> You may have to wait *awhile.* (Adverb.)
> You may have to wait for a *while.* (Noun; object of *for.*)
> I ran into him a *while* back.

Bad-badly. To describe the way a person feels, use the adjective *bad* (not the adverb *badly*) after the verb *feel.*

> I feel *bad* (**NOT** badly) about the mistake.
> **BUT:** He was hurt *badly* in the accident.

Avoid using *badly* for *a great deal* or *very much.*

> Mr. Tead wants *very much* (**NOT** badly) to meet Mr. Scott.

Because. (See *Reason is because.*)

Because of. (See *Due to-because of-on account of.*)

Being that. Do not use for *since* or *because.* For example, "*Because* (**NOT** being that) I was late, I could not get a seat."

Beside-besides

> I sat *beside* (next to) Mr. Parrish's father at the luncheon.
> *Besides* (in addition), we need your support of the measure.

Between-among. Ordinarily, use *between* when referring to *two* persons or things and *among* when referring to *more than* two persons or things.

> The territory is divided evenly *between* the two salesmen.
> The profits are to be evenly divided *among* the three partners.

Use *between* with more than two persons or things when they are being considered in pairs as well as in a group.

> There are distinct differences *between* New York, Chicago, and Dallas.
> In packing china, be sure to place paper *between* the plates. (**NOT:** between *each* of the plates.)

Between you and me (not *I*). (See ¶ 1047*b*.)

Both-each. *Both* means "the two considered together." *Each* refers to the individual members of a group considered separately.

> *Both* designs are acceptable.   The designs are *each* acceptable.

Both alike. *Both* is unnecessary. For example, "The dresses are *alike.*" (NOT: both alike.)

Bring-take. *Bring* indicates motion toward the speaker. (HINT: Connect the *i* in *bring* with *I*, the speaker.) *Take* indicates motion away from the speaker. (HINT: Connect the *a*'s in *take* and in *away.*)

> Please *bring* me the morning paper.
>
> Please *take* this file to Mr. Walter.

See note under *Come-go.*

But what. Prefer *that.* For example, "I do not doubt *that* (NOT but what) he will be elected."

Cannot help but. This expression is a confusion of two others, namely, *can but* and *cannot help.*

> I *can but* try.
>
> I *cannot help* feeling sorry for her. (NOT: cannot help but feel.)

Class. (See *Kind.*)

Come-go. The choice between verbs depends on the location of the speaker. *Come* indicates motion *toward; go,* motion *away from.* (See also *Bring-take.*)

> When Bellotti *comes* home, I will *go* to the airport to meet him.
>
> *A salesman speaking over the phone to a customer:* Perhaps it is not convenient for you to *come* to the store tomorrow.
>
> *Anyone outside the store speaking:* Perhaps it is not convenient for you to *go* to the store tomorrow.

NOTE: When writing about your travel plans to a person at your destination, adopt that person's point of view and use *come.*

> *Midwesterner to Californian:* I am *coming* to California during the week of the 11th and hope to see you sometime that week. I will *bring* the plans with me if they are ready.

However, if you are telling your travel plans to someone who is *not* at your destination, observe the regular distinction between *come* and *go.*

> *Midwesterner to Midwesterner:* I am *going* to California during the week of the 11th and will try to see Spenser sometime that week. I will *take* the plans with me if they are ready.

Come and. In written material prefer *come to* to the colloquial *come and.* For example, "Come to (NOT and) see me."

Data-datum. (See ¶ 1017.)

Different-differently. When the meaning is "in a different manner," use the adverb *differently.*

I wish the story had ended *differently*.

I understand it *differently*.

My mother looked at the episode *differently*.

After linking verbs and verbs of the senses, the adjective *different* is correct. (See ¶ 1058.)

That music sounds completely *different*.

The salesclerk looked *different* in her new hairdo.

He seems (appears) *different* since his promotion.

Done. Do not use *done* in the past tense; use *did*. For example, "I *did* it." (NOT: I *done* it.)

Don't (do not). Do not use *don't* with *he, she,* or *it;* use *doesn't*.

He *doesn't* talk easily.	BUT: I *don't* think so.
She *doesn't* take her work seriously.	They *don't* want to help.
It *doesn't* seem right to penalize him.	We *don't* understand.

Doubt that-doubt whether. Use *doubt that* in negative statements and in questions. Use *doubt whether* in all other cases. (See also *If-whether*.)

We do not *doubt that* he is capable.

Is there any *doubt that* the letter was mailed?

I *doubt whether* I can go.

Due to-because of-on account of. *Due to* introduces an adjectival phrase and should modify nouns. It is normally used only after some form of the verb *to be* (*is, are, was, were,* etc.).

Her success is *due to* conscientiousness. (Modifies *success*.)

Because of and *on account of* introduce adverbial phrases and should modify verbs.

He resigned *because of* (OR *on account of*) ill health. (Modifies *resigned*.)

Each-both. (See *Both-each*.)

Each other-one another. Use *each other* to refer to two persons or things; *one another* for more than two.

The two partners had great respect for *each other*.

The four winners congratulated *one another*.

Equally as good. Use either *equally good* or *just as good*.

His pen is newer, but mine is *equally good*. (NOT: equally as good.)

My pen is *just as good* as his. (NOT: equally as good.)

Etc. This abbreviation means "and other things." Therefore, do not use *and* before it. A comma both precedes and follows *etc.* (see ¶ 149). Avoid *etc.* in sentences where phrases such as *and the like* or *and so on* will do as well.

Everyday-every day

The new stenographer soon mastered the *everyday* (ordinary or daily) routine of the office.

He has called *every day* (each day) this week.

Everyone-every one

Everyone (everybody) likes to be recognized for his ability.

Every one of the men (each person in the group) was paid.

NOTE: Spell *every one* as two words when it is followed by *of.*

Except. When *except* is a preposition, be sure to use the objective form of a pronoun that follows. For example, "Everyone has been transferred *except* Frank and *me.*" (NOT: except Frank and I.)

Fewer-less. *Fewer* refers to number and is used with *plural* nouns. *Less* refers to degree or amount and is used with *singular* nouns.

Fewer accidents (a smaller number) were reported than was expected.

Less effort (a smaller degree) was put forth by the organizers, and thus *fewer* people (a smaller number) attended.

NOTE: The expression *less than* (rather than *fewer than*) precedes plural nouns.

Less than five customers have asked for refunds.

Former. Refers to the first of two persons or things. When more than two are mentioned, *first* is preferred to *former.* (See also *Latter.*)

This style is made in wool and in cotton, but I prefer the *former.*

This style is made in wool, in cotton, and in Orlon, but I prefer the *first.*

From-off. Use *from* (not *off*) with persons.

I got this bracelet *from* Margaret. (NOT: off Margaret.)

Good-well. *Good* is an adjective. *Well* may be used as an adverb or (with reference to health) as an adjective.

Marie got *good* grades in school. (Adjective.)

I will do the job as *well* as I can. (Adverb.)

He admits he does not feel *well* today. (Adjective.)

The guards look *good* in their new uniforms. (Adjective.)

NOTE: To feel *well* means "to be in good health." To feel *good* means "to be in good spirits."

Hardly. Since *hardly* is negative in meaning, do not use another negative with it.

You *could hardly* (NOT couldn't hardly) expect that to happen.

Have got. In written material use *have* in place of the colloquial *have got.* For example, "They *have* (NOT have got) a television set."

Healthy-healthful. People are *healthy;* a climate or food is *healthful.*

Help. Do not use *from* after *help.* For example, "I couldn't *help* (**NOT** help from) telling her she was wrong."

If-whether. *If* is often used colloquially for *whether* in such sentences as "He doesn't know *whether* he will be able to leave tomorrow." In written material, prefer *whether,* particularly in such expressions as *see whether, learn whether, know whether,* and *doubt whether.*

Imply-infer. *Imply* means "to suggest"; a person implies something by *his own* words or actions.

>   Frank *implied* that you would not be invited.

Infer means "to deduce" or "to arrive at a conclusion"; a person infers something from *another person's* words or actions.

>   I *inferred* from Frank's remarks that you would not be invited.

In-into-in to

>   The correspondence is *in* the file. (*In* implies position within.)
>   He walked *into* the outer office. (*Into* implies entry or change of form.)
>   All sales reports are to be sent *in to* the sales manager. (*In* is an adverb in the verb phrase *are to be sent in; to* is a simple preposition.)
>   Mr. Green came *in to* see me. (*In* is part of the verb phrase *came in; to* is part of the infinitive *to see.*)

In regards to. Substitute *in regard to, with regard to,* or *as regards.*

Indifferent-in different

>   She was *indifferent* (not caring one way or the other) to the opportunity for a transfer.
>   He liked our idea, but he wanted it expressed *in different* (in other) words.

Indirect-in direct

>   *Indirect* (not direct) lighting will enhance the appearance of this room.
>   This order is *in direct* (the preposition *in* plus the adjective *direct*) conflict with the policy of this company.

Its-it's. (See ¶ 1048*d.*)

Kind. *Kind* is singular; therefore, write *this kind, that kind, these kinds, those kinds* (but not *these kind, those kind*). The same distinctions hold for *class, type,* and *sort.*

Kind of-sort of. In written material use *somewhat* or *rather* instead of the colloquial expression *kind of* or *sort of.*

>   I was *somewhat* (**NOT** kind of, sort of) bored.
>   She seemed *rather* (**NOT** kind of, sort of) tired.

Kind of a. The *a* is unnecessary. For example, "That *kind of* (**NOT** kind of a) material is very expensive."

Kindly. Often meaningless in letters when no act of kindness is intended. Such expressions as *Thank you very much* or *Will you please* are preferable.

Last-latest. *Last* means "after all others"; *latest*, "most recent."

> Mr. Long's *last* act before leaving was to recommend Mr. Holt's promotion.
>
> This is the *latest* bulletin from the Weather Bureau.

Latter. Refers to the second of two persons or things mentioned. When more than two are mentioned, *last* is preferable to *latter*. (See also *Former*.)

> July and August are both vacation months, but the *latter* is more popular.
>
> June, July, and August are all vacation months, but the *last* is the most popular.

Lay-lie. *Lay* (principal parts: *lay, laid, laid, laying*) means "to put" or "to place." It signifies that someone is placing something in a reclining position. This verb requires an object to complete its meaning.

> Please *lay* the *box* on the shelf.
>
> I *laid* the *letter* on his desk.
>
> I *had laid* two other *letters* there yesterday.
>
> He is always *laying* the *blame* on his assistants. (Puts the blame.)
>
> The dress *was laid* in the box. (A passive construction implying that someone *laid the dress* in the box.)

Lie (principal parts: *lie, lay, lain, lying*) means "to recline, rest, or stay" or "to take a position of rest." It refers to a person or thing as either assuming or being in a reclining position. This verb cannot take an object.

> The invalid *lies* on a couch.
>
> Our dog *lay* before the fire all evening.
>
> That beautiful dress *has lain* on the dirty floor.
>
> Today's mail is *lying* on the table in the reception room.

TEST: In deciding whether to use *lie* or *lay* in a sentence, substitute the word *place* for the word in question. If it does not fit, then use some form of *lie*.

> I will (*lie* or *lay?*) down now. (You could not say, "I will place down now." Therefore, the word must be *lie*.) I will *lie* down now.
>
> I (*laid* or *lay?*) the pad on his desk. I *placed* (*laid*) the pad on his desk.

NOTE: When the verb *lie* means "to tell a falsehood," it has regularly formed principal parts (*lie, lied, lied, lying*) and is seldom confused with the verbs just described.

Learn-teach. *Learn* (principal parts: *learn, learned, learned, learning*) means "to acquire knowledge." *Teach* (principal parts: *teach, taught, taught, teaching*) means "to impart knowledge to others."

> I *learned* my lesson well.   An excellent instructor *taught* me.
>
> I was *taught* to do that a different way, but I now *teach* according to the new method.

Leave-let. *Leave* (principal parts: *leave, left, left, leaving*) means "to move away," "to abandon," or "to depart." *Let* (principal parts: *let, let, let, letting*) means "to permit" or "to allow."

> I now *leave* you to your own devices. (Abandon you.)
> Mr. Maxwell *left* on the morning train. (Departed.)
> *Let* me see the last page. (Permit me.)

TEST: In deciding whether to use *let* or *leave*, try substituting *permit*. If *permit* fits, use *let;* if not, use *leave*.

Like-as, as if. *Like* is correctly used as a preposition.

> Mary looks *like* her mother.   My sister looks *like* me.

Although *like* is now widely used as a conjunction in colloquial speech, prefer *as* or *as if* in written material.

> Mary looks *as* (**NOT** like) her mother did at her age.
> It looks *as if* (**NOT** like) it will rain.

May-can (might-could). *May* and *might* imply permission or possibility; *can* and *could,* ability or power.

> You *may* send us a dozen cans of paint on trial. (Permission.)
> The report *may* be true. (Possibility.)
> *Can* he present a workable plan? (Has he the ability?)
> Mr. Pratt said I *might* (permission) have the time off if I *could* (power) finish my work in time.

Maybe-may be

> If we don't receive a letter today, *maybe* (an adverb meaning "perhaps") we should wire the company.
> Mr. Brown *may be* (a verb) in his office tomorrow.

Most. Do not use for *almost.* For example, *"Almost all* the paper is gone" **OR** *"Most* of the paper is gone." (**BUT NOT:** *Most all* of the paper is gone.)

Nobody-no body

> There was *nobody* (no person) at the information desk when I arrived.
> *No body* (no group) of employees is more cooperative than yours.

NOTE: Spell *no body* as two words when it is followed by *of.*

None-no one. (See also ¶ 1012, note.)

> *None* of the offers proved acceptable.
> *No one* in the room could answer the question.

Number. (See *Amount-number.*)

Of-have. Do not use *of* instead of *have* in verb forms. The correct forms are *could have, would have, should have, might have, may have, must have, ought to have,* etc.

Off. Do not use *off of* or *off from* in place of *off*.

The papers fell *off* the desk. (**NOT:** off of the desk.)

On–onto–on to

Next place the carbon sheet *on* the onionskin. (*On* implies position or movement over.)

He lost control of the car and drove *onto* the sidewalk. (*Onto* implies movement toward and then over.)

Let's go *on to* the next problem. (*On* is an adverb in the verb phrase *go on*; *to* is a preposition.)

He then went *on to* tell about his experiences in Asia. (*On* is part of the verb phrase *went on*; *to* is part of the infinitive *to tell*.)

On–upon–up on

His statements were based *on* (**OR** *upon*) experimental data. (*On* and *upon* are interchangeable.)

To reach those shelves, step *up on* the chair. (*Up* is part of the verb phrase *step up*; *on* is a preposition.)

One another. (See *Each other–one another*.)

Only. The adverb *only* is negative in meaning. Therefore, do not use another negative with it unless you want a positive meaning. (See ¶ 1064 for the placement of *only* in a sentence.)

I use this letterhead *only* for foreign correspondence. (I do not use this letterhead for anything else.)

BUT: I do not use this letterhead *only* for foreign correspondence. (I use it for a number of other things as well.)

Opposite. When used as a noun, *opposite* is followed by *of*.

Her opinion is the *opposite of* mine.

In other uses, *opposite* is followed by *to* or *from* or by neither.

Her opinion is *opposite to* (**OR** *from*) mine.

She lives *opposite* the school.

Party. Do not use for *person*, except in legal work.

Per–a. *Per*, a Latin word, is frequently used in business to mean "by the," as in *$5 per hundredweight* or *60 miles per hour*. Whenever possible, substitute *a* or *an*; for example, *at the rate of 75 cents an hour, 30 cents a gallon*. Do *not* use *per* in the sense of "according to" or "in accordance with."

We are sending you samples *in accordance with* (**NOT** as per) your request.

Raise–rise. *Raise* (principal parts: *raise, raised, raised, raising*) means "to cause to lift" or "to lift something." This verb requires an object to complete its meaning.

Mr. Pinelli *raises* a good question.

The teacher *raised* the *shade* in the late afternoon.

Most growers *have raised* the *price* of coffee.

We are *raising money* for the United Fund.

Our rent *has been raised*. (A passive construction implying that someone *has raised* the rent.)

Rise (principal parts: *rise, rose, risen, rising*) means "to ascend," "to move upward by itself," or "to get up." This verb cannot be used with an object.

Mr. Chairman, I *rise* to a point of order.

The sun *rose* at 6:25 this morning.

The river *has risen* to flood level.

The temperature *has been rising* all day.

TEST: Remember, you cannot "rise" anything.

Real-really. *Real* is an adjective; *really*, an adverb. Do not use *real* for *very* or *really*.

The ring is set with *real* diamonds. (Adjective.)

I was *really* ashamed of her. (Adverb.)

It was *very* nice of you to call. (**NOT:** real nice.)

Reason is because. Substitute *reason is that*. For example, "The *reason* for such low sales *is that* (**NOT** because) prices are too high."

Retroactive to (not *from*). For example, "Salaries of all secretaries will be increased $5 a week *retroactive to* January 1."

Same. Do not use for *it*. For example, "We will alter the suit and have *it* (**NOT** same) ready for you by Saturday."

Scarcely. The adverb *scarcely* is negative in meaning. Therefore, do not use another negative with it. (See ¶ 1064 for the placement of *scarcely*.)

She *scarcely* recognized (**NOT** didn't scarcely recognize) me.

Set-sit. *Set* (principal parts: *set, set, set, setting*) means "to place something somewhere." This verb requires an object to complete its meaning.

Shall I *set* another *place* at the table?

I *set* my *suitcase* down and hailed a taxicab.

I *have set* my *alarm* for six o'clock.

The crew *was setting* the *stage* for the evening performance.

The vase *was set* on the mantle. (A passive construction implying that someone *set* the vase on the mantle.)

NOTE: *Set* has a few other meanings in which the verb does *not* require an object, but these meanings are seldom confused with *sit*.

They *set* out on the trip in high spirits.

The sun *set* at 5:34 p.m. Wednesday.

Do not disturb the gelatin dessert until it *has set*.

Sit (principal parts: *sit, sat, sat, sitting*) means "to be in a position of rest" or "to be seated." This verb cannot be used with an object.

[*Continued on page 184.*]

Here we *sit,* waiting for a decision.

I *sat* next to Bertrand at the board meeting.

They *had sat* at the station a full hour.

They *will be sitting* in the orchestra.

TEST: Remember, you cannot "sit" anything.

Shall–will. The auxiliary verb *shall* has largely given way to the verb *will* in all but the most formal writing and speech. Some business firms, however, still prefer a formal style and require that the distinction between *shall* and *will* be observed. The following rules reflect both general and formal usage:

a. To express simple future time:

(1) In *ordinary* circumstances, use *will* with all three persons.

I (OR we) *will* be glad to help you if we can.

You *will* want to study his recommendations before the meeting.

He (OR she, it, they) *will* arrive tomorrow morning.

(2) In *formal* circumstances, use *shall* with the first person (*I, we*) and *will* with the second and third persons (*you, he, she, it, they*).

I (OR we) *shall* be glad to answer all inquiries promptly.

You *will* meet her at the reception this evening.

They (OR he, she) *will* not find the trip too tiring.

NOTE: In formal situations, do not say "I will" unless you really mean "I am determined" or "I am willing."

I *shall* appreciate an early reply.

b. To indicate *determination, promise, desire, choice,* or *threat:*

(1) In *ordinary* circumstances use *will* with all three persons.

(2) In *formal* circumstances, use *will* for the first person (*I, we*) and *shall* for the second and third persons (*you, he, she, it, they*).

In spite of the risk, I *will* go where I please. (Determination.)

We (OR I) *will* not be coerced. (Determination.)

He (OR they) *shall* not work in my department. (Determination.)

I *will* send my check by the end of the week. (Promise.)

We (OR I) *will* report you to the authorities if this is true. (Threat.)

You *shall* obey me! (Threat.)

He *shall* study, or he *shall* leave college. (Threat.)

c. To indicate *willingness* (to be willing, to be agreeable to) in both *ordinary* and *formal* circumstances, use *will* with all persons.

Yes, I *will* meet you at six o'clock.

Yes, he *will* meet you at six o'clock.

Should–would. *Should* and *would* follow the same rules as *shall* and *will* (see entry above) in expressions of future time, determination, and willingness. The distinctions concerning ordinary and formal usage also apply here.

ORDINARY: I *would* like to hear from you.
FORMAL: I *should* like to hear from you.

ORDINARY: We *would* be glad to see him.
FORMAL: We *should* be glad to see him.

ORDINARY: I *would* be pleased to serve on that committee.
FORMAL: I *should* be pleased to serve on that committee.

a. Always use *should* in all persons to indicate "ought to."

I *should* study tonight.
You *should* report his dishonesty to the manager.
He *should* pay his debts.

b. Always use *would* in all persons to indicate customary action.

Every day I *would* swim in the lake.
They *would* only say "No comment."
She *would* practice day after day.

c. Use *should* in all three persons to express a condition in an *if* clause.

If he *should* win the prize, he will share it with his sister.
If you *should* miss the train, please wire me at once.

d. Use *would* in all three persons to express willingness in an *if* clause.

If he *would* apply himself, he could win top honors easily.
If you *would* consider delaying your decision, I am sure I could offer you a more attractive set of terms.

So–so that. *So* as a conjunction means "therefore"; *so that* means "in order that."

The work is now finished, *so* you can all go home. (See also ¶ 179.)
Please finish what you are doing *so that* we can all go home.

Someone–some one

Someone (somebody) called you early this morning.
Some one of the stenographers (some person in the group) mislaid the carbon copy of that letter.

NOTE: Spell *some one* as two words when it is followed by *of*.

Sometime–sometimes–some time

The order will be shipped *sometime* (at some unspecified time) next week.
Sometimes (now and then) reports are misleading.
It took me *some time* (a period of time) to complete the job. (NOTE: If the word *little* can be mentally inserted between *some* and *time*, the two-word phrase is correct.)

Sort. (See *Kind.*)

Sort of. (See *Kind of–sort of.*)

Sure–surely. *Sure* is an adjective; *surely,* an adverb.

> I am *sure* that I did not make that mistake. (Adjective.)
> You can *surely* count on our help. (Adverb.)

Do not use *sure* as an adverb; use *surely* or *very.*

> I was *very* glad to be of help. (NOT: sure glad.)

Sure and. In written material prefer *sure to* to the colloquial *sure and.* For example, "Be *sure to* turn left at the corner."

Than–then. *Than* is a conjunction introducing a subordinate clause of comparison. *Then* is an adverb meaning "at that time" or "next."

> The compulsory retirement age is considerably lower now *than* it was *then.*
> He *then* asserted that he could do the job better *than* we. (See ¶ 1049 for the case of pronouns following *than.*)

That–which–who. (See ¶ 1054.)

Them. Never use as an adjective. For example, "Do not file today's letters with *those* others." (NOT: them others.)

These sort–these kind. Incorrect; the correct forms are *this* sort, *this* kind. (See also *Kind.*)

This here. Do not use for *this.* For example, "*This* (NOT this here) typewriter is out of order."

Toward–towards. Both forms are correct.

Try and. In written material use *try to* rather than the colloquial *try and.* For example, "Please *try to* be here on time." (NOT: try and be here.)

Type. (See *Kind.*)

Unique. Do not use in sense of "unusual." A unique thing is one that is alone of its kind (see ¶ 1063f).

Up. Many verbs (for example, *end, rest, confess, settle, burn, drink, eat*) contain the idea of "up"; therefore, the adverb *up* is unnecessary. In the following sentences, *up* should be omitted.

> I'd like to settle (up) my bill.
> The electrician will connect (up) the fan.
> Let's divide (up) the sandwiches.
> Can you help me lift (up) this case?
> I will call him (up) tomorrow.

Very. This adverb can be used to modify an adjective, another adverb, a present participle, or a "descriptive" past participle.

> We are *very happy* with the outcome. (Modifying an adjective.)
> Strike the keys *very lightly.* (Modifying an adverb.)
> It is a *very disappointing* showing. (Modifying a present participle.)
> I was *very pleased* with the pictures. (Modifying a descriptive past participle.)

When the past participle expresses action rather than description, insert an adverb like *much* after *very*.

> They are *very much opposed* to your plan. (*Opposed* is part of the complete verb *are opposed* and expresses action rather than description.)

Ways. Do not use for *way* in referring to distance. For example, "I live a short *way* (NOT ways) from here."

Whether. (See *If–whether*.)

Who–which–that. (See ¶ 1054.)

Who–whom. (See ¶ 1053.)

Whoever–who ever

> *Whoever* (anyone who) is elected secretary should write that letter at once.
> *Who ever* made such a statement? (*Ever* is an adverb.)

Would have. Do not use for *had* in a clause beginning with *if*. For example, "If you *had* (NOT would have) come early, you could have seen him."

You was. Incorrect; use *you were*. (See ¶ 1001a.)

Section 12
DICTATION AND TRANSCRIPTION TECHNIQUES

TAKING DICTATION

1201 Start each day's dictation on a new notebook page.

1202 Write the date in longhand in the lower left corner of each notebook page that you use during the day; for example, *Jan. 11, 1970.*

1203 Use a fountain pen or a ball-point pen so that your notes will be more legible, but have several well-sharpened pencils at hand for emergency use.

1204 Number the notes for each letter, starting with *1* each day. As your employer hands you the letter or other material about which he has just dictated, number it to correspond with your notes. This will speed the identification of background material as you transcribe.

1205 Use encircled letters to indicate changes in the notes. For example, write Ⓐ at the point in the notes where the first change is to be made; then key the notes for the change in the same way, (A). If the dictator custom-arily makes many changes during dictation, keep one notebook column free for writing these changes.

1206 Write the following in longhand:

a. The addressee's name, unless you are familiar with the correct spelling or can easily confirm it by checking other correspondence; for example, ec *welford.*

b. Street names, unless you know or can easily confirm the spelling.

c. Any unusual words or trade names.

1207 Underscore in your notes as follows:

a. Draw one line under words that are to be underscored in typewritten material or italicized in printed material.

b. Draw two lines under words that are to be typed or printed in all-capital letters.

1208 Use a distinctive mark, such as a double line, to indicate the end of the notes for each dictated item.

1209 Leave a few blank lines between items of dictation so that you will have space to write any special instructions the dictator may give you—for example, *Transcribe first.*

1210 Mark the notes for telegrams and top-priority letters *RUSH* (using a colored pencil if one is available).

1211 Flag *RUSH* dictation by folding back the corner of the notebook page so that it projects beyond the edge of the cover.

1212 Be efficient in turning notebook pages. One method is to keep both hands on the notebook, using your left hand to keep the book steady and your left thumb to move the page gradually upward as you approach the bottom of the page. (If you are left-handed, you naturally will use your right hand and right thumb.)

1213 Watch for subdivisions of thought as you are taking dictation and para-graph accordingly.

1214 Do not interrupt the dictator unless he is so far ahead of you that you are losing the meaning of the dictation. Check doubtful words or sentences immediately after the dictator has finished the individual item of dicta-tion. Read back the sentence containing the questioned word. If you are uncertain about an entire sentence, read back the sentence immediately preceding the one in question and as much of the one in question as you can.

TRANSCRIBING

1215 Check to see which items, if any, are to receive priority treatment. (See ¶¶ 1210–1211.)

1216 Check for special instructions from the dictator before you begin to transcribe (see ¶ 1209). Always make at least one carbon copy of the correspondence (see also ¶¶ 1306–1309, 1455–1456).

1217 Confirm spellings, numbers, and similar details before you start transcribing.

1218 Transcribe directly from your notes. Develop the ability to read ahead as you transcribe in order to foresee such special problems as errors in grammar, incomplete sentences, and changes in the dictation (see ¶ 1205).

1219 If possible, do not make a paragraph more than eight to ten lines long. Avoid dividing the letter into a great many very short (two- or three-line) paragraphs.

1220 Consider the advantages of displaying numbered or lettered items (as illustrated in Letter Style 7, page 215) instead of running them together in a paragraph.

1221 Proofread the letter before removing it from the machine. Check carefully for typing accuracy as well as for correct meaning. If you merely scan the copy, you are likely to miss word substitutions, such as *than* for *that* or *now* for *not,* or you may miss simple omissions. Be sure that you have incorporated all the changes requested by the dictator (see ¶ 1205).

1222 Cancel the transcribed notes with a diagonal line.

1223 Check your notebook at the end of each day to be sure that you have transcribed all your notes. If any are left, give them top priority the next day.

1224 Keep a rubber band around the notebook at the last page transcribed so that you will know immediately where to resume transcribing or writing during the day or at the beginning of the next day.

SUBMITTING YOUR WORK

1225 Check to see that each transcript is clean (no smudges, fingerprints, or obvious erasures) before you submit it to the dictator.

1226 Follow this procedure when you submit transcripts to the dictator for his signature:

a. Place the *unfolded* letter together with any enclosures under the flap of the envelope. Have the address side of the envelope on top.

b. Assemble each carbon copy that is to be signed in the same way you arranged the original letter. Place the carbon copies under the original copy.

c. Attach the file copy to the letter or other correspondence, if any, to which it is related. The file copy is usually placed on top.

d. Put all the transcripts to be signed in a folder (often labeled "For Your Signature"), and place the folder on the dictator's desk. If the dictator customarily initials file copies, present them in a separate folder labeled "File Copies."

USING THE DICTIONARY

1227 A dictionary is your most indispensable reference book because you will need to consult it frequently in order to ensure accuracy and acceptability in the use of words. When you choose a dictionary, select one that is reliable and up to date. (Several good ones are listed in Section 20 on pages 264–265.) Then become thoroughly familiar with the features of your dictionary.

Section 13
TYPING
TECHNIQUES

MAKING CORRECTIONS

1301 Erasing. When you erase:

a. Move the carriage to the extreme right or left so that the eraser crumbs will fall on the desk, not into the typewriter.

b. Roll the paper forward two or three lines, and hold it firmly against the platen, or cylinder.

c. Place a stiff card or a metal erasing guard between the original copy and the first sheet of carbon paper.

d. Using a clean typewriter (ink) eraser, erase the error with several light strokes that follow the grain of the paper. Brush or blow away any erasure crumbs that do not fall off the paper.

e. Remove the card or metal shield, and place it between the first carbon copy and the second sheet of carbon paper.

f. Using a clean pencil eraser or other soft rubber eraser, erase the error on the carbon copy. Be sure to brush or blow the erasure crumbs from the carbon copy and the sheet of carbon paper facing it.

g. Follow steps e and f for each carbon copy in the pack.

h. Remove the card or metal shield, and reposition the carriage so that the printing point indicator is at the point where you are ready to begin typing the correction.

i. On a manual machine, type the correction lightly two or three times until it matches the other copy on the page. On an electric machine, reduce the pressure before you type the correction and be sure to return the pressure point indicator to its normal setting after you make the correction.

1302 **Crowding.** When typing a correction that contains one letter more than the erased word, such as *that* for *may*, select a method below that is appropriate for your machine.

a. Using the *backspace* method on a manual machine: Move the carriage to the position at which the *m* was typed. Depress and hold the backspacer halfway down, type the *t*, and release the backspacer; repeat this procedure for each remaining letter in the correction—*h, a,* and *t.*

NOTE: If you are using a manual machine with a half-space key, use that key in place of the backspacer key.

b. Using the *space bar* method on a manual machine: Move the carriage to the space preceding the erased *m*. Hold the space bar down, type the *t*, and release the space bar; repeat this procedure for each remaining letter in the correction—*h, a,* and *t.*

c. Using the *half-spacing* method on an electric machine: Move the carriage to the position of the erased *m*. Bracing your hand against the machine and pressing your fingertips against the end of the carriage, push the carriage back a half space (this will not be necessary if your machine has a half-spacer key), type the *t*, and release the carriage; repeat this procedure for each remaining letter in the correction—*h, a,* and *t.*

1303 **Spreading.** When typing a correction that contains one letter less than the erased word, such as *the* for *when*, select a method below that is appropriate for your machine.

a. Using the *backspace* method on a manual machine: Move the carriage to the position of the erased *w*. Space once, depress and hold the backspacer halfway down, type the *t*, and release the backspacer; repeat this procedure for each remaining letter in the correction—*h* and *e*. (If your machine has a half-space key, use it in place of the backspacer key.)

b. Using the *space bar* method on a manual machine: Move the carriage to the position of the erased *w*. Hold the space bar down, type the *t*, and release the space bar; repeat this procedure for each remaining letter in the correction—*h* and *e.*

c. Using the *half-spacing* method on an electric machine: Move the carriage to the position of the erased *w*. Space once, half-space as described in ¶ 1302c, type the *t*, and release the carriage; repeat this procedure for each remaining letter in the correction—*h* and *e.*

1304 **Reinserting Pages.** When reinserting a page to type a correction or add an insertion, follow this procedure:

a. Before inserting the page, type a line of copy on a piece of scratch paper and note where the bottom of such letters as *a, m, n,* and *l* appear in relation to the top of the aligning scale. Move the carriage right or left until the letter *l* appears over the aligning scale, and note where the vertical part of the letter appears in relation to one of the vertical lines on the aligning scale.

[Continued on page 192.]

b. Remove the scratch paper, and insert the page on which the correction is to be typed. Using the paper release and the variable linespacer, align the paper on the basis of your observations in a.

c. Test the alignment of the page by setting the ribbon at the stencil position and lightly typing over a period or a comma. If necessary, use the paper release and the variable linespacer to further adjust the page.

MAKING SYMBOLS NOT ON THE TYPEWRITER

1305 Typewriters used for typing technical material usually contain special keys for the symbols that occur most frequently. If your typewriter does not have these special keys, you may either insert them with a pen or construct them on the typewriter, as shown in the chart on page 193.

PREPARING CARBON COPIES

1306 When assembling a carbon pack:

a. Use carbon paper that has the upper left and lower right corners cut off diagonally. (Reason: It is easier to remove the carbons later on. To do so, grasp the upper left corner of the sheets with one hand and either shake out the carbons or, if the carbons extend below the typed sheets, pull out the carbons from the bottom with your other hand.)

b. Place the *glossy* side of the carbon against the paper on which the copy is to be made. (Including the letterhead or other sheet on which the original is to be typed, the pack will contain one more sheet of typing paper than of carbon paper.)

c. Pick up the pack, and holding it loosely, tap the left and top edges against your desk until the sheets are even.

1307 When inserting a carbon pack into the machine:

a. Hold the pack so that the *glossy* side of the carbons is toward you, and with the line reset (ratchet release) engaged, roll the pack into the machine. (Using the line reset prevents slippage when you insert the pack into the machine or when you turn it back to make corrections.)

b. Use an envelope or a sheet of paper to guide a thick carbon pack into the machine. If you use an envelope, place the pack under the flap of a large envelope and then roll them both into the machine far enough to permit removing the envelope from the front of the cylinder. If you use a sheet of paper as a guide, insert the sheet about halfway into the machine. Place the pack between the guide sheet and the cylinder, and then roll them forward until the guide sheet can be removed from the front of the cylinder.

1308 After the carbon pack has been inserted into the machine:

a. Check to be sure that the printed side of the letterhead and the dull side of the carbon sheets are toward you.

[*Continued on page 194.*]

MAKING SYMBOLS NOT ON THE TYPEWRITER

Symbol	Example	Directions
Cents	He charges 2¢	Small letter *c* intersected by diagonal
Asterisk	✻ ✻ ✻ ✻ ✻	Capital *A* typed over small *v*
Caret	They try$\overset{\text{so}}{/}$hard	Underscore and diagonal (center word above diagonal)
Brackets	He /Johnston/	Diagonals with underscores facing inside
Roman numerals	Chapter XVIII	Capitals *I, V, X, L, C, D,* and *M*
Pounds sterling	£8 is English	Capital *L* typed over small *f*
Degrees	Freezing——32°	Small letter *o* raised slightly (turn cylinder by hand)
Military zero	Leave at Ø1ØØ	Numeral 0 intersected by diagonal
Times, by	Is it 4 x 5?	Small letter *x*
Equals	11 x 11 = 121	Two hyphens, one below the other (turn cylinder by hand)
Divided by	120 ÷ 10 = 12	Colon intersected by hyphen
Plus	87 ≠ 18 = 105	Hyphen intersected by diagonal
Minus	140 − 56 = 84	Hyphen
Superior numbers	$8^2 - 5^2 = 29^2$	Number or letter typed above line (turn cylinder by hand)
Inferior numbers	H_2O is water.	Number or letter typed below line (turn cylinder by hand)
Square root	√90000 is 300	Small letter *v* off-positioned to meet diagonal, followed by underscores on line above
Divide into	45)9045 = 201	Right parenthesis, followed by underscores on line above
Feet, inches	Mary is 5' 2"	For feet, apostrophe; for inches, quotation mark
Minutes, seconds	Time: 3' 15"	For minutes, apostrophe; for seconds, quotation mark
Ellipsis marks	He . . . also He I	Within sentences, three spaced periods; at end of sentence, four spaced periods
Section	Ŝ 201 or Ŝ201	Capital *S* intersected by raised capital *S*
Paragraph	₽ 202 or ₽202	Capital *P* intersected by small *l*
Bar graph line	mmmmmmmmmmmm	Small letter *m, w, o,* or *x* typed in a solid row

Adapted from John L. Rowe et al., *Gregg Typing, 191 Series*, Book 1, "General Typing," 2d ed., Gregg Division, McGraw-Hill Book Company, New York, 1967, p. 106.

b. Be sure that the pack is straight in the machine.

c. Operate the paper release before you start typing in order to release the tension on the papers and to prevent the carbon sheets from making marks on the copies.

1309 When reusing carbon paper, rotate the sheets from the front to the back of carbon packs and turn them from the top to the bottom so that the wear will be more evenly distributed.

TYPING CARDS AND POSTCARDS

1310 Use the cardholders to keep the card in position, and adjust the paper bail rolls in case you need to type near the bottom of the card.

1311 When typing on a stiff or smooth card, advance the card at the end of each typed line by using the cylinder knob instead of the carriage-return lever or key. It may also be necessary to hold the card with one hand as you turn the cylinder knob in order to ensure even line spacing.

1312 When typing on a standard-size postcard (5½ by 3¼ inches):

a. Set margins for a 4½-inch writing line, leaving side margins of ½ inch each.

b. Type the date on the third line from the top of the card, beginning at the center.

c. Omit the name and address of the person to whom the card is being sent.

d. Type the salutation (*Dear Sir, Dear Mrs. Davis,* etc.) on the second line below the date, beginning at the left margin. If it is necessary to conserve space, omit the salutation.

e. Begin typing the message, using single spacing, on the second line below the salutation.

f. Type the closing lines starting on the second line below the last line of the message; begin each line at the center. In order to leave a bottom margin of ½ inch, omit the following elements if necessary: the complimentary closing (for example, *Sincerely yours*), the handwritten signature, and reference initials.

▶ See ¶ 1474 for the procedure in addressing postcards; ¶ 1475 for the procedure in chain-feeding envelopes (the same procedure is used for chain-feeding postcards).

TYPING STENCILS

1313 Set the ribbon control at the stencil position. Clean the keys thoroughly.

1314 Carefully read the instructions that accompany the package of stencils.

1315 Assemble and insert the stencil pack into the machine as follows:

a. Insert the cushion sheet smoothly between the stencil and the backing sheet. Do not use a torn or badly worn cushion sheet.

b. Hold the stencil pack at the bottom in order to keep the cushion sheet from slipping as you insert the pack into the machine. If the stencil does not feed in easily, depress the paper release briefly. Be sure the stencil is not wrinkled.

c. Straighten the stencil in the machine.

1316 Compare the typed draft and the markings on the stencil to determine:

a. At what points to set margins and tab stops (note the scale across the top of the stencil).

b. On what line to start typing (note the numbers down the side of the stencil).

1317 Make the necessary machine adjustments and begin typing. On a manual machine, type with an even touch and at a rate a little slower than your normal speed. Type punctuation marks and such letters as *o* and *e* with a light touch; type capital letters and the small letters *w* and *m* with a heavier touch. If you are using an electric machine, set the pressure dial at a lower figure before you start typing.

1318 To make a correction:

a. Roll the stencil forward a line or two.

b. Rub the burnisher supplied with the correction fluid or a smooth paper clip over the error, being careful not to tear the stencil.

c. Apply a *thin* coating of correction fluid and let it dry. Replace the cap on the bottle of correction fluid at once.

d. Roll the stencil back to the line in which the error appeared. To avoid wrinkling the stencil (particularly when it is being rolled back several lines), hold the lower edge of the sheets in the stencil pack firmly and use the line reset (ratchet release) as you roll the stencil back slowly.

1319 On a major stencil-typing project, make a carbon copy of each stencil that you can use in proofreading or as a reference pending the duplicating of the material. To make a copy, place a carbon sheet and a piece of paper between the backing sheet and the cylinder.

TYPING DITTO MASTERS

1320 Remove the protective tissue between the master sheet and the attached carbon sheet. Do not detach the carbon sheet.

1321 Insert the master set (open end first) so that the master sheet faces you in front of the cylinder. Using a heavy backing sheet between the back of the carbon sheet and the cylinder will enable you to duplicate more and clearer copies.

1322 Leave the ribbon in the regular position. If you are using a manual machine, type with a very sharp, smooth touch. On an electric machine, reduce the pressure two or three points. (Note that the carbon prints on the reverse side of the master sheet as you type.)

1323 To correct an error:

a. Roll the papers forward several lines and bend the master sheet toward you so that you can see the error.

b. *Lightly* scrape off the carbon of the error, using a single-edged razor blade or a desk knife.

c. Tear a piece off the corner of the carbon sheet, and with the glossy side facing you, place it over the spot where the correction is to be typed.

d. Slowly roll the papers back, using the line reset (ratchet release) to prevent slippage.

e. Type the correction right over the error and remove the slip of carbon.

f. To correct a long error, such as a whole line, retype the line correctly in an unused part of the master; cut out both the correct and the incorrect lines; and tape the correct line in the position originally filled by the incorrect line.

1324 To display some portions of the material in a different color, place a sheet of colored duplicating carbon between the master sheet and the carbon sheet attached to the master, being sure that the glossy side faces you. Type the copy that is to be displayed, and then remove the extra carbon sheet before you resume typing the other copy.

TYPING OFFSET MASTERS

1325 Use a carbon, not a cloth, ribbon and be sure to clean the keys thoroughly before you start typing.

1326 Use special offset master paper or a good quality of white paper that has a fairly hard, smooth finish.

1327 Type with an even, sharp (but not heavy) touch.

1328 Erase errors with a soft rubber eraser, being careful not to roughen the surface of the paper and being sure to blow or brush away erasure crumbs. To remove all traces of the error, apply a very thin coat of whiting fluid (a number of brands are available at stationery and office supply stores).

1329 Handle the master (often referred to as "camera copy") *very* carefully to avoid smudging the copy. Since all marks (except those made with a pencil that has nonreproducing lead) will appear on the printing plate, be sure to remove or "white out" all fingerprints, smudges, and other marks that inadvertently appear on the sheet. Then, to protect the copy, either *lightly* coat it with a commercial protective plastic spray or place a sheet of tissue paper over it.

Section 14
LETTERS
AND MEMOS

LETTERHEAD OR RETURN ADDRESS

1401 Ordinarily business letters are written on stationery with a printed letterhead containing at least these elements: company name; street address; city, state, and ZIP Code; area code and telephone number. When using plain paper instead of printed letterhead stationery, include either a typewritten letterhead or a return address on the first page of the letter. (See also ¶ 1468.)

a. If you use a *typewritten letterhead,* center the following information in four double-spaced lines, beginning on the sixth line from the top of the page: (1) the company name; (2) the street address; (3) the city state, and ZIP Code; (4) the telephone area code and number.

TURPIN & KELLY, INC.

2550 Mulberry Street

New York, New York 10012

(212) 555-3600

b. If you use a *return address,* type the street address on the thirteenth line from the top of the page and the city, state, and ZIP Code on the fourteenth line. Except in the full-blocked and simplified letter arrangements (see Letter Styles 3 and 7 on pages 213 and 215), start each line of the return address at the center of the page or position the longest line so that it ends at the right margin (as shown below).

2550 Mulberry Street
New York, New York 10012

DATE LINE

1402 In business correspondence:

a. The date line consists of the *name of the month,* written in full—never abbreviated or represented by figures; the *day,* written in figures and followed by a comma; and the *complete year;* for example, *December 8, 1972.* Never use the styles *12/8/72, 2/8/72,* or *'72* because the dates they represent are easily confused.

b. When using letterhead stationery (printed or typewritten), position the date on the fifteenth line from the top of the page or three lines below the letterhead, whichever is lower. The date line usually begins at the center of the page or ends at the right margin; however, it may be positioned in some other attractive relationship to the letterhead design. In the full-blocked and simplified arrangements (see Letter Styles 3 and 7), the date line begins at the left margin.

c. When using a return address, type the date on the line below the city and state and begin it at the same point as the other lines in the return address. (**EXCEPTION:** In the indented style treat the date as another line of the return address by indenting it the same number of spaces as the city and state.)

1403 In military correspondence:

a. The date line usually consists of the day, the month, and the year, in that order; for example, *15 June 1972.*

b. The month may be abbreviated to the first three letters of the complete name, for example, *15 Jun 1972,* even though the name of the month is not ordinarily abbreviated. Note that a period is not used after the abbreviation and that no commas are used in a military-style date line.

1404 In correspondence from some foreign countries, the date may be written with the month between the day and the year; for example, *10 August 1974.*

PERSONAL OR CONFIDENTIAL NOTATION

1405 If a letter is of a personal or confidential nature, type the word *Personal* or *Confidential* in all-capital letters and underscore it. Position this notation on the second line below the date, at the *left* margin.

INSIDE ADDRESS

1406 a. The inside address of a business letter must contain at least the following information: (1) the name of the person or the company to whom you are writing, or both; (2) the street address; (3) the city, state, and ZIP Code (see Letter Styles 2 and 3). It may include such additional information as the person's job title and his department (see Letter Style 4).

b. The inside address should begin on the third line below the personal or confidential notation, if used, or on the fifth line below the date.

c. The inside address should be single-spaced unless the whole letter is double-spaced.

▶ See ¶¶ 1407–1429 for additional details concerning the parts of inside addresses; see also Letter Styles 1 to 7, pages 212–215, for the arrangement of inside addresses.

NAME OF PERSON AND TITLE

1407 When writing the name of a person in an inside address or elsewhere be sure to follow the spelling and capitalization that the owner of the name uses. In order to verify the correctness of a name, you may need to consult original correspondence from that person, a mailing list, a directory, or the person who dictated the letter you are typing.

a. Give particular attention to the variations in the spelling of such names as these:

Berns, Burns, Byrnes, Byrns   Magowan, McGowan
Clark, Clarke   Reilley, Reilly, Riley

b. Note the differences in spelling, capitalization, and spacing in names containing the prefixes *Mac* and *Mc*.

Macmillan, MacMillan, Mac Millan, Macmillen, MacMillen
McMillan, Mc Millan, McMillen, McMillin

c. In names containing the prefix *O'*, always capitalize the *O* and the letter following the apostrophe; for example, *O'Brian* or *O'Brien*.

d. Watch for differences in spacing and capitalization in names containing the prefixes *d', da, de, del, della, di, du, la, le, van, von*, etc.

D'Amato, Damato   de laFuente, DeLaFuente, De laFuente
D'Amelio, d'Amelio   van Auken, Van Auken, VanAuken

NOTE: When a surname with an uncapitalized prefix stands alone (that is, without a first name, a title, or initials preceding it), capitalize the prefix to prevent a misreading.

George de Luca   Mr. de Luca   G. R. de Luca
BUT: I hear that *De Luca* is leaving the company.

e. Do not abbreviate or use initials unless the person to whom you are writing uses an abbreviation or initials; for example, do not write *Mr. Wm. B. Sachs* or *Mr. W. B. Sachs* if the person to whom you are writing used *William B. Sachs*.

NOTE: When names that contain prefixes and particles are to be typed in all-capital letters, follow these principles: If there is no space after the prefix, capitalize only the initial letter of the prefix. If space follows the prefix, capitalize the entire prefix.

Normal Form   **All-Capital Form**
MacDonald   MacDONALD
BUT: Mac Donald   MAC DONALD

1408 In an inside address, always use a title before the name of a person unless the abbreviation of an academic degree, such as *M.D.* or *Ph.D.*, or the abbreviation *Esq.* (which stands for *Esquire* and which is sometimes used after the name of a lawyer) is to appear after the name.

a. If the person has no special title, such as *Dr., Professor,* or *Honorable,* use the courtesy title *Mr., Mrs.,* or *Miss.* Use *Master* before the name of a young boy.

[Continued on page 200.]

b. If there is no way to determine whether the person is a man or a woman, use the title *Mr.*

c. If there is no way to determine the marital status of a woman, use the title *Miss.* (The abbreviation *Ms.,* meaning "Miss" or "Mrs.," is also acceptable in ambiguous situations.)

d. If a letter is intended for two or more men, use the title *Messrs.* (plural of *Mr.*); for two or more married women, use *Mesdames* (plural of *Mrs.*); for two or more unmarried women, use *Misses* (plural of *Miss*). (See ¶ 617.)

e. Long titles, such as *Lieutenant, Governor,* and *Superintendent,* should be spelled out in formal correspondence. They may be abbreviated in informal correspondence.

f. *The Reverend* and *The Honorable* are titles of respect, not of rank or office. They should be spelled out in formal correspondence, but they may be abbreviated in informal correspondence; for example, *Rev. James Lee, Hon. Shirley Chisholm.*

g. If a letter is being addressed to more than one person, be sure to use the appropriate title with each name when a plural title, such as *Messrs.* or *Professors,* does not apply to all the persons.

> Dr. and Mrs. Herbert Booth

If a letter is being addressed to two persons with different surnames, type each name on a separate line.

> Dr. Paul J. Rogers
> Mr. James A. Davis

1409 When *Jr., Sr.,* or a roman numeral such as *III* is typed after a name, use a comma before *Jr.* or *Sr.* but not before a roman numeral. (Even the comma before *Jr.* and *Sr.* is increasingly being dropped.)

1410 Abbreviations of academic degrees, such as *M.D.,* and of religious orders, such as *S.J.,* are typed after names and preceded by a comma.

1411 A title of position, such as *Vice President* or *Vocational Director,* should be included in an inside address when possible. If the title is short, it may be typed on the same line as the person's name and preceded by a comma. If the title is long, type it on the line following the name; if the title runs on to a second line, indent the turnover two spaces.

Mr. J. C. Lee, President	Mrs. Helen Hansen	Mr. Ralph Nielsen
	Executive Vice President	Vice President and
		General Manager

NOTE: Capitalize a title that accompanies a name in an address.

1412 Never use two titles that mean the same thing with a name; for example, *Dr. George M. Wharton, Ph.D.,* would be incorrect. Address the letter to *Dr. George M. Wharton* or to *George M. Wharton, Ph.D.*

NAME OF FIRM

1413 When writing the name of a firm in an inside address or elsewhere, always use the official name and follow the company's style for spelling, punctuation, capitalization, spacing, and abbreviations. The letterhead of incoming correspondence is the best source for this information. Note the variations in style in these names:

> Time Inc.
> Thyme Inc.
>
> Chas. H. Bohn & Co., Inc.
> Consolidated Edison Company of New York, Inc.
>
> Standard Duplicating Machines Corp.
> H. Wilson Corporation
>
> Faber & Faber, Ltd.
> Abelard-Schuman, Limited
>
> Mekler/Ansell Associates Inc.
> Post-Keyes-Gardner Inc.
>
> Merrill Lynch, Pierce, Fenner & Smith Inc.
> Webster Sheffield Fleischmann Hitchcock & Brookfield

1414 If the official form cannot be ascertained from incoming correspondence, follow these general rules:

a. Use the ampersand (&) rather than *and* when the company name consists of the names of persons.

> Curtis & Hall, Inc.   **BUT:** Acme Lead and Tin Company

b. Write *Inc.* for *Incorporated* and *Ltd.* for *Limited,* and precede the abbreviation by a comma.

c. As a rule, spell out *Company* or *Corporation;* if the name is extremely long, however, use the abbreviation *Co.* or *Corp.*

d. Do not capitalize the word *the* at the beginning of a name unless you are sure it is part of the official name; for example, *The Rand Corporation.*

e. Use an apostrophe if the name includes a singular possessive noun or an irregular plural noun; for example, *Harper's Bazaar, The Children's Shop.* Do not use an apostrophe if the name includes a regular plural noun; for example, *American Bankers Association.*

1415 Ordinarily, type the firm name on a line by itself.

BUILDING NAME

1416 If the name of a building is included in the inside address, type it on a line by itself immediately above the street address.

STREET ADDRESS

1417 Always type the street address on a line by itself.

1418 Use figures for house, building, apartment, room, or rural route numbers. Do not include the abbreviation *No.* or the symbol *#* before such numbers. **EXCEPTION:** For clarity, the word *One* instead of the figure *1* is generally used in a house or building number; for example, *One Park Avenue*.

1419 Numbers used as street names are written as follows:

a. Spell out the numbers 1 through 10; for example, *177 Second Avenue*.

b. Use figures for numbers over 10; for example, *27 East 22d Street* or *27 East 22 Street*. The ordinal sign *st, d,* or *th* may be omitted so long as a word such as *East* or *West* separates the street number from the building number. If no such word intervenes, use the ordinal sign for clarity; for example, *144 65th Street*.

1420 Do not abbreviate *North, South, East, West, Northeast, Southwest,* or a similar word when it appears before the street name; for example, *330 West 42 Street*.

1421 Type an abbreviation representing a section of a city after the street name and use a comma before it; for example, *2012 Massachusetts Avenue, N.W.*

1422 Use the word *and,* not an ampersand (*&*), in a street address; for example, *Tenth and Market Streets*.

1423 Avoid abbreviating such words as *Street* and *Avenue* whenever possible. If it is necessary to abbreviate the word in the envelope address, then abbreviate it in the inside address as well. The following abbreviations should be used:

Alley	Al.	Lane	La.	Road	Rd.
Avenue	Ave.	Near	nr.	South	S.
Between	bet.	North	N.	Southeast	S.E.
Boulevard	Blvd.	Northeast	N.E.	Southwest	S.W.
Court	Ct.	Northwest	N.W.	Square	Sq.
Drive	Dr.	Opposite	opp.	Street	St.
East	E.	Park	Pk.	Terrace	Ter.
Heights	Hts.	Place	Pl.	West	W.

CITY, STATE, AND ZIP CODE

1424 The city, state, and ZIP Code must always be typed on one line, immediately following the street address. Type the name of the city, followed by a comma and one space; the state, followed by one space but no comma; and the ZIP Code. (See Letter Style 3.)

1425 When writing the name of a city in an address:

a. Never use an abbreviation (for example, *Chic.* for *Chicago*).

b. Never abbreviate the words *Fort, Mount, Point,* or *Port.* Write the name of the city in full. For example: *Fort Dodge, Mount Vernon, Point Pleasant, Port Huron.*

c. Abbreviate the word *Saint* in the names of American cities; for example, *St. Louis, St. Paul.*

1426 In an address, the name of the state may be spelled out or abbreviated as follows:

	New	Old		New	Old
Alabama	AL	Ala.	Missouri	MO	Mo.
Alaska	AK	. . .	Montana	MT	Mont.
Arizona	AZ	Ariz.	Nebraska	NE	Nebr.
Arkansas	AR	Ark.	Nevada	NV	Nev.
California	CA	Calif.	New Hampshire	NH	N.H.
Canal Zone	CZ	C.Z.	New Jersey	NJ	N.J.
Colorado	CO	Colo.	New Mexico	NM	N. Mex.
Connecticut	CT	Conn.	New York	NY	N.Y.
Delaware	DE	Del.	North Carolina	NC	N.C.
District	DC	D.C.	North Dakota	ND	N. Dak.
of Columbia			Ohio	OH	. . .
Florida	FL	Fla.	Oklahoma	OK	Okla.
Georgia	GA	Ga.	Oregon	OR	Oreg.
Guam	GU	. . .	Pennsylvania	PA	Pa.
Hawaii	HI	. . .	Puerto Rico	PR	P.R.
Idaho	ID	. . .	Rhode Island	RI	R.I.
Illinois	IL	Ill.	South Carolina	SC	S.C.
Indiana	IN	Ind.	South Dakota	SD	S. Dak.
Iowa	IA	. . .	Tennessee	TN	Tenn.
Kansas	KS	Kans.	Texas	TX	Tex.
Kentucky	KY	Ky.	Utah	UT	. . .
Louisiana	LA	La.	Vermont	VT	Vt.
Maine	ME	. . .	Virgin Islands	VI	V.I.
Maryland	MD	Md.	Virginia	VA	Va.
Massachusetts	MA	Mass.	Washington	WA	Wash.
Michigan	MI	Mich.	West Virginia	WV	W. Va.
Minnesota	MN	Minn.	Wisconsin	WI	Wis.
Mississippi	MS	Miss.	Wyoming	WY	Wyo.

a. Though they may be used in other situations, the new two-letter state abbreviations were created by the U.S. Postal Service specifically for use in address blocks on envelopes. However, for the sake of consistency, the style used in the envelope address should be used in the inside address of a letter.

b. Writers who regard the two-letter abbreviations as too informal to be used on all correspondence may elect to spell out state names in most cases and to use the abbreviations only in informal correspondence.

c. Always type the two-letter state abbreviations in capital letters, with no periods after or space between the letters.

d. When an address is written in a sentence, spell out the name of the state; leave one space between the state and the ZIP Code.

My address next month will be 501 South 71 Court, Miami, Florida 33144, but mail sent to my office will reach me just as easily.

1427 Do not include the name of a county or an area (such as *Long Island*) in an address.

1428 In a Canadian address, spell out or abbreviate the name of the province.

	New	Old		New	Old
Alberta	AB	Alta.	Nova Scotia	NS	N.S.
British Columbia	BC	B.C.	Ontario	ON	Ont.
Labrador	LB	Lab.	Prince Edward	PE	P.E.I.
Manitoba	MB	Man.	Island		
New Brunswick	NB	N.B.	Quebec	PQ	Que. OR
Newfoundland	NF	Nfld.			P.Q.
Northwest	NT	N.W.T.	Saskatchewan	SK	Sask.
Territories			Yukon Territory	YT	Y.T.

1429 In a foreign address, type the name of the country on a separate line in all-capital letters. Do not abbreviate the name of the country. EXCEPTION: *U.S.S.R.* (*Union of Soviet Socialist Republics*).

```
Mr. Ralph P. Williams          Mr. H. Andrew Koyama
Robinson & Young, Ltd.         1-504 Kitaisogo-Danchi
50 York Street                 Isogo-Ku
Toronto 1, Ontario             Yokohama
CANADA                         JAPAN
```

ATTENTION LINE

1430 When a letter is addressed to a company, an attention line may be used to direct the letter to a particular person or department. The attention line should be typed on the second line below the inside address. It may start at the left margin, it may be indented the same as the paragraphs, or it may be centered. It may be typed in all-capital letters, or it may be typed in capital and small letters, with the complete line or only the word *Attention* underscored. The word *Attention* should not be abbreviated; it need not be followed by the word *of* or a colon. (See also Letter Style 2.) Two common typewritten styles are as follows:

```
ATTENTION SALES MANAGER        Attention Mr. Ellery
```

▶ See ¶ 1434, note, for the salutation to use with an attention line.

SALUTATION

1431 Type the salutation, beginning at the left margin, on the second line below the attention line (if used) or on the second line below the inside address. Follow the salutation with a colon unless you are using open punctuation (see Letter Style 3) or you are typing a social-business letter (see ¶ 1481*b*).

1432 Abbreviate only the titles *Mr., Mrs., Messrs.,* and *Dr.* (In formal correspondence, the title *Doctor* may be spelled out.) All other titles, such as *Professor* and *Father*, should always be written out. (See ¶ 1801 for military titles.)

1433 Capitalize the first word as well as any nouns and titles in the salutation; for example, *Dear Sir, My dear Mr. Brand, Right Reverend* and *dear Sir.*

1434 The following are approved forms of salutation:

To one person
Customary:	Dear Mr. Smith:	Dear Miss Simpson:
More formal:	My dear Mr. Smith:	My dear Miss Simpson:
Formal and impersonal:	Dear Sir:	Dear Madam:
Very formal (official):	Sir:	Madam:

CAUTION: Never write just *Dear Miss;* always include a surname.

To two men
Customary:	Dear Mr. Brown and Mr. Jones:
	OR Gentlemen:
More formal:	My dear Messrs. Brown and Jones:

To two women
Customary—Married:	Dear Mrs. Brown and Mrs. Jones:
Unmarried:	Dear Miss Allen and Miss Davis:
More formal—Married:	My dear Mesdames Brown and Jones:
Unmarried:	My dear Misses Allen and Davis:
To a man and a woman:	Dear Miss Allen and Mr. Kent:
To an organization:	Gentlemen:
To an organization composed entirely of women:	Mesdames: OR Ladies:

NOTE: When an attention line is used (see ¶ 1430), the salutation must always be *Gentlemen* (or, if appropriate, *Mesdames* or *Ladies*). Reason: The letter is addressed to an organization, not to one person.

SUBJECT LINE

1435 **a.** Type the subject line (if given) on the second line below the salutation. You may start it at the left margin, indent it the same as the paragraphs, or center it. Type it either in all-capital letters or in capital and small letters that are underscored.

MORAN LEASE   <u>Introductory Offer to New Subscribers</u>

b. The term *Subject:* or (in legal correspondence) *In re:* often precedes the actual subject. (See also Letter Style 3.)

SUBJECT: MORAN LEASE   <u>In re: Moran Lease</u>

BODY OF LETTER

1436 Begin the body of the letter on the second line below the subject line, if used, or on the second line below the salutation. EXCEPTION: In the simplified letter (see Letter Style 7), the body starts on the third line.

1437 In the semiblocked and indented letter styles (see Letter Styles 2 and 5), indent the first line of each paragraph. (Although five spaces is the usual indention, some writers prefer to indent up to ten spaces.) In the other letter styles (see Letter Styles 1, 3, 4, 6, and 7), start each paragraph at the left margin.

NOTE: Always indent the first line of each paragraph in any double-spaced letter.

1438 Except for very short letters, use single spacing and leave one blank line between paragraphs.

COMPLIMENTARY CLOSING

1439 Type the complimentary closing on the second line below the last line of the body of the letter. If the full-blocked or square-blocked letter style is used, start the closing at the left margin (see Letter Styles 3 and 4). Otherwise, start the closing at the center or at the point at which the date line begins.

1440 Capitalize only the first word of a complimentary closing. Place a comma at the end of the line (except when open punctuation is used).

1441 If the dictator does not dictate the complimentary closing, use one of these:

a. Personal in tone: *Sincerely, Cordially, Sincerely yours, Cordially yours.*

b. More formal in tone: *Yours truly, Yours very truly, Very truly yours, Very sincerely yours, Very cordially yours.*

c. If an informal closing phrase, such as *Best wishes* or *Kindest regards,* is used instead of a regular complimentary closing, type the phrase in the complimentary-closing position and follow it by a comma. (Stronger punctuation, such as a question mark, an exclamation point, or a dash, may be used if appropriate.) If both a complimentary closing and an informal closing phrase are used, type the complimentary closing in its regular position, and type the informal phrase at the end of the last paragraph or as a separate paragraph with the appropriate terminal punctuation.

NOTE: Once a pattern of informal phrases is begun with a customer, it should not be discontinued without good reason. Otherwise, if a closing returns to a more formal phrasing, the customer will wonder what has happened.

COMPANY SIGNATURE

1442 A company signature may be used to emphasize the fact that a letter represents the views of the company as a whole (and not merely the individual who has written it). If included, the company signature should be typed on the second line below the complimentary closing. Begin the company signature at the same point as the complimentary closing (except when the indented style is used).

WRITER'S NAME AND TITLE

1443 Type the writer's name on the fourth line below the company signature, if used, or on the fourth line below the complimentary closing. Except in the indented style (see Letter Styles 5 and 6), start typing at the same point as the company signature or complimentary closing.

1444 In addition to the writer's name, type his title or the name of his department or both. Good visual balance will dictate the best arrangement (see the four variations below). If a title takes two or more lines (as in the fourth example), block all the lines at the left.

James Mahoney, Director   Ernest L. Welhoelter
Data Processing Division   Head, Sales Department

Charles Saunders   Franklin Browning
Assistant Manager   Vice President and
Circulation Department   General Manager

1445 Never type *Miss* or *Mr.* in the signature line unless the writer's given name might be that of either a man or a woman; for example, *Mr. Evelyn Shaw, Miss Reed Noyes.* It is assumed that a woman is *Miss* unless *Mrs.* is clearly indicated in some way.

1446 An unmarried woman may include *Miss,* within parentheses, in her *handwritten* signature, or she may simply sign her name.

Sincerely yours,   Sincerely yours,

(Miss) Constance Booth   *Constance Booth*

Constance Booth   Constance Booth

1447 A married woman or a widow may include *Mrs.* in either her handwritten or her typewritten signature. If included in her handwritten signature, *Mrs.* is enclosed in parentheses (see illustration at left in *a*). If included in her typewritten signature, *Mrs.* is typed without parentheses (see illustration at right in *a*). Her typewritten signature may consist of:

a. Her first name plus her husband's surname. These are the styles commonly used in business.

Cordially yours,   Cordially yours,

(Mrs.) Nancy Wells   *Nancy Wells*

Nancy Wells   Mrs. Nancy Wells

b. Her first name plus her maiden surname plus her husband's surname. This is the style used by many professional women.

Cordially yours,

Nancy Ross Wells

Mrs. Nancy Ross Wells

[Continued on page 208.]

c. Her husband's first name and initial plus his surname. This is the style that married women or widows use socially; it is usually not used in business.

Cordially yours,

Nancy Wells

Mrs. John A. Wells

1448 A divorcee may use one of these styles:

a. Her first name plus her maiden surname plus her ex-husband's surname.

Yours very truly,

Elsie Hoyt Prince

Mrs. Elsie Hoyt Prince

b. Her maiden surname plus her ex-husband's surname.

Yours very truly,

Elsie Hoyt Prince

Mrs. Hoyt Prince

c. Either of the forms used by an unmarried woman (see ¶ 1446) if she has resumed her maiden name.

1449 A secretary who signs mail for her employer may use either of the following styles, depending on the wishes of her employer and the circumstances involved.

Sincerely yours,   Sincerely yours,

Dorothy Cook   *R. H. Benedict*
                                          DC

Secretary to Mr. Benedict   R. H. Benedict, Manager

1450 If the person who signs for another is not actually the secretary, either of the following forms may be used:

Sincerely yours,   Sincerely yours,

Mabel Phillips   *R. H. Benedict*
                                          mp

For Mr. Benedict   R. H. Benedict, Manager

REFERENCE INITIALS

1451 The initials of the typist or those of the typist and the dictator are usually typed at the left margin, on the second line below the dictator's name and title. In a square-blocked letter (see Letter Style 4), the reference initials are typed at the right margin, on the same line as the dictator's name. When used, the initials of the dictator precede those of the typist. The following are commonly used styles:

```
APG/mm      MFF:CCR      STG:ebh      JDeL:C      lba      t
```

NOTE: If the dictator's name is not typed in the signature line (see Letter Style 6), and especially if the handwritten signature is illegible, it is advisable to type the dictator's name before the initials of the typist; for example, *B. S. Dixon:RP* or *BSDixon*/rp.

1452 When the letter is written by someone other than the person who signs it, use the writer's and the typist's initials (not the signer's and the typist's).

Sincerely yours,

Herbert Heymann

Herbert Heymann
President

PBR/jb

1453 Do not include reference initials in a personal letter.

ENCLOSURE NOTATION

1454 If an item is to be included in the envelope with the letter, indicate that fact by typing the word *Enclosure* (or the abbreviation *Enc.* or *Encl.*) at the left margin, on the line below the reference initials. If more than one item is to be enclosed, use the word *Enclosures* (or the abbreviation *Encs.* or *Encls.*) and indicate the number of items. The styles illustrated below are commonly used.

```
Enclosure          2 Enclosures      Enclosures:
Enc.               2 Encs.              1. Check
1 Enc.             Enc. 2               2. Invoice
1 Enclosure        Enclosures 2
Check Enclosed     Enclosures (2)
```

NOTE: In military correspondence, the word *Inclosure* and the abbreviations *Inc.* and *Incl.* are used.

CARBON COPY NOTATION

1455 If the writer wishes the addressee to know that one or more other persons will be sent a copy of the letter, type a *cc* (carbon copy) notation at the left margin, on the line below the enclosure notation (if used) or on the line below the reference initials. If several persons are to receive carbon copies, the names should be listed according to the rank of the persons or, if there is no difference in rank, alphabetically.

```
  cc Miss Johnson       CC:  Mr. A. C. Case       cc:  Wells, Inc.
                             Mr. R. G. Flynn
```

1456 If the addressee is not intended to know that one or more other persons are being sent a copy of the letter, type a *bcc* (blind carbon copy) notation in the upper left corner of the carbon copies only—never on the original copy. Any of the forms used for a regular *cc* notation may be used for a *bcc* notation.

MAILING NOTATION

1457 If a letter is to be delivered by messenger or by registered, certified, or special delivery mail, type the appropriate notation (for example, *SPECIAL DELIVERY*) at the left margin, on the line below the cc notation (or whatever notation was typed last). An acceptable alternative is to type the notation on the second line below the date, starting it at the same point as the date (see Letter Style 1).

POSTSCRIPT

1458 A postscript can be quite effective when it is used to express an idea that has been deliberately withheld from the body of a letter; stating this idea at the very end gives it strong emphasis. A postscript may also be used to express an afterthought; this usage, however, may not be effective if it suggests that the body of the letter was badly organized. When a postscript is used:

a. Start the postscript on the second line below the cc notation (or whatever notation was typed last). If the paragraphs are indented, indent the first line of the postscript; otherwise, begin it at the left margin (see Letter Style 1).

b. Type *PS:* or *P.S.* before the first word of the postscript. (Leave two spaces between the colon or period and the first word.)

c. Use *PPS:* or *P.P.S.* (or no abbreviation at all) at the beginning of an additional postscript, and treat the additional postscript as a separate paragraph.

TWO-PAGE LETTERS

1459 Use plain paper of the same quality as the letterhead (but never a letterhead) for the second and each succeeding page of a long letter.

1460 Use the same left and right margins that you used on the first page.

1461 On the seventh line from the top of the page, type a continuation-page heading consisting of the following: the name of the addressee, the page number, and the date. Either of the following styles is acceptable:

Mrs. L. R. Austin   2   September 30, 1970

OR: Mrs. L. R. Austin
    Page 2
    September 30, 1970

1462 Resume typing the message on the third line below the last line of the continuation-page heading.

a. Always type at least two lines of a paragraph at the top of a continuation page, and leave at least two lines of the paragraph at the bottom of the previous page.

b. Do not divide a paragraph that contains three or fewer lines.

c. Never use a continuation page to type only the closing section of a business letter. (The complimentary closing should always be preceded by at least two lines of the message.)

1463 Leave a bottom margin of at least 1 inch at the foot of each page of a letter (except the last page), and keep the bottom margin as uniform as possible on all pages except the last.

1464 Avoid dividing the last word on a page.

SPACING AND STYLES OF LETTERS

1465 Except for very short letters, always use single spacing. If you use double spacing, always indent the first line of each paragraph.

1466 A business letter is usually arranged in one of the following styles:

a. The *blocked* (modified block) and the *semiblocked* (modified block with indented paragraphs) are the most popular styles (see Letter Styles 1 and 2).

b. The *full-blocked* (extreme block) style is similar to the *simplified* letter recommended by the Administrative Management Society (AMS). (Compare Letter Style 3 with Letter Style 7.)

c. The *square-blocked* style (see Letter Style 4) permits typing more copy on a page.

d. The *indented style* (see Letter Style 5) is not used extensively.

e. The *hanging-indented* style (see Letter Style 6) is seldom used except in advertising letters.

PUNCTUATION PATTERNS

1467 The body of a business letter is always punctuated with normal punctuation (see Sections 1 and 2). The other parts of a letter may be punctuated according to one of the following patterns:

a. *Standard* (mixed) pattern (see Letter Styles 1, 2, 4, and 6). A colon is used after the salutation and a comma after the complimentary closing.

[Continued on page 216.]

Blocked
THE MOST FLEXIBLE
Letter Style

With foreign address, quotation, and postscript

March 10, 1972

REGISTERED

Mr. Philip Watkins
Watkins & Matthews, Ltd.
199 Wellington Street
Ottawa 2, Ontario
CANADA

Dear Mr. Watkins:

It is current practice in American business letters
to display quotations and similar data in a special
paragraph, like this:

    The paragraph is indented five spaces on
    both sides and is preceded and followed
    by one ordinary blank line space.

If it is necessary to use more paragraphs
for the quotation, then a standard single
blank line is left between paragraphs.

We show the mail service (on the second line below
the date) only if we are sending the correspondence
by some special service, such as special delivery
or registered, and we do so only to get the fact
indicated on our file copy of the correspondence.

    Sincerely yours,

    David of Collins

    Assistant Director
    Bureau of Information
    and Public Relations

DIC/urs

P.S. We treat postscripts in the same way that we
treat other paragraphs except that we precede each
postscript by PS: or P.S.

THE SEVEN LETTER STYLES

Letter Style 1. The blocked (or modified block) style is used more frequently in business than any other letter style. The paragraphs begin at the left margin, and punctuation is standard.

Full-Blocked
VIGOROUS, AGGRESSIVE
Letter Style   With subject line and open punctuation

March 6, 1972

Mr. Roger S. Patterson
Western Life Company
2967 East Fourth Street
Cincinnati, Ohio 45202

Dear Mr. Patterson

Subject: Form of a Full-Blocked Letter

This letter is set up in the full-blocked style, in which every line begins at the left margin. A few companies modify it by moving the date to the right, but most firms use it as shown here. Because this style is the fastest to type, it is considered very modern; it is natural, although not necessary, to use open punctuation with this style of letter.

This letter also illustrates one arrangement of the subject line, which may be used with any style of letter. Like an attention line, a subject line may be typed with underscores or capitals. In a full-blocked letter, it must be blocked; in other letter styles, it may be blocked or centered. It always appears after the salutation and before the body, for it is considered a part of the body.

Legal firms and the legal departments of companies sometimes prefer to use the Latin terms Re or In Re instead of the English word Subject.

Sincerely,

Mary Ellen Smith

Mary Ellen Smith
Reference Department

urs
Enc.

Letter Style 3. The full-blocked (or extreme block) style is the fastest style to type because each line begins at the left margin. It is customary to use open punctuation with this letter style.

Semiblocked
CONSERVATIVE, EXECUTIVE
Letter Style   With attention line and cc notation

March 7, 1972

Savard, Foster & Company
171 Westminster Street
Providence, RI 02904

ATTENTION TRAINING DIRECTOR

Gentlemen:

For a letter design that is both standard and distinctive, try this style: semiblocked (one of the two most popular styles) with the paragraphs indented ten spaces (instead of the usual five).

This letter also shows you an alternative arrangement for the attention line: centered, in all capitals (instead of being blocked at the left margin and underscored). In two respects, however, the use of the attention line here is standard: it is accompanied by a salutation, it should be, by the salutation Gentlemen; and it is typed above the salutation.

Worth noting also in this letter are the following: (1) positioning the date at the center as an alternative to ending it at the right margin; (2) the use of standard punctuation, which calls for a colon after the salutation and a comma after the complimentary closing; and (3) the use of the cc notation to indicate the secondary position to whom copies of the letter are being sent.

Cordially,

Louise R. Adams

Louise R. Adams, Director

URS
cc Miss Filene
   Dr. Young

Letter Style 2. The semiblocked style (or modified block with indented paragraphs) is another popular letter style. It is the same as the blocked style except that the first line of each paragraph is indented.

March 8, 1972.

Miss June R. Zane,
2831 Browning Avenue,
Knoxville, Tennessee 27901.

Dear Miss Zane:

The indented style is one of the few that may be typed in either single or double spacing. The double-spaced form, therefore, is convenient when you have a short letter that must be stretched.

When you plan the placement of a double-spaced letter, you must remember that it will stretch out to twice its single-spaced length. This letter of 74 words, double-spaced, occupies as much space as would a single-spaced letter of 148 words.

Cordially yours,

Henry J Sullivan
District Manager.

HJS/urs.
cc Chicago Office.

Letter Style 5. The indented style may be typed with close punctuation as shown here or with standard punctuation. Both the inside address and closing lines, as well as the paragraphs, are indented.

March 7, 1972

Mrs. Truda Tracy George
President, Pi Omega Pi
California State College
San Diego, California 92101

Dear Mrs. George:

SUBJECT: THE SQUARE-BLOCKED LETTER

A square-blocked letter like this one is simply the familiar full-blocked letter with (1) the date moved to the right and typed on the same line with the start of the inside address to square off that corner and (2) the reference symbols also shifted to the right to square off that corner.

This arrangement has many advantages. It is almost as quick to type as the full-blocked style. Because it saves lines or space that are otherwise given to the drop-down date and below-the-letter reference initials, you can get seven or eight additional lines of typing on a page. You can see why this is popular among secretaries whose employers dictate rather long letters. Any letter looks shorter when typed in this style. It permits any kind of display, either centered or blocked.

When using this letter style, make it a rule not to use less than a 50-space line; otherwise, the first line of the inside address might run into the date at the right margin. For an ordinary letter, where you do not need to save space, you must mind yourself to start two or three lines lower on the page, lest your letter look too high on the stationery.

One limitation of the square-blocked letter style is the way it restricts the notation, if you use enclosures. If you want to enumerate the enclosures, however, the display would have to be at the left, and then the perfect balance of the squared corners would be lost.

Fraternally yours,

Elsie Dodds Frost
Mrs. Elsie Dodds Frost

urs
Enclosures

Letter Style 4. The square-blocked style permits more copy to be typed on a page. As a space-saving device, the date, reference initials, and enclosure notation are typed in the right corner margins.

Simplified
THE EFFICIENCY EXPERT'S
Letter Style With open punctuation and full-blocked design

March 6, 1972

Mr. Richard W. Parker, Jr.
Humphrey Lumber Company
520 Southwest Park Avenue
Portland, Oregon 97208

THE SIMPLIFIED LETTER

You will be interested to know, Mr. Parker, that several years ago the Administrative Management Society (formerly NOMA) designed a new letter form called the simplified letter. This is a sample:

1. It uses the full-blocked form and open punctuation.

2. It contains no salutation or closing. (AMS believes such expressions to be meaningless.)

3. It displays a subject line in all capitals, both preceded and followed by two blank lines. Note that the word subject is omitted.

4. It identifies the signer by an all-capital line that is preceded by at least four blank lines and followed by one—if further notations are used.

5. It seeks to maintain a brisk but friendly tone, partly by using the addressee's name at least in the first sentence.

Perhaps, Mr. Parker, as some say, this form does not really look like a business letter but, its efficiency suggests that this style is worth a trial, especially where output must be increased.

Ralph E. Jones

RALPH E. JONES, TRAINING CONSULTANT

urs

Letter Style 7. The simplified letter is similar to the full-blocked letter, but the salutation and complimentary closing are omitted. The subject line and writer's identification are typed in all capitals. Punctuation is open.

Hanging-Indented
FOR SUPER-DISPLAY SALESMANSHIP
Letter Style With paragraphs and signer's name displayed

March 9, 1972

To All the Typists Who
Need a Way to Display
A Special Sales Letter
So It Looks Special

Dear Ready-for-Rescue:

Yes, this is a hanging-indented letter, with a key word at the start of the margin and the rest of each paragraph and with other lines indented.

Yes, this letter style takes attentive production. You leave a two-, three-, four-, or five-space indent. All lines except the first one in each paragraph.

Yes, the hanging-indented style is designed solely for display correspondence. Since the process is too slow and cumbersome for ordinary correspondence, the whole point of the display is to feature those paragraph starters, the letter has to be prepared especially to fit this arrangement.

Yes, indicating the signer's name in the reference position, as below, instead of below the space where he signs the letter, is a procedure that may be used. With such a signature, it is a good device to use when a signet-bar, a signature he likes but which is illegible.

Yours very truly,

L. T. Leslie

Vice President, Sales

LTLeslie/ars

Letter Style 6. The hanging-indented style is commonly used in sales letters. It is similar to the blocked style except all the lines in a paragraph after the first line and the writer's identification are indented.

b. *Open* pattern (see Letter Styles 3 and 7). No punctuation is used at the end of any line outside the body of the letter unless that line ends with an abbreviation.

c. *Close* (full) pattern (see Letter Style 5). Each line outside the body of the letter ends with a punctuation mark.

LETTER STATIONERY

1468 When typing a business letter:

a. Use letterhead, plain paper, and envelope stationery that is matched in size, weight, and color. The most commonly used sizes of stationery are given in the following table:

Name	Letterhead Size	Envelope No.	Envelope Size
Standard	8½ x 11	6¾ or	3⅝ x 6½
		10	4⅛ x 9½
Half sheets	8½ x 5½	6¾	3⅝ x 6½
Baronial	5½ x 8½	5⅜	4⅝ x 5¹⁵/₁₆
Monarch	7¼ x 10½	7	3⅞ x 7½

b. For carbon copies, use *manifold* (an inexpensive, lightweight paper available with either a glazed or an unglazed finish), *onionskin* (a stronger, more expensive paper available with either a smooth or a ripple finish), or *copy letterhead* (lightweight paper with the letterhead and the word *COPY* printed on it).

c. Use carbon paper of the weight and finish most appropriate for the number of copies you are making, as follows:

Copies	Weight	Finish
1–4	Standard	Hard
5–8	Medium	Hard
9–20	Light	Medium

NOTE: Many companies provide preassembled "snap-out" carbon packs in addition to loose sheets of carbon and copy paper. The sheets of copy paper are often of different colors in order to facilitate the routing of copies.

LETTER PLACEMENT

1469 On a standard typewriter, 1 inch equals:

a. Ten spaces if the machine has *pica* type. . . . .

b. Twelve spaces if the machine has *elite* type. . . . .

c. Six vertical line spaces.

NOTE: If you do not know whether your machine has pica type or elite type, type a series of periods and compare them with the ones above. (Proportional-spacing machines provide spacing different from that indicated in *a*, *b*, and *c* above.)

1470 The following letter-placement guide is generally used when business letters are typed on stationery measuring 8½ by 11 inches.

a. To determine the margins, estimate the number of words in the body of the letter and then select the appropriate line length and margins as shown in the following table:

LETTER-PLACEMENT GUIDE
(With center at 50 and inside address on fifth line below date)

Length of Letter	Words in Body	Length of Line in		Margins*
		Inches	Spaces	
Short	Up to 100	4	40 pica	30–75
			50 elite†	25–80
Average	100–200	5	50 pica	25–80
			60 elite	20–85
Long	200–300	6	60 pica	20–85
			70 elite†	15–90
Two-page	Over 300	6	60 pica	20–85
			70 elite†	15–90

NOTE: In some offices, one line length is used for all letters, regardless of their length.

*An additional five spaces has been added to the right margin setting in order to avoid frequent use of the margin release key.
†Rounded off.

b. For the spacing to be used between the parts of a letter, see the paragraphs in which the various letter parts are described. (For example, see ¶ 1402 for the positioning of the date line.)

1471 To *lengthen* a very short letter, use any combination of the following spacing techniques:

a. Lower the date (from three to five lines).

b. Allow five to six blank lines between the date and the inside address.

c. Use 1½ lines before and after the salutation, between the paragraphs, between the body and the complimentary closing, and between the complimentary closing and the company name.

d. Allow four to six blank lines for the signature.

e. Place the signer's name and title on separate lines.

f. Lower the reference initials one or two lines.

1472 To *condense* a long one-page letter, use any combination of the following spacing techniques:

a. Raise the date.

b. Allow only two or three blank lines between the date and inside address.

[Continued on page 218.]

   c. Omit the company name, if permitted.

   d. Allow only two blank lines for the signature.

   e. Raise the reference initials one or two lines.

1473 To insert paper into the machine so that the center of the sheet will always be at a preselected centering point:

   a. Select a centering point, such as 50 or 40, and position the carriage so that the printing-point indicator is at that point on the carriage-position scale.

   b. Fold a sheet of paper in half lengthwise, make a crease at the fold, unfold the sheet, and then insert it into the machine.

   c. Using the paper release, loosen the paper and slide it right or left until the crease is at the center of the printing-point indicator.

   d. Set the paper guide at the left edge of the paper.

   e. Note and remember the point at which the paper guide appears on the paper-guide scale. Then, always check to see that the paper guide is set at that point before you insert paper into the machine.

No. 6¾ envelope, with mailing notation.

Ralph L. Landers
172 Western Drive
San Jose, CA 95117

REGISTERED

Mr. John R. Reardon, Treasurer
Blake, Walsh & Taylor Company, Inc.
598 East 77 Street
Los Angeles, CA 90052

No. 10 envelope, with attention line.

SPLANE & GARDNER, INC.
29 EAST CANYON AVENUE
SANTA FE, NEW MEXICO 87501

Attention Manager, Sales Department

Lewis & Erickson Products, Inc.
398 North Michigan Avenue
Chicago, Illinois 60603

ADDRESSING ENVELOPES

1474 When addressing an envelope:

a. Always use single spacing and blocked style (see illustrations on page 218).

b. Always type the city, state, and ZIP Code on one line. Leave one space between the state and the ZIP Code.

c. When using a large (No. 10) envelope, start the address on line 14, about 4 inches from the left edge. When using a small (No. 6¾) envelope or when addressing a postcard, start the address on line 12, about 2 inches from the left edge.

d. If a printed return address does not appear on the envelope, type a return address in the upper left corner, beginning on line 3 about ½ inch from the left edge of the envelope. The return address should contain at least the following information, arranged in three lines: (1) the name of the writer or his company; (2) the street address; and (3) the city, state, and ZIP Code.

e. Type an attention line or a notation such as *Personal* or *Confidential* below the return address. It should begin on line 9 or at least two lines below the return address. Begin each word with a capital letter, and use underscoring.

f. If a special mailing procedure is used, type the appropriate notation (such as *SPECIAL DELIVERY* or *REGISTERED*) in all capitals in the upper right corner of the envelope, beginning on line 9. The notation should end about ½ inch from the right margin.

1475 To chain-feed envelopes:

a. After addressing the first envelope, roll it back until only ½ inch or so shows in front of the cylinder.

[*Continued on page 220.*]

Chain-feeding envelopes. Each new envelope is inserted from the front, with its bottom edge placed between the previous envelope and the cylinder.

Courtesy International Business Machines Corporation

b. Insert the next envelope from the front, placing its bottom edge between the first envelope and the cylinder.

c. Turn the cylinder toward you to remove the first envelope and to bring the second one into typing position.

FOLDING AND INSERTING LETTERS

1476 Always check for enclosures before folding letters. Remember that carbon copies may require the same (or occasionally different) enclosures.

1477 To fold a letter for insertion into a small business envelope:

a. Fold from the lower edge of the letter, bringing the bottom edge to within ½ inch or so of the top edge before you crease the letter (see illustration below).

b. Fold from the right edge, making the fold a little less than one-third the width of the sheet before you crease it.

c. Fold from the left edge, bringing it to within ½ inch or so of the crease you made in step *b* before you crease the sheet again.

d. Insert the left creased edge into the envelope first. This will leave the crease you made in step *b* near the flap of the envelope.

1478 To fold a letter for insertion into a large envelope:

a. Fold from the lower edge, bringing the bottom of the letter up approximately one-third the length of the sheet before you make the crease (see illustration below).

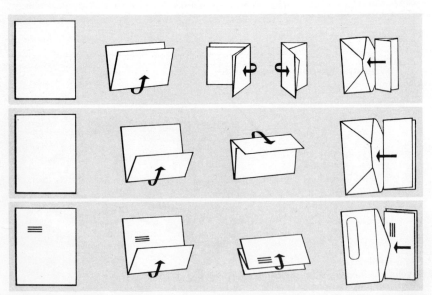

Folding and inserting letters. These diagrams show the proper way to fold a letter for insertion into a No. 6¾ envelope (*top*), a No. 10 envelope (*center*), and a window envelope (*bottom*).

b. Fold from the top edge, bringing it to within ½ inch or so of the crease you made in step *a* before you make the second crease.

c. Insert the crease you made in step *b* into the envelope first. This will leave the crease you made in step *a* near the flap of the envelope.

1479 To fold a letter for insertion into a window envelope:

a. Fold from the lower edge of the letter, bringing it up approximately one-third the length of the sheet before you make the crease (see illustration on page 220).

b. Fold the top edge of the letter *back* to the edge of the crease you made in step *a*. (The letterhead and inside address should now be facing you.)

c. Insert the letter with the letterhead near the flap of the envelope and the inside address toward the *front* of the envelope. (The inside address should now be readable through the window of the envelope.)

INTEROFFICE CORRESPONDENCE

1480 When typing a memorandum on a printed form, such as the one illustrated on page 222:

a. Set the left margin stop either at a point two or three spaces after the longest guide word in the left half of the printed heading (for example, after *Subject*) or at the point where the printed guide words begin.

b. Set a tab stop two or three spaces after the longest guide word in the right half of the printed heading (for example, after *From*).

c. Set the right margin stop to leave a right margin equal to the left margin.

d. Type in the appropriate information after each printed guide word. Make sure that the typewritten fill-ins align *at the bottom* with the printed guide words.

e. Begin typing the message on the third or fourth line below the last fill-in line in the heading. (An interoffice memorandum ordinarily does not include a salutation; the printed heading takes the place of the inside address, date line, and various other parts of a regular business letter.) Use single spacing, and either block or indent the paragraphs.

f. Type the dictator's name, initials, or title (whichever he prefers to use) on the second line below the last line of the message, beginning at the tab stop you set in step *b*. (The dictator normally does not sign a memorandum.)

g. Type the reference initials (see ¶ 1451) on the second line below the dictator's name, initials, or title; block them at the left margin.

h. Type the enclosure notation, if used, on the line below the reference initials, beginning at the left margin.

i. Type the carbon copy notation, if used, on the line below the enclosure notation, if used, or on the line below the reference initials.

Interoffice Memorandum

TO	Lawrence R. Jensen	FROM	Robert C. Nelson
SUBJECT	Form for Memorandums	DATE	January 17, 1972

Interoffice memorandums are used for correspondence between persons, departments, and branch offices in the same firm.

The left margin stop is set either at a point two or three spaces after the longest printed guide word in the left half of the heading or at the point where the printed guide words begin. The right margin should be the same width as the left margin.

A tab stop is set two or three spaces after the longest printed guide word in the right half of the heading.

The dictator's name, initials, or title is typed on the second line below the body of the memorandum. It should begin at the tab stop that has been set in the right half of the heading.

Reference initials and enclosure and carbon copy notations are used as in letters.

RCN

CS
cc Mr. Kendrick

SOCIAL-BUSINESS CORRESPONDENCE

1481 Social-business correspondence usually differs from that of regular business correspondence in such details as these:

a. The inside address may be typed at the bottom of the letter, beginning at the left margin on the fifth line below the typewritten signature.

b. The salutation is usually very informal (for example, *Dear Betty* or *Dear Jack*) and is followed by a comma instead of a colon.

c. Numbers are often written according to the "word style" (see ¶¶ 404–407).

d. The complimentary closing is usually very informal (for example, *Regards* or *Yours*).

e. The writer's typewritten signature may be omitted, depending upon how well the writer knows the addressee.

f. The reference initials are omitted, and even though an enclosure may be mentioned in the letter, the enclosure notation is usually omitted.

g. Carbon copy and other notations rarely appear in social-business letters.

1482 Always consult a standard book of etiquette (see Section 20 for the names of several good ones) when typing an invitation, an announcement, or a similar communication.

Section 15
TELEGRAMS

Since the procedures for sending domestic and international telegrams and radiograms change from time to time, consult your local telegraph agency for the latest information.

DOMESTIC SERVICES

A domestic telegram may be sent to a person or firm in the continental United States, Canada, or Mexico. Distance is no longer a factor in computing rates for domestic telegraph services within the United States; in general, a standard charge applies regardless of where the wire originates or where it is to be sent. The two classes of domestic services are the telegram and the overnight telegram. In addition, special domestic services are available.

1501 Telegram. A telegram is the quickest but most expensive service. It should be used only when delivery the same day is essential. A message is accepted at any time of day or night and is delivered usually within two hours. The minimum charge is for a 15-word message, with an additional charge for each extra word.

NOTE: Time-zone differences must be considered in determining whether a fast-service telegram is feasible. (The standard time zones in the United States are shown in the illustration on page 224.) For example, if a message is to be sent from San Francisco to New York, it may be received too late for delivery the same day; the overnight telegram described in ¶ 1502 would be more practical.

1502 Overnight Telegram. An overnight telegram is a less expensive service. A message may be sent at any time up to midnight for delivery the following morning, usually by the time businesses open. The minimum charge is for 100 words, with an additional charge for each extra word. This service should be used when a message is lengthy, when delivery the same day is not necessary, or when it is near closing time at the point of destination.

1503 Special Domestic Services. The charges for special services vary and should be checked with your local telegraph agency. Among the services are:

a. Money orders. Telegraphic money orders can be filed at any Western Union office and are paid at the destination.

b. Hotel reservations. Reservations at hotels in the United States may be made by sending a telegram, with a choice of accommodations, to the Western Union Hotel Reservations Desk.

c. Will-call telegrams. If a traveler is expecting a telegram to be sent to him en route, he must go to the local telegraph agency office to col-

Courtesy American Telephone and Telegraph Company

This time-zone map shows the different time zones in the continental United States and in Canada. It also shows the telephone area codes.

lect the message. If a will-call telegram is not picked up within seventy-two hours, the agency will notify the sender by a free-service message.

d. Gift services and greetings. Western Union will deliver such gifts as candy, flowers, and perfume for holidays and other special occasions. They will also provide special holiday and anniversary greetings.

e. Messenger service. Special messengers may be engaged through Western Union to deliver or pick up items within a city.

INTERNATIONAL SERVICES

An international telegram may be sent to a person or firm in all foreign countries. The two classes of international services are the full-rate telegram and the letter telegram. Special international services are also available, including ship radiograms.

1504 Full-Rate Telegram (FR). A full-rate international telegram provides the fastest but most expensive service to foreign countries. Delivery is usually the same day. The minimum charge is for 7 words.

1505 Letter Telegram (LT). The letter telegram is a deferred foreign service. It is normally delivered the following morning, depending on which city and country are involved. The minimum charge is for 22 words. A letter telegram usually costs half the amount of a full-rate telegram of the same length.

1506 Special International Services. The following special services are available:

a. Code address. Abbreviated code names for companies and their cities may be registered by calling the telegraph company, or they may be registered at the Central Bureau for Registered Addresses. There is a yearly charge.

b. Secret language. Full-rate international telegrams may utilize codes, ciphers, codes combined with ciphers, or plain language combined with codes or ciphers. (Letter telegrams must be written in plain language.) Among the best-known standard or public codes are the Western Union Code, A.B.C. Code, Bentley's Code, and Acme Code.

c. Ship radiogram. The ship radiogram is used for sending messages to and from ships at sea. Two classes of ship radiograms are available: the standard *full-rate* classification, which has a minimum charge for 5 words, and the *press* classification (limited to official members of the press), which has a minimum charge for 10 words. Ship radiograms may be written in code or plain language.

WORD COUNTING

The charge for both domestic and international telegrams is based on the number of chargeable words, but the method of computing words differs.

1507 Domestic Telegrams

a. The name and address of the addressee and the signature are transmitted free. A business signature may include both the employee's name and the name of his company, the name of his department, or his title without extra charge.

b. Dictionary words from the English, German, French, Italian, Dutch, Portuguese, Spanish, and Latin languages are counted as one word each regardless of length. Any word or combination of letters not included in the dictionary is counted at the rate of one word for each five letters or less.

c. Each initial is counted as one word unless the letters are written together. For example, *R. C. Adams* would be counted as three words; *RC Adams,* as two words.

d. Common abbreviations typed together with or without periods are counted at the rate of one word for each five letters or less; for example, *c.o.d.* or *COD; r.p.m.* or *rpm.* Contractions should not be used because the words that make up a contraction are counted as separate words.

e. Standard punctuation marks (the period, decimal point, comma, colon, semicolon, question mark, apostrophe, parentheses, dash, hyphen, and quotation marks) are neither counted nor charged for in the message. (Such words as *stop* and *quote* are counted as one word each and should not be used in place of punctuation marks.)

[Continued on page 226.]

f. Groups of figures and letters and such symbols as $, /, #, &, ' (for feet), and " (for inches) are counted at the rate of one word for each five characters or less. For example, #8159 has five characters and is counted as one word; $750.35 has six characters and is counted as two words (the decimal is classified as a punctuation mark and is therefore not counted as a character). Since the percent symbol is transmitted as o/o, it is counted as three characters. The symbols ¢ and @ cannot be transmitted and must be written as words.

1508 International Telegrams

a. Each word in the address and signature is counted and charged for. Therefore, firms doing frequent foreign business usually have one-word registered addresses (see ¶ 1506a).

b. Each dictionary word is counted at the rate of fifteen, or a fraction of fifteen, letters to the word. Code or cipher language (in full-rate messages only) is counted at the rate of five, or a fraction of five, characters to the word.

c. Each punctuation mark is counted as one word.

d. Groups of figures and letters are counted at the rate of five characters to the word. Any punctuation included in a group of figures is counted as one character in the group, not as a separate word.

TYPING THE TELEGRAM

1509 Western Union provides free telegraph forms for all types of service. You should observe the following points in typing telegrams:

a. Always make at least one carbon copy. If your company asks you to send a confirmation copy by mail to the addressee and another to the accounting department, two additional copies will be needed.

b. Set the left margin stop at the *S* in *SVC.* and tab stops at the *R* in *CHARGE* and at the *T* in *OVERNIGHT,* as shown in the illustration on page 227. (This will automatically clear all the printed guide words in the form.)

c. If you are sending an overnight telegram, type an *x* in the box in the upper right side of the form. (If you do not check *Overnight Telegram,* the message will be sent by the faster, more expensive service.)

d. If the message is to be sent collect, type *Collect* in the block headed *Pd. or Coll.*

e. If the message is to be charged to your company's account, tab to the first stop and type *Sender* in the block headed *Charge to the Account Of.*

f. Tab to the second stop and type the date in the space provided in the upper right side of the form.

g. Type the name and full address (or code address) of the person to whom the telegram is to be sent in the upper left side of the form, beginning at the left margin. Be sure the addressee's name and address are accurate and as complete as possible. If the telegram is going to a large office building, include the room or floor number if known.

NO. WDS.–CL. OF SVC.	PD. OR COLL.	CASH NO.	CHARGE TO THE ACCOUNT OF	OVER NIGHT TELEGRAM

western union — **Telegram**

CHARGE TO THE ACCOUNT OF ▲ Sender

☐ OVER NIGHT TELEGRAM
UNLESS BOX ABOVE IS CHECKED THIS MESSAGE WILL BE SENT AS A TELEGRAM

Send the following message, subject to the terms on back hereof, which are hereby agreed to   December 10, 19 72

TO   John Miller, Report Delivery

CARE OF OR APT. NO.

Gaines Company

STREET & NO.   388 Wayne Avenue

TELEPHONE   721-6898

CITY & STATE   Denver, Colorado

ZIP CODE   80205

> Sending advance copy of new catalog air express. Do not release
> before January 1.
>
>   Alan B. Mercer
>   C. H. Walters, Inc.

SENDER'S TEL. NO. 849-3322   NAME & ADDRESS   C. H. Walters, Inc.
                                              378 Jones Street
                                              Berkeley, California 94704

WU 1207 (R 5-69)

Courtesy The Western Union Telegraph Company

h. Tab to the second stop and type the addressee's telephone number and his ZIP Code in the upper right side of the form. This should be done as you are typing the address.

i. Type the message single-spaced, beginning at the left margin on the third or fourth line below the city and state. (If your machine has 1½-line spacing, you may type on the lightly printed lines; otherwise, ignore the lines. They are used mainly for handwritten messages.) Be sure that the message is stated briefly but clearly. Use standard punctuation marks for clarity (see ¶ 1507e).

j. Tab to the first stop and type the sender's signature on the second line below the message. On the next line type the name of his company. This information will be transmitted with the message. (Do not include any information in the space provided for the message that you do not want to have transmitted.)

k. Type the sender's telephone number in the space provided at the bottom of the form, beginning at the left margin.

l. Tab to the first stop and type your company's name and address in the space provided.

1510 If the sender requests a report of the delivery of the message, type the words *Report Delivery* after the addressee's name in the address block (see illustration above). The receiving office will then wire back, at an additional charge, a copy of the telegram showing when and to whom the telegram was delivered.

Section 16
REPORTS AND MANUSCRIPTS

TYPING THE MANUSCRIPT

PAPER, CARBONS, AND RIBBON

1601 Use a good quality of bond paper, usually $8\frac{1}{2}$ by 11 inches. Type on only one side of the paper.

1602 Make at least one carbon copy.

1603 Use a black record ribbon so that the copy will be clear and permanent.

MARGINS

1604 Use the following margins for all typed reports and manuscripts:

a. Top margin of first page. Leave 2 inches (12 blank lines) at the top of the first page when it contains the title of the report or manuscript. Center the title and type it in all-capital letters. Center the author's name on the second line below the title. (If a subtitle is to be included in the heading, center it on the second line below the main title; then type the author's name on the second line below the subtitle.) On the third line below the author's name, begin typing the first line of the body of the manuscript.

b. Top margin of other pages. Leave 1 inch (6 blank lines) at the top. Type the page number on the seventh line from the top, and begin typing the text on the third line below the page number.

c. Left margin. Leave $1\frac{1}{4}$ inches at the left (elite: 15 spaces; pica: 13 spaces). If the pages are to be bound in a notebook or binder, leave $1\frac{1}{2}$ inches (elite: 18 spaces; pica: 15 spaces).

d. Right margin. Leave $1\frac{1}{4}$ inches at the right (or 1 inch if the pages are to be bound).

e. Bottom margin. Leave 1 to $1\frac{1}{2}$ inches (6 to 9 blank lines).

1605 A ruled backing sheet will help keep margins uniform on all pages.

a. Draw a rectangle with *heavy* lines (black ink is most visible) to indicate the type area within the rectangle and the margins outside.

b. Place this sheet between the original copy and the back of the first carbon sheet; the rulings will show through the original copy to serve as a guide.

Page 5

A quote that would fill three or fewer full lines when it is typed is shown in quotation marks, but a longer quote must be given special display: it is single-spaced and is indented five spaces from each side margin, as shown below.

3. Footnotes. The credits in a report are numbered in the order in which they occur. Each must be explained in a matching footnote at the bottom of the same page.

Each footnote is arranged as ". . . a separate paragraph. It is indented. It is single-spaced. It is numbered."[3] The footnotes must be kept apart from the body of the report:

Separate a footnote from the text above it by a 2-inch line of underscores--that would be 20 pica spaces long or 24 elite spaces long. Be sure, also, to single-space before typing the line so that one blank space will be left between the typed line and the first footnote below the line.[4]

IV. Summary

The rules for typing a term paper may vary from school to school, but in most regards the rules are fairly standard.

As long as the typist remembers to display headings so that they stress the outline of the report, to arrange pages with proper margins, to set up tables with care, and to give full credit for borrowed thoughts and words, he will find that typing a term paper is easy to manage.

[3]Alan C. Lloyd and Russell Hosler, Personal Typing, 3d ed., McGraw-Hill Book Company, New York, 1968, p. 115.
[4]Ibid., p. 116.

The top margin on the other pages of the manuscript is much narrower. A properly typed quotation and two footnotes are also shown.

HOW TO TYPE A TERM PAPER

A Special Report

by Gordon McCrea

I. Introduction

Many persons learn to typewrite so that they may use the skill in typing term papers and other formal reports that are assigned to them in high school and college. The purpose of this report is to review how such papers should be typed.

II. Investigation

The information in this report comes from two sources:

A. SOURCES OF INFORMATION

1. Interviews. The subject was discussed with several persons, including a free-lance typist, two college students, two high school teachers, and a college instructor.

2. Readings. Ideas and details were drawn also from a magazine article, from two typewriting textbooks, and from a booklet published by the English department of a college.

B. ORGANIZATION OF FINDINGS

The findings deal with four topics: the use of a clear outline, the general arrangement of pages, and the treatment of quotations and other references.

The four topics are discussed in the following sections.

The first page of a properly typed manuscript will look like this. Notice the margins and the spacing above and below the headings.

SPACING AND PARAGRAPHS

1606 Observe these rules of spacing and indentation:

a. Leave two blank lines between the last line in the title block and the first line of text. (See ¶ 1604a.)

b. Double-space all text matter, and indent paragraphs five spaces.

c. Single-space tabulations, outlines, and quoted material typed as an extract (see illustration on page 229). Indent this copy five or more spaces from each margin. If a whole paragraph is quoted in an extract, indent the first word an additional five spaces.

d. A centered heading displayed on a line by itself should be preceded by two blank lines and followed by one blank line.

e. A side heading displayed on a line by itself should be preceded by two blank lines and followed by one blank line. (When a side heading comes directly below a centered heading, leave only one blank line above the side heading.)

f. A run-in heading (that is, a heading run into the start of a paragraph) should be indented five spaces from the left. The run-in heading should be underscored and followed by a period. The text then begins two spaces after the period.

PAGING

1607 Number the pages as follows:

a. When the first page contains the title of the manuscript or the report, it is accounted for in the numbering but the number is not typed on the page.

b. The numbers of all other pages should be typed in the upper right corner. Place the number at the right margin on the seventh line from the top. (The word *Page* may precede the number.)

c. After typing the page number, begin the first line of text on the third line below (on line 10).

d. When it is necessary to save space, the page number may be typed on line 4 (instead of line 7) and the first line of the text typed on line 6.

NOTE: An acceptable variation is to type all page numbers at the bottom of the page. In this case, begin the text on the seventh line from the top of the page, (2) type the last line of text on the ninth line ($1\frac{1}{2}$ inches) from the bottom of the page, and (3) leaving two blank lines, type the page number on the sixth line from the bottom, centered between the margins.

1608 Start each chapter of a report or manuscript on a fresh page. When the chapter title appears at the top of a page, type the page number at the foot of the page (as described in ¶ 1607, note, above).

FOOTNOTES

1609 **a.** Footnotes serve two functions: (1) they convey subordinate ideas which the writer feels might be distracting if incorporated within the main text; (2) they serve as references, identifying the source of a statement quoted or cited in the text. (The second kind of footnote is often called a *reference footnote*. See also ¶ 1612.)

b. Footnotes are ordinarily keyed by number to a word, phrase, or sentence in the text.

c. Footnotes customarily appear at the foot of the same page as the textual matter to which they refer. In typing each page, be sure to allow sufficient space at the bottom for any footnotes that may be required. Estimate three to four lines for each reference footnote: this estimate allows for space above and below each footnote.

FOOTNOTE REFERENCES IN THE TEXT

1610 **a.** To indicate the presence of a footnoted comment or reference at the bottom of the page, type a superior (raised) figure immediately following the appropriate word, phrase, or sentence in the text. Do not leave any space between the superior figure and the preceding word. However, if any punctuation occurs at the same point, the superior figure should occur immediately after the punctuation mark.

His latest article, "Everyone Loses,"[1] was published about three months ago.

NOTE: To type a superior number, turn the cylinder back slightly with one hand and type the number with the other hand.

b. Number footnotes consecutively throughout; do not begin renumbering with 1 on each new page. However, if the material consists of chapters (or equivalent divisions), begin a new sequence of numbers with each new chapter.

c. Footnotes are sometimes keyed by symbol rather than by number, particularly in tables where there are only a few footnotes and the tabular matter itself consists of numbers. In such cases footnotes may be identified by the following sequence of symbols: *, **, ***.

PLACEMENT OF FOOTNOTES

1611 **a.** To separate footnotes from the text above, type an underscore line 2 inches long (20 strokes on a pica machine, 24 strokes on an elite). Type the underscore one line below the last line of text, starting at the left margin. (See illustration at right on page 229.)

b. Start the first footnote on the second line below the underscore line.

c. Type each footnote single-spaced, and leave a blank line between footnotes.

d. Indent the first line of each footnote five spaces. Additional lines within the same footnote should begin at the left margin.

PATTERNS FOR REFERENCE FOOTNOTES

1612 The following patterns (and examples) provide guidelines for constructing the kinds of reference footnotes that most commonly occur. These
patterns can be modified as necessary to fit the varying needs of individual circumstances. For detailed information about specific elements
within footnotes, see the following paragraphs:

▶ Footnote number: see ¶ 1613.
Names of authors: see ¶ 1614.
Underscoring titles of complete works: see ¶ 288.
Quoting titles of *parts* of complete works: see ¶¶ 242–244.
Capitalization in titles: see ¶¶ 351–352.
Publisher's name: see ¶ 1615.
Place of publication: see ¶ 1616.
Date of publication: see ¶ 1617.
Page numbers: see ¶ 1618.
Subsequent references in footnotes: see ¶¶ 1619–1620.

a. Book Title: Basic Pattern

[1]Author, book title, publisher, place of publication, date of publication,
page number [if reference is being made to a specific page].

[1]John Kenneth Galbraith, The Affluent Society, Houghton
Mifflin Company, Boston, 1958, p. 101.

NOTE: If any of these elements have already been identified in the text
(for example, the author's name and the book title), they need not be
repeated in the footnote. Moreover, if reference is made to the book as
a whole rather than to a particular page, omit the page number.

According to Professor J. K. Galbraith, in his widely acclaimed book The Affluent Society, ". . . it falls within
the power of the modern large corporation to mitigate or
eliminate (with one exception) every important risk to which
business enterprises have anciently been subject."[1]

---

[1]Houghton Mifflin Company, Boston, 1958, p. 101.

b. Book Title: With Subtitle

[1]Author, book title: subtitle, publisher, place, date, page number.

[1]Vito Tanzi, The Individual Income Tax and Economic
Growth: An International Comparison, The Johns Hopkins
Press, Baltimore, 1969, p. 36.

NOTE: Do not show the subtitle of a book unless it is significant in identifying the book or in explaining its basic nature. If a subtitle is shown,
separate it from the main title with a colon and extend the underscore
(without a break) to the end of the subtitle.

c. Book Title: With Series Designation

[1]Author, book title, series designation, publisher, place, date, page number.

[1]John Robert Gregg et al., Gregg Dictation, Diamond Jubilee Series, McGraw-Hill Book Company, New York, 1963, p. 49.

NOTE: Do not show the series designation unless it is significant in identifying the book. If included, the series designation follows the main title and is set off by commas. Extend the underscore (without a break) to the end of the series designation.

d. Book Title: With Edition Number

[1]Author, book title, edition number [if not the first edition], publisher, place, date, page number.

[1]Fred L. Whipple, Earth, Moon, and Planets, 3d. ed., Harvard University Press, Cambridge, Mass., 1968, pp. 5-6.

NOTE: Use an edition number only when the book is not in the first edition. If included, the edition number follows the main title and any related elements, such as the subtitle, the series designation, or the volume number and title. (For examples see ¶ 1612e below.) The following abbreviated forms are commonly used: *2d ed., 3d ed., 4th ed.,* or *rev. ed.* (for "revised edition").

e. Book Title: With Volume Number and Volume Title

[1]Author, book title, volume number, "volume title," edition number [if not the first edition], publisher, place, date, page number.

[1]E. Lipson, The Economic History of England, Vol. 1, "The Middle Ages," 12th ed., Adam & Charles Black, London, 1959, pp. 511-594.

[2]John L. Rowe et al., Gregg Typing, 191 Series, Book 2, "Vocational Office Typing," 2d. ed., McGraw-Hill Book Company, New York, 1967, pp. 247 ff.

NOTE: As a rule, do not show the volume title in a footnote unless it is significant in identifying the book. When the volume title is included, both the volume number and the volume title follow the book title (and subtitle or series designation, if any) but precede the edition number. The volume number is usually preceded by the abbreviation *Vol.* or by the word *Book* or *Part* (depending on the actual designation). The volume number may be arabic or roman, depending on the style used in the actual book.

▶ See also ¶ 1612f.

f. Book Title: Volume Number (Without Volume Title)

[1]Author, book title, publisher, place, date, volume number, page number.

[1]Robert E. Spiller et al. (eds.), Literary History of the United States, The Macmillan Company, New York, 1948, Vol. II, pp. 639–651. OR: . . . II, 639–651.

NOTE: When the volume number is shown without the volume title, it follows the date of publication. When the volume number and page number occur one after the other, they may be styled as follows:

STYLE FOR ROMAN VOLUME NUMBER: STYLE FOR ARABIC VOLUME NUMBER:

Vol. III, p. 197   OR   III, 197   Vol. 5, pp. 681–684   OR   5:681-684

Do not use the latter forms (with figures alone) if there is a chance your reader will not understand them.

g. Book Title: With Chapter Reference

[1]Author, book title, publisher, place, date, chapter number, "chapter title" [if significant], page number.

[1]Will Durant and Ariel Durant, Rousseau and Revolution, Simon and Schuster, New York, 1967, Chap. II, "The Seven Years' War," pp. 38–64.

NOTE: When a footnote refers primarily to the title of a book, a chapter number and a chapter title are not usually included. If considered significant, however, these details can be inserted just before the page numbers. The word *chapter* is usually abbreviated as *Chap.*, the chapter number is arabic or roman (depending on the original), and the chapter title is enclosed in quotation marks.

h. Selection in Anthology

[1]Author of selection, "title of selection," **in** editor of anthology **(ed.),** book title, publisher, place, date, page number.

[1]William Jennings Bryan, "Imperialism," in Ernest J. Wrage and Barnet Baskerville (eds.), American Forum: Speeches on Historic Issues, 1788–1900, Harper & Brothers, New York, 1960, pp. 358–368.

i. Selection From Collected Works of One Author

[1]Author, "title of selection," book title, publisher, place, date, page number.

[1]T. S. Eliot, "The Love Song of J. Alfred Prufrock," Collected Poems, 1909–1935, Harcourt, Brace and Company, New York, 1936, pp. 11–17.

j. Article in Newspaper

[1]Author [if known], "article title," name of newspaper, date, page number, column number.

[1]Harlan S. Byrne, "Merger Come-Ons," The Wall Street Journal, June 6, 1969, p. 1, col. 6.

NOTE: If a particular issue of a newspaper is published in several sections and the numbering begins anew with each section, include the section number before the page number.

[2]William Beecher, "Trying to Tighten the Purse Strings," The New York Times, June 8, 1969, Sec. 4, p. 2, cols. 6–7.

k. Article in Popular Magazine

[1]Author [if known], "article title," name of magazine, date, page number.

[1]"Fabric Softeners," Consumer Reports, May, 1969, pp. 254–257.

l. Article in Technical or Scholarly Journal

[1]Author, "article title," title of journal [often abbreviated], series number [if given], volume number, issue number [if given], page number, date.

[1]Ellen Z. Fifer, "Hang-Ups in Health Planning," Journal of Public Health, Vol. 59, No. 5, pp. 765–769, May, 1969.

OR: [1]Ellen Z. Fifer, "Hang-Ups in Health Planning," JPH, 59(5):765–769, May, 1969.

NOTE: Titles of journals are often abbreviated in footnotes whenever these abbreviations are likely to be familiar to the intended readership or are clearly identified in a bibliography at the end. Moreover, volume numbers and page numbers may be expressed in a short form so long as this style will be clearly understood by the reader. For example:

STYLE FOR ROMAN VOLUME NUMBER:

Vol. IX, pp. 217-243 (full form) OR IX, 217-243 (short form)

STYLE FOR ARABIC VOLUME NUMBER:

Vol. 3, pp. 381-392 (full form) OR 3:381-392 (short form)

If a series number or an issue number is also included, use the following style:

Ser. 8, Vol. 5, pp. 213-219 OR (8) 5:213-219
Vol. 59, No. 5, pp. 765-769 OR 59(5):765-769

m. Bulletin, Pamphlet, or Monograph

[1]Author [if given], "article title" [if appropriate], <u>title of bulletin</u>, series title and series number [if appropriate], sponsoring organization, place, date, page number.

[1]"The Third Quarter Balance of Payments," <u>Business and Economic Review</u>, The First National Bank of Chicago, January, 1969, pp. 6–7. (Here the place of publication is incorporated in the name of the sponsoring organization.)

[1]<u>Environmental Health Planning Guide</u>, U.S. Public Health Service Publication No. 823, Washington, 1967, pp. 21–22. (Here the name of the sponsoring organization is incorporated in the series designation.)

[2]Author [if given], "article title" [if appropriate], <u>title of bulletin</u>, volume number and issue number, page number, sponsoring organization, place, date.

[2]<u>Washington Report</u>, Vol. 8., No. 21, p. 3, Chamber of Commerce of the United States, Washington, May 26, 1969.

OR: [2]<u>Washington Report</u>, 8(21):3, Chamber of Commerce . . . (See note at the foot of page 235.)

NOTE: Because the pertinent data used to identify bulletins, pamphlets, and monographs varies widely, adapt either of the two patterns shown above as necessary to fit each particular situation.

n. Unpublished Dissertation or Thesis

[1]Author, "title of thesis," **unpublished doctoral dissertation OR unpublished master's thesis** [identifying phrase to be inserted], name of academic institution, place, date, page number.

[1]David Harry Weaver, "An Experimental Study of the Relative Impact of Controllable Factors of Difficulty in Typewriting Practice Material," unpublished doctoral dissertation, Syracuse University, Syracuse, N.Y., 1966, p. 121.

ELEMENTS OF FOOTNOTES

1613 Footnote Number

a. Make sure that the number at the start of a footnote corresponds to the appropriate superior number in the text above.

b. Indent the footnote number five spaces, and (1) type it as a superior number without any space following it or (2) type it on the line (like an ordinary number) followed by a period and one space.

[1]Carl B. Kaufmann, <u>Man Incorporate</u>, Doubleday & Company, Inc., Garden City, N.Y., 1967, pp. 52 ff.

OR: 1. Carl B. Kaufmann, <u>Man Incorporate</u>, Doubleday & Company, Inc., Garden City, N.Y., 1967, pp. 52 ff.

1614   Names of Authors

a. Type an author's name (first name first) exactly as it appears on the title page of a book or in the heading of an article.

[1]Arthur M. Schlesinger, Jr., A Thousand Days, Houghton Mifflin Company, Boston, 1965, p. 31.

b. When two authors share a common surname, show the surname with each author's listing.

[2]John W. Wyatt and Madie B. Wyatt, Business Law, 3d ed., McGraw-Hill Book Company, New York, 1966, pp. 98 ff.

c. When there are three or more authors, list only the first author's name followed by *et al.* (meaning "and others"). Do not underscore *et al.*

[3]M. Herbert Freeman et al., Accounting 10/12, McGraw-Hill Book Company, New York, 1968, pp. 54–55.

NOTE: If desired, the names of all the authors may be given. This style, if adopted for a given manuscript, should be used consistently throughout.

d. When an organization (rather than an individual) is the author of the material, show the organization's name in the author's position.

[4]Committee for Economic Development, The Schools and the Challenge of Innovation, McGraw-Hill Book Company, New York, 1969, p. 28.

However, if the organization is both the author and the publisher, show the organization's name only once—as the publisher.

[5]Patterson's American Education, 1966–67, Educational Directories Inc., Mount Prospect, Ill., 1966, Vol. LXIII.

e. When a work such as an anthology carries an editor's name rather than an author's name, list the editor's name in the author's position, followed by the abbreviation *ed.* in parentheses. (If the names of two or more editors are listed, use the abbreviation *eds.* in parentheses.)

[6]John A. Myers, Jr. (ed.), Predicting Managerial Success, Foundation for Research on Human Behavior, Ann Arbor, Mich., 1968, p. 13.

If a *reference work* carries the name of an editor rather than an author, the editor's name is usually omitted.

[7]Webster's Third New International Dictionary, G. & C. Merriam Company, Springfield, Mass., 1966, pp. 30a–31a.

1615   Publisher's Name

a. List the publisher's name exactly as it appears on the title page. If a division of the publishing company is also listed on the title page, it is not necessary to include this information in the footnote. Publishers, however, often do so in references to their own materials.

b. Omit the publisher's name from footnote references to magazines, newspapers, and journals.

1616 Place of Publication

a. As a rule, list only the city of publication (for example, *New York, Cleveland, Washington, Toronto*). If the city is not well known or is likely to be confused with another city of the same name, add the state or the country (for example, *Cambridge, Mass.; Cambridge, England*). If the title page lists several cities in which the publisher has offices, use only the first city named.

b. Omit the place of publication from footnote references to magazines, newspapers, and journals.

1617 Date of Publication

a. For books, show the year of publication. (If this date does not appear on the title page, use the most recent year shown in the copyright notice.)

b. For monthly periodicals, show both the month and the year. (See ¶ 1612*k* for an example.)

c. For weekly or daily periodicals, show the month, day, and year. (See ¶ 1612*j* for examples.)

1618 Page Numbers

a. Page references in footnotes occur in the following forms:

> p. 30   p. v   pp. 301 f. (meaning "page 301 and the following page")
> pp. 30–31 pp. v–vii pp. 301 ff. (meaning "page 301 and the following pages")

b. In a range of page numbers the second number is sometimes abbreviated; for example, *pp. 981–983* may be expressed as *pp. 981–83*. (See ¶ 464.)

SUBSEQUENT FOOTNOTE REFERENCES

1619 When a footnote refers to a work that was fully identified in the footnote *immediately preceding,* it may be shortened by use of the abbreviation *ibid.* (meaning "in the same place"). *Ibid.* replaces all those elements that would otherwise be carried over intact from the previous footnote.

> [1]David Ogilby, <u>Confessions of an Advertising Man</u>, Atheneum, New York, 1963, pp. 46–51.

> [2]Ibid., p. 63. (*Ibid.* represents all of the elements in the previous footnote except the page number.)

> [3]Ibid. (Referring to page 63 in the same work. Here *ibid.* represents everything in the preceding footnote, including the page number.)

NOTE: Do not underscore *ibid.*

1620 **a.** When a footnote refers to a work fully identified in an earlier footnote but not the one immediately preceding, it may be shortened as follows:

> [1]Author's surname, page number.

> [8]Ogilvy, p. 79. (Referring to the work fully identified before; see footnote 1 in ¶ 1619 above.)

b. When previous reference has been made to different authors with the same surname, the use of a surname alone in a subsequent reference would be confusing. Therefore, the basic pattern in ¶ 1620*a* must be modified as follows:

¹Author's initial(s) plus surname, page number.

OR: ²Author's full name, page number.

¹Cecil Williams, <u>The Foundations of Intelligence</u>, Comet Press Books, New York, 1953, p. 86.

²John K. Williams, <u>The Wisdom of Your Subconscious Mind</u>, Prentice–Hall, Inc., Englewood Cliffs, N.J., 1964, pp. 137–139.

³C. Williams, p. 88.

⁴J. K. Williams, p. 145.

c. If previous reference has been made to different works by the same author, any subsequent reference should contain the title of the specific work now being referred to. When feasible, this title may be shortened to a key word or phrase; the word or phrase should be sufficiently clear, however, so that the full title can be readily identified in the bibliography or in an earlier footnote.

¹Author's surname, <u>book title</u> [shortened if feasible], page number.

¹Clinton Rossiter, <u>Seedtime of the Republic</u>, Harcourt, Brace and Company, New York, 1953, p. 70.

²Clinton Rossiter, <u>1787: The Grand Convention</u>, The Macmillan Company, New York, 1966, p. 163.

³Rossiter, <u>Seedtime</u>, p. 73.

If referring to an article in a periodical, refer to the periodical title rather than the article title.

¹Author's surname, <u>periodical title</u> [shortened if feasible], page number.

⁴John Kenneth Galbraith, "How to Control the Military," <u>Harper's</u>, June, 1969, p. 33.

⁵V. S. Pritchett, . . .

⁶Galbraith, <u>Harper's</u>, p. 35. (Referring to the work identified in footnote 4 above.)

d. A more formal style in subsequent references involves the use of the abbreviations *loc. cit.* ("in the place cited") and *op. cit.* ("in the work cited").

¹Author's surname, **loc. cit.** (This pattern is used when reference is made to the *very same page* in the work previously identified.)

²Author's surname, **op. cit.,** page number. (This pattern is used when reference is made to a *different page* in the work previously identified.)

[Continued on page 240.]

[1]John Kenneth Galbraith, <u>The Great Crash: 1929</u>, 2d
ed., Houghton Mifflin Company, Boston, 1961, p. 65.

[2]Jan Tinbergen and J. J. Polak, <u>The Dynamics of
Business Cycles</u>, The University of Chicago Press, Chicago,
1950, p. 83.

[3]Galbraith, op. cit., p. 67. (Referring to a different page in
The Great Crash.)

[4]Tinbergen and Polak, loc. cit. (Referring to the same page
in *The Dynamics of Business Cycles.*)

NOTE: Do not underscore *loc. cit.* or *op. cit.* in footnotes.

BIBLIOGRAPHIES

1621 A bibliography at the end of a manuscript or a report typically lists all
the works consulted in the preparation of the material as well as all the
works that were previously cited in the footnotes. The format of a bibliography is also used for any list of titles, such as a list of recommended
readings or a list of new publications.

1622 **a.** A bibliography should begin on a fresh sheet under the centered heading *BIBLIOGRAPHY* (or some other title, if appropriate).

b. Center the bibliography vertically on the page, or start with the heading on line 13.

c. Use the same left and right margins and the same placement of the
page number as on other pages in the manuscript.

1623 Each entry should be typed single-spaced. Leave two blank lines between
the heading and the first entry. Leave one blank line between each of
the other entries.

1624 Each entry within the bibliography should begin at the left margin. Use
a uniform indentation of four, five, or ten spaces for additional lines
within each entry.

1625 Entries in bibliographies contain the same elements and follow the same
style as footnotes except that:

a. Entries are not numbered.

b. The name of the author is listed in inverted order (last name first).
When an entry includes two or more authors' names, only the first author's name is inverted. When an organization is listed as the author,
do not invert the name. (For examples, see the first four entries in the
illustration on page 241.)

c. Page numbers are included in bibliographic entries only when the
material being cited is part of a larger work. In such cases show the range
of pages (for example, *pp. 215-232*) on which the material appears. (For
an example, see the seventh entry in the illustration on page 241.)

1626 **a.** Entries in a bibliography are listed alphabetically by author.

b. Entries lacking an author are alphabetized by title. Disregard the words *The* or *A* at the beginning of a title in determining alphabetical sequence. (For an example, see the ninth entry in the illustration below. Note that this entry is alphabetized on the basis of *Guide,* following *Galbraith.*)

1627 When a bibliography contains more than one work by the same author, replace his name with a long dash (six hyphens) in all of the entries after the first. List his works alphabetically by title. (For examples, see the fifth, sixth, and seventh entries in the illustration below. Note that these titles are alphabetized on the key words *Affluent, Great,* and *How.*)

29

BIBLIOGRAPHY

Auerback, Jerold S., Jr., <u>Labor and Liberty</u>, The Bobbs-Merrill Company, Inc., Indianapolis, 1966.

Blaustein, Arthur I., and Roger R. Woock (eds.), <u>Men Against Poverty: World War III</u>, Random House, New York, 1968.

Committee for Economic Development, <u>The Schools and the Challenge of Innovation</u>, McGraw-Hill Book Company, New York, 1969.

Freeman, M. Herbert, et al., <u>Accounting 10/12</u>, McGraw-Hill Book Company, New York, 1968.

Galbraith, John Kenneth, <u>The Affluent Society</u>, Houghton Mifflin Company, Boston, 1958.

------, <u>The Great Crash: 1929</u>, 2d ed., Houghton Mifflin Company, Boston, 1961.

------, "How to Control the Military," <u>Harper's</u>, June, 1969, pp. 31-46.

------ and Molinder S. Randhawa, <u>The New Industrial State</u>, Houghton Mifflin Company, Boston, 1968.

<u>A Guide to Graduate Study: Programs Leading to the Ph.D. Degree</u>, 3d ed., American Council on Education, Washington, 1965.

Section 17
TABLES

GENERAL GUIDELINES

1701 Before typing any tabular material, plan the horizontal and vertical placement carefully.

a. If the table is to appear on the same page with straight copy, it should be centered horizontally within the established margins and should be set off by three blank lines from the straight text above or below.

[Continued on page 242.]

b. If the table is to appear on a page by itself, it should be centered horizontally within the established margins and also centered vertically on the page. To determine vertical placement on a full page, see ¶ 1707. To determine horizontal placement, use either the backspace method (see ¶ 1708) or the mathematical method (see ¶ 1709).

1702 Use the following style for elements in a table:

a. Title of table. Type in all-capital letters and center.

b. Subtitle of table. Type in capital and small letters and center.

c. Column heads. Type in capital and small letters and center over the column text (see ¶¶ 1711–1712). Underscore each line of the column head in unruled tables.

d. Table text. Use single or double spacing in the table text, but treat all tables in the same context consistently. Since the proportions of any table will vary depending on whether the table text is single- or double-spaced, use the spacing that will produce the more attractive appearance in the space available. If column heads are used, center the text in each column under the head.

NOTE: If the title, subtitle, or column head requires more than one line, use single spacing for each additional line. If any item in the table text requires more than one line, use single spacing and indent the extra line two spaces.

1703 For the proper spacing between elements in a table, see page 243.

1704 If the table requires rules, either of these two methods may be used:

a. Insert all rules on the typewriter, using the underscore. Place a horizontal rule above and below the column heads and at the bottom of the table; do not underscore the column heads. These rules should extend to the full width of the table. As shown in examples 3 and 4 on page 243, type each rule on the line immediately following the preceding copy. This creates the appearance of a blank line above the underscore. Leave one blank line between an internal rule and any table copy that follows; leave three blank lines between the bottom rule and any straight copy that follows. If vertical rules are to be used to separate the columns, insert the page sideways after you have finished typing the table text and type the vertical rules, using the underscore. Do not type rules on the side margins of the table—the sides should remain open.

b. Insert all rules with a ball-point pen and a ruler after the typing has been completed. Be sure to leave adequate space for these rules when typing the table.

1705 a. In columns of dollar amounts, the dollar signs should align in the first space to the left of the longest amount in the column (see illustration on page 247). Insert a dollar sign only before the first amount at the head of the column and before the total amount.

b. If all the amounts in a column are whole dollar amounts, omit the decimal and zeros; for example, type *$656* rather than *$656.00.* However,

ALTERNATIVE ARRANGEMENTS OF TABLES

1

TITLE OF TABLE
1 blank line →

Subtitle of Table
2 blank lines →

Column Head	Column Head
Column text	Column text
xxxxxxxxxxx	xxxxxxxxxxx
xxxxxxxxxxx	xxxxxxxxxxx
xxxxxxxxxxx	xxxxxxxxxxx

1 blank line →

2

TITLE OF TABLE
2 blank lines →

Column Head	Column Head
Column text	Column text
xxxxxxxxxxx	xxxxxxxxxxx
xxxxxxxxxxx	xxxxxxxxxxx
xxxxxxxxxxx	xxxxxxxxxxx
xxxxxxxxxxx	xxxxxxxxxxx

1 blank line →

3

TITLE OF TABLE
1 blank line →

Subtitle of Table

Type under-score on line immedi-ately follow-ing

1 blank line

Column Head	Column Head

1 blank line

Column text	Column text
xxxxxxxxxxx	xxxxxxxxxxx
xxxxxxxxxxx	xxxxxxxxxxx
xxxxxxxxxxx	xxxxxxxxxxx

4

TITLE OF TABLE

Type under-score on line immedi-ately follow-ing

1 blank line

Column Head	Column Head

1 blank line

Column text	Column text
xxxxxxxxxxx	xxxxxxxxxxx
xxxxxxxxxxx	xxxxxxxxxxx
xxxxxxxxxxx	xxxxxxxxxxx
xxxxxxxxxxx	xxxxxxxxxxx

5

TITLE OF TABLE
1 blank line →

Subtitle of Table
2 blank lines →

```
Table text ........... xxxxx
xxxxxxxxxxxxxx ....... xxxxx
xxxxxxxxxxxxxxxxx ... xxxxx
xxxxxxxxxxxx ......... xxxxx
```

6

TITLE OF TABLE
2 blank lines →

```
Table text . . . . . . xxxxx
xxxxxxxxxxxxxx . . . . xxxxx
xxxxxxxxxxxx . . . . . xxxxx
xxxxxxxxxxx . . . . . xxxxx
xxxxxxxxxxxxxxxx . . . xxxxx
xxxxxxxxxx . . . . . . xxxxx
```

if any amount in a column includes cents, use the decimal and zeros with all whole-dollar amounts for consistent appearance (see ¶ 423).

c. If the column of dollar amounts has a *total* line, type a line of underscores after the last amount as wide as the longest number in the column (including the dollar sign). Then type the dollar sign and total amount below (see illustration on page 247).

1706 Whenever the items in the first column of a table vary widely in length, you may use leaders (rows of periods that lead the eye across the page) to facilitate the reading of the table. The shortest line of leaders should have at least three periods. A line of leaders should be preceded and followed by one blank space. Leaders may be formed by typing periods in solid sequence, without spacing, or by alternately typing periods and spaces. The first method is faster, but the second is neater. If spaces are used, all the periods in the leader lines must align. Illustrations of closed and spaced leaders are shown in examples 5 and 6 on page 243.

VERTICAL PLACEMENT

1707 To center a table vertically on a full 8½- by 11-inch sheet, follow this procedure:

a. Count the number of lines in the table. Be sure to include the blank lines.

b. Subtract the number of lines in the table from the total number of lines available on the page. (There are 6 standard typewriter lines to an inch; there are 66 lines on an 8½- by 11-inch sheet of paper.)

c. Divide the difference by 2 to find the number of the line on which to start typing the table; if there is a fraction in your answer, count the fraction as the next whole number (for example if your answer is 12½, count it as line 13.)

NOTE: The bottom margin will be one or two lines deeper than the top margin. However, the table will appear to be centered on the page.

▶ See ¶ 1713a for an example.

HORIZONTAL PLACEMENT

1708 Backspace Method

a. Select the key item (longest item) in each column, whether it occurs in the column head or in one of the items below the column head.

b. Determine the number of spaces to be left between columns. Normally leave six blank spaces between each column; in financial statements, two blank spaces between columns of dollar amounts is sufficient.

c. Determine the centering point on the page. If the left and right margins have been established in advance, the centering point will fall halfway between these margins. If the left and right margins have not been established and are to be equal, use the exact center of the page as the centering point.

d. Clear all tab stops and the margin stops on the typewriter.

e. From the centering point, backspace three spaces for each of the six-space blank areas between columns; then backspace once for each pair of strokes in the combined key items. Set the left margin stop at this point (the beginning of the first column).

NOTE: If the left margin is less than 1 inch wide, you may reduce the width of the table by leaving three, four, or five blank spaces between columns instead of the usual six blank spaces. If you decide to use fewer than six spaces between columns, repeat step e so that the table will appear centered within the new margins.

f. From the left margin of the table, space forward once for each stroke in the first column plus once for each of the six spaces between columns and set a tab stop at this point (the beginning of the second column).

g. Repeat step f until the tab stops have been set for each of the remaining columns.

1709 Mathematical Method

a. Count the longest item in each column, whether it occurs in the column head or as one of the items below the column head.

b. Total the number of strokes needed for all the columns.

c. To this total, add six spaces for each area between columns. (See ¶ 1708b and e, note, for variations in spacing.)

d. Determine the centering point on the page. (See ¶ 1708c.)

e. Clear all tab stops and the margin stops on the typewriter.

f. From the centering point, backspace half the total spaces (the columns plus the blank spaces between columns) and set the left margin stop at this point.

g. From the left margin, space forward once for each stroke in the first column plus once for each of the six spaces between columns and set a tab at this point (the beginning of the second column).

h. Repeat step g until the tab stops have been set for each of the remaining columns.

▶ See ¶ 1713b and c for an example.

COLUMN HEADS

1710 A long column head should be broken into no more than two or three lines. Clear abbreviations are usually permissible in long column heads.

1711 To center a *narrow* column head:

a. Take the number of strokes in the longest line in the column head and subtract it from the number of strokes in the longest line in the body of the column.

[Continued on page 246.]

b. Divide the difference by 2 (drop any fraction) to find the number of spaces to indent the longest line in the column head. Center the other lines in the column head in relation to the longest line.

▶ For an example, see the head in the first column of the table on page 247; see also the analysis in ¶ 1713*d* (1).

NOTE: If all the column heads are short, you may align each line in the column head at the left with the column text (instead of centering the column head over the column text).

1712 To center a *wide* column head:

a. Type the longest line in the column head six spaces following the preceding column. Center the other lines in the column head in relation to the longest line.

b. Take the number of strokes in the longest line in the body of the column and subtract it from the number of strokes in the longest line in the column head.

c. Divide the difference by 2 (drop any fraction) to find the number of spaces to indent the body of the column. Set a tab stop here so that you can begin all lines in the body of the column at this point.

▶ For an example, see the head in the last column of the table on page 247; see also the analysis in ¶ 1713*d* (3).

EXAMPLE OF TABLE PLACEMENT

1713 The table at the top of page 247 has been used to illustrate how to plan the placement of a table on an 8½- by 11-inch sheet of paper.

a. Vertical placement

Number of lines available on sheet	66
Total number of lines in table (typed and blank)	18
Lines available for margins (66 − 18)	48
Line on which to start typing (48 ÷ 2 = 24)	24

b. Horizontal placement by mathematical method

Longest item in each column:	Column 1	13
	Column 2	9
	Column 3	9
	Column 4	11
Total number of strokes		42
Plus 6 spaces for each area between columns		18
Total width of table		60

c. Setting margins and tab stops

(1) Clear all tab stops and the margin stops on the typewriter.

(2) To find the left margin, backspace half the width of the table from the centering point on the page (in this case the exact center of the page), or 30 times (60 ÷ 2); set the margin stop.

ANALYSIS OF SALES QUOTAS

From January 1 Through March 31

Branch	Last Year	This Year	Increase in Sales
Chicago	$ 78,000	$ 84,000	$ 6,000
Cincinnati	57,000	65,000	8,000
Los Angeles	83,000	91,000	8,000
Memphis	48,000	53,000	5,000
New Orleans	45,000	51,000	6,000
New York	89,000	96,000	7,000
Philadelphia	83,000	88,000	5,000
San Francisco	76,000	85,000	9,000
Seattle	62,000	69,000	7,000
TOTALS	$620,000	$682,000	$61,000

(3) To set the tab stop for the second column, space once from the margin stop for each stroke in the first column (13) plus 6 spaces for the area between the first and second columns, or 19 times (13 + 6); set the tab stop.

(4) To set the tab stop for the third column, space once from the second column tab stop for each stroke in the second column (9) plus 6 spaces for the area between the second and third columns, or 15 times (9 + 6); set the tab stop.

(5) To set the tab stop for the fourth column, space once for each stroke in the third column (9) plus 6 spaces for the area between the third and fourth columns, or 15 times (9 + 6); set the tab stop.

d. Making adjustments for column heads

(1) The head for the first column is 7 spaces narrower than the column text (13 − 6). Indent 3 spaces (7 ÷ 2; drop the fraction) from the left margin stop before typing the head.

(2) Heads for the second and third columns are 1 space wider than the column text (9 − 8). In this case do not indent the column text since the amount of indention would be less than 1 space (1 ÷ 2).

(3) The fourth column has a two-line head. The first line is 6 spaces wider than the second line (11 − 5). First type the wider line of the column head. Then center the narrower line under it by indenting 3 spaces·(6 ÷ 2). Also, the first line in the column head is 4 spaces wider than the column text (11 − 7). To center the column text below the head, indent 2 spaces (4 ÷ 2) to the right and reset the tab stop.

Section 18
FORMS OF ADDRESS

1801 The following forms of address are correct for government officials; military and naval personnel; Roman Catholic, Protestant, and Jewish dignitaries; and education officials. In the salutations that follow the forms of address, the most formal ones are listed first.

NOTE: The masculine forms of address have been given throughout. When an office is held by a woman, make the following substitutions:

FOR: Mr.	USE: Mrs. OR Miss
Sir:	Madam:
Dear Sir:	Dear Madam:
My dear Mr. . . . (surname):	My dear Mrs. (OR Miss) . . . (surname):
My dear Mr. Secretary:	My dear Madam Secretary:
My dear Mr. Mayor:	My dear Madam Mayor:

Government Officials

PRESIDENT OF THE UNITED STATES
The President
The White House
Washington, D.C. 20500

Mr. President:
The President:
My dear Mr. President:

VICE PRESIDENT OF THE UNITED STATES
The Vice President
The United States Senate
Washington, D.C. 20510

OR: The Honorable . . . (full name)
Vice President of the United States
Washington, D.C. 20501

Sir:
Mr. Vice President:
My dear Mr. Vice President:

CHIEF JUSTICE OF THE UNITED STATES
The Chief Justice of the
United States
Washington, D.C. 20543

OR: The Chief Justice
The Supreme Court
Washington, D.C. 20543

Sir:
My dear Mr. Chief Justice:

CABINET MEMBER
The Honorable . . . (full name)
Secretary of . . . (department)
Washington, D.C.   ZIP Code

OR: The Secretary of . . . (department)
Washington, D.C.   ZIP Code

Sir:
Dear Sir:
My dear Mr. Secretary:

UNITED STATES SENATOR
The Honorable . . . (full name)
The United States Senate
Washington, D.C. 20510

Sir:
Dear Sir:
My dear Senator:
Dear Senator . . . :

UNITED STATES CONGRESSMAN
The Honorable . . . (full name)
House of Representatives
Washington, D.C. 20515

OR: The Honorable . . . (full name)
Representative in Congress
City, State

Sir:
Dear Sir:
My dear Mr. . . . :
Dear Mr. . . . :

GOVERNOR
In Massachusetts, New Hampshire, and by courtesy in some other states:

> His Excellency the Governor
> of . . .
> State Capital, State

In other states:

> The Honorable . . . (full name)
> Governor of . . .
> State Capital, State
>
> Sir:
> Dear Sir:
> My dear Governor:
> Dear Governor . . . :

STATE SENATOR
> The Honorable . . . (full name)
> The State Senate
> State Capital, State
>
> Sir:
> Dear Sir:
> My dear Senator:
> Dear Senator . . . :

STATE REPRESENTATIVE OR ASSEMBLYMAN
> The Honorable . . . (full name)
> House of Representatives
> (**OR** The State Assembly)
> State Capital, State
>
> Sir:
> Dear Sir:
> My dear Mr. . . . :
> Dear Mr. . . . :

MAYOR
> The Honorable . . . (full name)
> Mayor of . . . (city)
> City, State

OR: The Mayor of the City of . . .
> City, State
>
> Sir:
> Dear Sir:
> My dear Mr. Mayor:

> Dear Mr. Mayor:
> Dear Mayor . . . :

Military and Naval Personnel
The addresses of both officers and enlisted men in the Armed Forces should include title of rank, full name followed by the initials USA, USN, etc., and address. Below are some specific examples together with the appropriate salutations.

ARMY OFFICERS
> Lieutenant General . . . (full
>   name), USA
> Address
>
> Sir:
> Dear Sir:
> My dear General . . . :
> (**NOT:** My dear Lieutenant General
>   . . . :)
> Dear General . . . :

For officers below the rank of Captain, use:

> Dear Sir:
> My dear Lieutenant . . . :
> Dear Lieutenant . . . :

NAVAL OFFICERS
> Admiral . . . (full name), USN
> Address
>
> Sir:
> Dear Sir:
> My dear Admiral . . . :
> Dear Admiral . . . :

For officers below the rank of Commander, use:

> Dear Sir:
> My dear Mr. . . . :
> Dear Mr. . . . :

ENLISTED MEN
> Sergeant . . . (full name), USA
> Address
>
> Seaman . . . (full name), USN
> Address

[Continued on page 250.]

Dear Sir:
My dear Sergeant (OR Seaman) . . . :
Dear Sergeant (OR Seaman) . . . :

Roman Catholic Dignitaries

CARDINAL
His Eminence . . . (given name)
    Cardinal . . . (surname)
Address

Your Eminence:

ARCHBISHOP AND BISHOP
The Most Reverend . . . (full
    name)
Archbishop (OR Bishop) of
    . . . (place)
Address

Your Excellency:

MONSIGNOR
The Right Reverend Monsignor
    . . . (full name)
Address

Right Reverend Monsignor:
Dear Monsignor . . . :

PRIEST
Reverend . . . , (full name,
    followed by initials of order)
Address

Reverend Father:
Dear Father . . . :

MOTHER SUPERIOR
The Reverend Mother Superior
Convent of . . .
Address

OR: Reverend Mother . . . , (name,
    followed by initials of order)
Address

Reverend Mother:
Dear Reverend Mother:
My dear Reverend Mother . . . :
Dear Reverend Mother . . . :

SISTER
Sister . . . , (name, followed by
    initials of order)
Address

My dear Sister:
Dear Sister:
My dear Sister . . . :
Dear Sister . . . :

Protestant Dignitaries

PROTESTANT EPISCOPAL BISHOP
The Right Reverend . . . (full name)
Bishop of . . . (place)
Address

Right Reverend and dear Sir:
My dear Bishop . . . :
Dear Bishop . . . :

PROTESTANT EPISCOPAL DEAN
The Very Reverend . . . (full name)
Dean of . . .
Address

Very Reverend Sir:
My dear Mr. Dean:
My dear Dean . . . :
Dear Dean . . . :

METHODIST BISHOP
The Reverend . . . (full name)
Bishop of . . .
Address

Reverend Sir:
Dear Sir:
My dear Bishop . . . :
Dear Bishop . . . :

CLERGYMAN WITH DOCTOR'S DEGREE
The Reverend Dr. . . . (full name)
Address

OR: The Reverend . . . (full name), D.D.
Address

Reverend Sir:
Dear Sir:
My dear Dr. . . . :
Dear Dr. . . . :

CLERGYMAN WITHOUT DOCTOR'S DEGREE
The Reverend . . . (full name)
Address

Reverend Sir:
Dear Sir:
My dear Mr. . . . :
Dear Mr. . . . :

Jewish Dignitaries

RABBI WITH DOCTOR'S DEGREE
> Rabbi . . . (full name), D.D.
> Address

OR: Dr. . . . (full name)
> Address

> Reverend Sir:
> Dear Sir:
> My dear Rabbi (OR Dr.) . . . :
> Dear Rabbi (OR Dr.) . . . :

RABBI WITHOUT DOCTOR'S DEGREE
> Rabbi . . . (full name)
> Address

OR: Reverend . . . (full name)
> Address

> Reverend Sir:
> Dear Sir:
> My dear Rabbi . . . :
> Dear Rabbi . . . :

Education Officials

PRESIDENT OF A COLLEGE OR UNIVERSITY
> . . . , (full name, followed by
>   highest degree)
> President, . . . (name of college)
> Address

OR: Dr. . . . (full name)
> President, . . . (name of college)
> Address

> Dear Sir:
> My dear President . . . :
> Dear Dr. . . . :

PROFESSOR
> Professor . . . (full name)
> Department of . . .
> . . . (name of college)
> Address

OR: . . . , (full name, followed by
>   highest degree)
> Department of . . .
> . . . (name of college)
> Address

OR: Dr. . . . (full name)
> Professor of . . . (subject)
> . . . (name of college)
> Address

> Dear Sir:
> My dear Professor (OR Dr.) . . . :
> Dear Professor (OR Dr.) . . . :
> Dear Mr. . . . :

SUPERINTENDENT OF SCHOOLS
> Mr. (OR Dr.) . . . (full name)
> Superintendent of . . . Schools
> Address

> Dear Sir:
> My dear Mr. . . . :
> Dear Mr. (OR Dr.) . . . :

MEMBER OF BOARD OF EDUCATION
> Mr. . . . (full name)
> Member, . . . (name of city)
>   Board of Education
> Address

> Dear Sir:
> My dear Mr. . . . :
> Dear Mr. . . . :

PRINCIPAL
> Mr. (OR Dr.) . . . (full name)
> Principal, . . . (name of school)
> Address

> Dear Sir:
> My dear Mr. . . . :
> Dear Mr. (OR Dr.) . . . :

TEACHER
> Mr. (OR Dr.) . . . (full name)
> . . . (name of school)
> Address

> Dear Sir:
> My dear Mr. . . . :
> Dear Mr. (OR Dr.) . . . :

Section 19
GLOSSARY OF GRAMMATICAL TERMS

1901 This glossary provides brief definitions of all the grammatical terms that have been used elsewhere in this manual.

Adjective. A word that answers the question *what kind* (*excellent* results), *how many* (*four* acres), or *which one* (the *latest* data). An adjective may be a single word (a *wealthy* man), a phrase (a man *of great wealth*), or a clause (a man *who possesses great wealth*). An adjective modifies the meaning of a noun (fresh *fish*) or a pronoun (unlucky *me*, *I* was wrong).

Adjective, predicate. (See *Complement.*)

Adjective clause, phrase. (See *Clause; Phrase.*)

Adjectives, comparison of. (See *Comparison.*)

Adverb. A word that answers the question *when, where, why, in what manner,* or *to what extent.* An adverb may be a single word (speak *clearly*), a phrase (speak *in a clear voice*), or a clause (speak *as clearly as you can*). An adverb modifies the meaning of a verb, an adjective, or another adverb.

> He signed the note *slowly.* (Modifies the verb *signed.*)
> We moved to a *rapidly* growing suburb. (Modifies the adjective *growing.*)
> She agreed *most* reluctantly. (Modifies the adverb *reluctantly.*)

Adverbial clause, phrase. (See *Clause; Phrase.*)

Adverbial conjunctive (or **connective**). An adverb that connects the main clauses of a compound sentence; for example, *however, therefore, nevertheless, hence, moreover, otherwise, consequently.* (See also ¶ 178.)

Adverbs, comparison of. (See *Comparison.*)

Antecedent. A noun or a noun phrase to which a pronoun refers.

> He is the *person who* dictated the letter.
> *Owning your own home* has *its* advantages.

Appositive. A noun or a noun phrase that identifies another noun or pronoun that immediately precedes it.

> Mr. Mead, *our purchasing agent,* would like to meet you.
> We *employees* ought to discuss the proposal carefully.
> Dennis Taylor, *the man with the British accent,* is actually an American.

Article. Classed as an adjective. The *definite* article is *the;* the *indefinite,* *a* or *an.*

Case. The form of a noun or of a pronoun that indicates its relation to other words in the sentence. There are three cases: nominative, objective, and possessive. *Nouns* have the same form in the nominative and objective cases but a special ending for the possessive. The forms for *pronouns* are:

Nominative	Objective	Possessive
I, we	me, us	my, mine, our, ours
you	you	your, yours
he, she, it	him, her, it	his, hers, its
they	them	their, theirs
who	whom	whose

Nominative case. Used for the subject or the complement of a verb.

He sings well. (Subject.)   It is *I.* (Complement.)

Objective case. Used for (1) the object of a verb, (2) the object of a preposition, (3) the subject of an infinitive, (4) the object of an infinitive, or (5) the complement of the infinitive *to be.*

Tom hit *him.* (Object of the verb *hit.*)

John beckoned to *me.* (Object of the preposition *to.*)

The president encouraged *him* to run for office. (Subject of the infinitive *to run.*)

You ought to see *him* today. (Object of the infinitive *to see.*)

He believed me to be *her.* (Complement of the infinitive *to be.*)

Possessive case. Used to show ownership. See ¶¶ 629–650 for the formation of the possessives of nouns.

Clause. A group of related words that contains a subject and a predicate. An *independent* clause (also known as a *main clause* or *principal clause*) expresses a complete thought and can stand alone as a sentence. A *dependent* clause (also known as a *subordinate clause*) does not express a complete thought and cannot stand alone as a sentence.

I will go (independent clause) if the occasion demands my presence (dependent clause).

Adjective clause. A dependent clause that modifies a noun or a pronoun in the main clause. Adjective clauses are joined to the main clause by relative pronouns (*which, that, who, whose, whom*).

The charge, *which includes painting,* seems reasonable. (Modifies *charge.*)

The plan *that was recommended* did not prove practicable. (Modifies *plan.*)

Adverbial clause. A dependent clause that functions as an adverb in its relation to the main clause. Adverbial clauses indicate time, place, manner, cause, purpose, condition, result, reason, or contrast.

[Continued on page 254.]

These orders can be filled *as soon as stock is received.* (Time.)

I was advised to move to a locality *where the climate is dry.* (Place.)

She worked *as though her life depended on it.* (Manner.)

Please write me at once *if you have any suggestions.* (Condition.)

Because our plant is closed in August, we cannot accept your order. (Reason.)

The material you first shipped us was too thin, *whereas this is too thick.* (Contrast.)

Coordinate clauses. Clauses of the same rank. They may be independent or dependent clauses.

George will oversee the day-to-day operations, and Frank will be responsible for the finances. (Coordinate independent clauses.)

When you have read the chapter carefully and *you can answer all the questions correctly,* you ought to try these special problems. (Coordinate dependent clauses.)

Elliptical clause. A clause from which key words have been omitted. (See ¶¶ 102, 110, 130*b*.)

Now, for the next topic.   *Really?*   *If possible,* arrive at one.

Essential (or **restrictive**) **clause.** A dependent clause that cannot be omitted without changing the meaning of the main clause. Essential clauses are *not* set off by commas.

The magazine *that came yesterday* contains some beautiful illustrations.

Nonessential (or **nonrestrictive**) **clause.** A dependent clause that adds descriptive information but could be omitted without changing the meaning of the main clause. Such clauses are separated from the main clause by commas.

His latest book, *which is based on his experiences in the Far East,* has sold quite well.

Noun clause. A dependent clause that functions as a noun in the main clause.

That the plan was a failure cannot be denied.

Whether the proposal will be accepted remains to be seen.

Comparison. The forms of an adjective or adverb that indicate degrees in quality, quantity, or manner. There are three degrees: positive, comparative, and superlative.

Positive. The simple form; for example, *old, beautiful* (adjectives); *soon, quietly* (adverbs).

Comparative. Indicates a higher or lower degree of quality or manner than is expressed by the positive degree. It is used when two things are compared. It is regularly formed by adding *er* to the positive degree (*older, sooner*). In longer words, it is formed by adding *more* or *less* to the positive (*more beautiful, less beautiful; more quietly, less quietly*).

Superlative. Denotes the highest or lowest degree of quality or manner and is used when more than two things are compared. It is regularly formed by adding *est* to the positive degree (*oldest, soonest*). In longer words, it is formed by adding *most* or *least* (*most beautiful, least beautiful; most quietly, least quietly*).

Complement. A word or phrase that completes the sense of the verb. It may be an object, a predicate noun, or a predicate adjective.

Object. Follows a transitive verb. (See *Verb*.)

I have already mailed the *letter*.

Predicate noun. Follows a linking verb. It explains the subject and is identical with it. (Also called a *predicate complement, subject complement,* and *predicate nominative.*)

Miss Stewart is our *office manager*. (*Office manager* refers to *Miss Stewart*.)

Predicate adjective. Completes the sense of a linking verb. (Also called a *predicate complement.*)

The charge is *excessive*. (The adjective *excessive* refers to *charge*.)

NOTE: In this manual, *complement* is used to refer only to a predicate noun or adjective following a linking verb. The term *object* is used to denote the complement of a transitive verb.

Conjunction. A word or phrase that connects words, phrases, or clauses.

Coordinating conjunction. Connects words, phrases, or clauses of equal rank. The coordinating conjunctions are *and, but, or,* and *nor.*

Correlative conjunctions. Coordinating conjunctions used in pairs; for example, *both . . . .and, not only . . . but (also), either . . . or, neither . . . nor, whether . . . or (not).*

Subordinating conjunction. Used to join subordinate clauses to main clauses. A few common ones are *when, where, after, before, if, whether, since,* and *though.* (See also ¶ 133.)

Conjunctive adverb. See *Adverbial conjunctive.*

Connective. A word that joins words, phrases, or clauses. The chief connectives are conjunctions, adverbial conjunctives, prepositions, and relative pronouns.

Consonants. The letters *b, c, d, f, g, h, j, k, l, m, n, p, q, r, s, t, v, w, x, y, z. The letters w* and *y* sometimes function as vowels (as in *saw* and *hay*).

Contraction. A shortened form of a word in which an apostrophe indicates the omitted letters; for example, *don't* for *do not; o'clock* for *of the clock.*

Dangling modifier. A modifier that is attached to no word in a sentence or to the wrong word. (See ¶ 1074.)

Direct address. A construction in which a speaker or a writer addresses another person directly. For example, "What do you think, *Fred?*"

Elliptical expressions. Condensed expressions from which key words have been omitted. (See also *Clause; Sentence.*)

Gender. The characteristic of nouns and pronouns that indicates whether the thing named is *masculine* (*man, boy, stallion, he*), *feminine* (*woman, girl, mare, she*), or *neuter* (*book, flower, concept, it*). Nouns that refer to either males or females are said to have a *common* gender (*person, child, horse*).

Gerund. A verb form ending in *ing* and used as a *noun.* (See also *Phrase, gerund.*)

Selling is fun. (Subject of sentence.)

I enjoy *selling.* (Direct object of *enjoy.*)

She is experienced in *selling.* (Object of preposition *in.*)

Dangling gerund. A prepositional-gerund phrase that is attached to no word in a sentence or to the wrong word. (See ¶ 1074c.)

Infinitive. The form of the verb usually introduced by *to* (see ¶¶ 1041–1043). An infinitive may be used as a noun, an adjective, or an adverb. Like any verb, it can have a subject, take an object, and be modified by an adverb.

NOUN: *To do her a favor* is a pleasure. (Subject.)

She asked *to see the book.* (Object.)

ADJECTIVE: I still have two more letters *to transcribe.* (Modifies *letters.*)

ADVERB: He resigned *to take another position.* (Modifies *resigned.*)

Interjection. A word that shows emotion; usually without grammatical connection to other parts of a sentence.

Oh, so that's what he meant.   *Hooray!* We win.

Modifier. A word, phrase, or clause that qualifies, limits, or restricts the meaning of a word. (See *Adjective; Adverb; Dangling modifier.*)

Mood (mode). The form of the verb that shows the manner of the action. There are three moods: indicative, imperative, and subjunctive.

Indicative. States a fact or asks a question.

The safe is open.   Is the safe open?

Imperative. Expresses a command or makes a request.

Answer that bell.   Please transcribe this letter at once.

Subjunctive. Used following clauses of necessity, demand, or wishing (see ¶¶ 1035–1036) and used in *if, as if,* and *as though* clauses that state conditions which are improbable, doubtful, or contrary to fact (see ¶¶ 1037–1040).

I demand that we *be* heard.   We urge that he *be* elected.

It is imperative that she *be* notified by Friday.

I wish I *were* going.

If he *were* appointed head of the department, I would quit.

Noun. The name of a person, place, object, idea, quality, or activity.

Abstract noun. The name of a quality or a general idea; for example, *courage, freedom.*

Collective noun. A noun that represents a group of persons, animals, or things; for example, *audience, company, flock.* (See ¶ 1018.)

Common noun. The name of a class of persons or things; for example, *child, house.* (See ¶¶ 306–309.)

Predicate noun. (See *Complement.*)

Proper noun. The official name of a particular person, place, or thing; for example, *Henry, San Diego, Library of Congress.* Proper nouns are capitalized. (See ¶¶ 303–305.)

Number. The characteristic of a noun, pronoun, or verb that indicates whether one person or thing (singular) or more than one (plural) is meant.

NOUN: girl, girls   PRONOUN: she, they   VERB: he *sings,* they *sing*

Object. The person or thing that receives the action of the verb. An object may be a word, a phrase, or a clause.

I bought a *radio.* (Word.)

She likes *to skate.* (Infinitive phrase.)

I did not realize *that it was so late.* (Clause.)

Direct object. The person or thing that is directly affected by the action of the verb. (The object in each of the three sentences above is a *direct* object.)

Indirect object. The person or thing indirectly affected by the action of the verb. The indirect object can usually be made the object of the preposition *to* or *for.*

He gave (to) *me* the book.

Ordinal number. The form of a number that indicates order or succession; for example, *first, second, twelfth.*

Parallel structure. (See ¶ 1073.)

Parenthetical elements. Words, phrases, or clauses that are not necessary to the completeness of the structure or the meaning of a sentence.

Participle. A word that may stand alone as an adjective or may be combined with helping verbs to form different tenses (see ¶¶ 1032–1033). There are three forms: present participle, past participle, and perfect participle.

Present participle. Ends in *ing;* for example, *making, advertising.*

Past participle. Regularly ends in *ed* (as in *asked* or *filed*) but may be irregularly formed (as in *lost, seen,* and *snug*). (See ¶ 1029a–b.)

[Continued on page 258.]

Perfect participle. Consists of *having* plus the past participle; for example, *having heated, having lost.*

When a participle functions as an *adjective,* it modifies a noun or a pronoun.

The *leaking* pipe caused trouble. (Modifies *pipe.*)

Saddened by his failure, he lost interest in his work. (Modifies *he.*)

Because a participle has many of the characteristics of a verb, it may take an object and be modified by an adverb. The participle and its object and modifiers make up a *participial phrase.*

Waving his hand, he drove quickly away. (Object is *hand.*)

Speaking quickly, she described the project in detail. (*Quickly* modifies *speaking.*)

Dangling participle. A participial phrase attached to no word in a sentence or to the wrong word. (See ¶ 1074a.)

Parts of speech. The eight classes into which words are grouped according to their uses in a sentence: verb, noun, pronoun, adjective, adverb, conjunction, preposition, and interjection.

Person. The characteristic of a word that indicates whether a person is speaking (*first person*), is spoken to (*second person*), or is spoken about (*third person*). Only personal pronouns and verbs change their forms to show person.

FIRST PERSON: *I* liked this book.   *We* liked this book.

SECOND PERSON: *You* liked this book.

THIRD PERSON: *He* liked this book.   *They* liked this book.

Phrase. A group of two or more words, not having a subject and a predicate, used as a noun, an adjective, or an adverb.

Adjective phrase. A phrase that functions as an adjective (such as an infinitive phrase, a participial phrase, or a prepositional phrase).

Adverbial phrase. A phrase that functions as an adverb (such as an infinitive phrase or a prepositional phrase).

Essential (or **restrictive**) **phrase.** A phrase that limits, defines, or identifies something; cannot be omitted without changing the meaning of the main clause.

The chapter *explaining the law* appears at the end of the book.

Gerund phrase. A gerund plus its object and modifiers; used as a noun.

Running your own business is not as easy as it looks.

Infinitive phrase. An infinitive plus its subject, object, and modifiers; may be used as a noun, an adjective, or an adverb. An infinitive phrase that is attached to no word in a sentence or to the wrong word is called a *dangling* infinitive (see ¶ 1074b).

To pass this subject requires conscientious study. (As a noun.)

We still have more checking *to do.* (An adjective modifying *checking.*)

He resigned *to enlist.* (An adverb modifying *resigned.*)

Nonessential (or **nonrestrictive**) **phrase.** A phrase that can be omitted without changing the meaning of the sentence.

Joan, *wishing to improve her typing skill,* registered for a second course.

Noun phrase. A phrase that functions as a noun (such as a gerund phrase, an infinitive phrase, or a prepositional phrase).

Participial phrase. A participle and its object and modifiers; used as an adjective.

We heard the rain *splashing on the window.*

The old man, *confused by the bright lights,* stepped in the path of the car.

I can now relax, *having finished the assignment.*

Prepositional phrase. A preposition and its object and modifiers; may be used as a noun, an adjective, or an adverb.

From New York to Denver is a long way to drive. (Noun.)

The package *on the large desk* is ready to be sent. (Adjective.)

He has gone *to Cleveland.* (Adverb.)

Prepositional-gerund phrase. A phrase that begins with a preposition and has a gerund as the object. (See ¶ 1074c.)

By rechecking the material before it is set in type, you avoid expensive corrections later on. (*By* is the preposition; *rechecking,* a gerund, is the object of *by.*)

Positive degree. (See *Comparison.*)

Predicate. That part of a sentence that tells what the subject does or what is done to the subject or what state of being the subject is.

Complete predicate. The complete predicate consists of a verb and its complement along with any modifiers.

Paul *has handled the job well.*

Simple predicate. The simple predicate is the verb alone, without regard for any complement or modifiers that may accompany it.

Paul *has handled* the job well.

Compound predicate. Two or more predicates in the same sentence.

Paul *has handled the job well* and *ought to be commended.*

Predicate adjective, complement, nominative, noun, object. (See *Complement.*)

Prefix. A letter, syllable, or word joined at the beginning of a word to change its meaning; for example, *a*float, *re*upholster, *under*nourished.

Preposition. A connective that shows the relation of a noun or pronoun to some other word in the sentence. The noun or pronoun following a preposition is in the objective case.

He has left the sales figures *with me.*

Principal parts. The forms of a verb from which all other forms are derived: the *present,* the *past,* the *past participle,* and the *present participle.* (See ¶¶ 1029–1034.)

Pronoun. A word used in place of a noun; for example, *I, he, it.*

DEMONSTRATIVE: *this, that, these, those*

INDEFINITE: *each, either, any, anyone, someone, everyone, few, all,* etc.

INTENSIVE: *myself, yourself,* etc.

INTERROGATIVE: *who, which, what,* etc.

PERSONAL: *I, you, he, she, it, we, they*

RELATIVE: *who, whose, whom, which, that,* and compounds with *ever* (such as *whoever*)

Punctuation. Marks used to indicate relationships between words, phrases, and clauses.

Terminal (or **end**) **punctuation.** The period, the question mark, and the exclamation point—the three marks that may indicate the end of a sentence.

Internal punctuation. The comma, the semicolon, the colon, the dash, parentheses, quotation marks, the underscore, the apostrophe, ellipsis marks, the asterisk, the diagonal, and brackets.

Question, direct. A question in its original form, as spoken or written.

He then asked me, "What is your opinion?"

Indirect question. A statement of the substance of a question without the use of the exact words of the speaker.

He then asked me what my opinion was.

Independent question. A question that represents a complete sentence but is incorporated in a larger sentence.

The main question is, Who will translate this idea into a clear plan of action?

Quotation, direct. A quotation of words exactly as spoken or written.

George said, "I plan to take a 10 p.m. flight."

Indirect quotation. A statement of the substance of a quotation without using the exact words.

He said that *he planned to take a 10 p.m. flight.*

Sentence. A group of words representing a complete thought and containing a subject and a verb (predicate) along with any complements and modifiers.

Simple sentence. A sentence consisting of one independent clause.

I have no unfiled correspondence.

Compound sentence. A sentence consisting of two or more independent clauses.

Our Boston office will be closed, and our Dallas office will be relocated.

Complex sentence. A sentence consisting of one independent clause and one or more dependent clauses.

We will make an exception to the rule if circumstances warrant.

Compound-complex sentence. A sentence consisting of two independent clauses and one or more dependent clauses.

I tried to handle the monthly report alone, but when I began to analyze the data, I realized that I needed your help.

Declarative sentence. A sentence that makes a statement.

All the newspapers were sold.

Elliptical sentence. A word or phrase that is treated as a complete sentence, even though the subject and the verb are only understood but not expressed.

Enough on that subject.   Why not?

Exclamatory sentence. A sentence that expresses strong feeling.

Don't remove these files!

Imperative sentence. A sentence that expresses a command or a request. (The subject *you* is understood if it is not expressed.)

Send a wire.   Please close the door.

Interrogative sentence. A sentence that asks a question.

When does the conference begin?

Sentence fragment. A phrase or clause that is incorrectly treated as a sentence. (See ¶ 102, note.)

Statement. A sentence that asserts a fact. See also the entry for *Declarative sentence* above.

Subject. A word, phrase, or clause that names the person, place, or thing about which something is said.

The book was printed in Chicago.
That the work will be completed by the first of the month is doubtful.

Compound subject. A subject consisting of two or more simple subjects joined by conjunctions.

Johnson and *Little* are planning to establish a partnership.

Suffix. A letter, syllable, or word added to the end of a word to modify its meaning; for example, friend*ly*, count*less*, receiver*ship*, lone*some*, thank*ful*.

Superlative degree. (See *Comparison*.)

Syllable. A single letter or a group of letters taken together to form one sound.

Tense. The property of a verb that expresses *time*.

The three primary tenses correspond to the three time divisions: *present* (*they think*), *past* (*they thought*), and *future* (*they will think*).

There are three *perfect* tenses, corresponding to the primary tenses: *present perfect* (*they have thought*), *past perfect* (*they had thought*), and *future perfect* (*they will have thought*).

There are six *progressive* tenses, corresponding to each of the primary and perfect tenses: *present progressive* (*they are thinking*), *past progressive* (*they were thinking*), *future progressive* (*they will be thinking*), *present perfect progressive* (*they have been thinking*), *past perfect progressive* (*they had been thinking*), *future perfect progressive* (*they will have been thinking*).

There are two *emphatic* tenses: *present emphatic* (*they do think*) and *past emphatic* (*they did think*).

Transitional phrases. Expressions that link independent clauses or sentences; for example, *as a result, therefore, on the other hand, nevertheless*.

Verb. A word used to express action or state of being. (See also *Mood*.)

The bell *rang*. (Action.)
The book *is* thick. (State of being.)

Auxiliary (helping) verb. A verb that helps in the formation of the particular form of another verb. The chief auxiliaries are *be, can, could, do, have, may, might, must, ought, shall, should, will, would*.

Intransitive verb. A verb that does not require an object to complete its meaning.

The clock *stopped* at 10:30.

Linking verb. A verb that connects a subject with a predicate adjective or noun. The various forms of *to be* are the most commonly used linking verbs. *Become, look, seem, appear,* and *grow* are often used as linking verbs. (See ¶ 1058.)

He *became* a mining engineer.

Principal parts of verbs. (See *Principal parts*.)

Transitive verb. A verb that requires an object to complete its meaning. (See also *Object*.)

The clerk *filed* the letter.

Verbal. A word that partakes of the nature of a verb but functions in some other way. (See *Gerund; Infinitive; Participle.*)

Voice. The property of a verb that indicates whether the subject acts or is acted upon.

> **Active voice.** A verb is in the active voice when its subject is the doer of the act.
>
> Frank *wrote* the report.
>
> **Passive voice.** A verb is in the passive voice when its subject is acted upon.
>
> The report *was written* by Frank.

Vowels. The letters *a, e, i, o,* and *u.* The letters *w* and *y* sometimes act like vowels (as in *awl* or in *cry*). (See also *Consonants.*)

Section 20
REFERENCE BOOKS

2001 Certain basic reference books are a "must" in almost any business office. These include a desk-sized dictionary, a secretarial handbook, and a telephone directory. In addition, each type of business has its own special reference sources. The public library also is a good source of information.

Almanacs
Information Please Almanac, Atlas and Yearbook, Simon and Schuster, New York. (Published annually.)
Reader's Digest Almanac and Yearbook, The Reader's Digest Association, Inc., Pleasantville, N.Y. (Published annually.)
The World Almanac and Book of Facts, Doubleday & Company, Inc., Garden City, N.Y. (Published annually.)

Biographical Information
Webster's Biographical Dictionary, G. & C. Merriam Company, Springfield, Mass., 1966.
Who's Who, St. Martin's Press, New York. (A biographical dictionary of notable persons, mostly British; published annually.)
Who's Who in America, Marquis-Who's Who Incorporated, Chicago. (A biographical dictionary of notable living Americans; published biennially. Similar biographical dictionaries covering persons in various fields are *Who's Who of American Women, Who's Who in Commerce and Industry,* etc.)

Book and Periodical Directories

N. W. Ayer & Son's Directory of Newspapers and Periodicals, N. W. Ayer & Son, Inc., Philadelphia. (Published annually.)

Books in Print, R. R. Bowker Company, New York. (An author-title-series index to the *Publishers' Trade List Annual;* published annually.)

Cumulative Book Index, The H. W. Wilson Company, New York. (A listing of currently published books in the English language; published monthly.)

The New York Times Index, The New York Times Company, New York. (Published semimonthly.)

Publishers' Trade List Annual, R. R. Bowker Company, New York. (Published annually.)

Readers' Guide to Periodical Literature, The H. W. Wilson Company, New York. (Published semimonthly, September-June; monthly, July-August.)

Business and Government Directories

Congressional Directory, U.S. Government Printing Office, Washington. (Published annually.)

Kelly's Directory of Manufacturers, Merchants, and Industrial Services, Kelly's Directories Limited, London. (Published annually.)

Martindale-Hubbell Law Directory, Martindale-Hubbell, Inc., Summit, N.J. (Published annually.)

Poor's Register of Corporations, Directors and Executives, Standard & Poor's Corporation, New York. (Published annually.)

Rand McNally Bankers Directory, Rand McNally & Company, Chicago. (Published semiannually.)

Thomas Register of American Manufacturers, Thomas Publishing Company, New York. (Published annually.)

Also consult local telephone directories (both alphabetic and classified) as well as local city directories and lists of city officials.

Dictionaries and Word Books

The American Heritage Dictionary of the English Language, American Heritage Publishing Co., Inc., and Houghton Mifflin Company, Boston, 1969.

Funk & Wagnalls New Standard Dictionary of the English Language, Funk & Wagnalls Company, New York, 1963. (Unabridged.)

Funk & Wagnalls Standard College Dictionary, Funk & Wagnalls Company, New York, 1963. (Desk-sized.)

Leslie, Louis A., *20,000 Words,* 5th ed., Gregg Division, McGraw-Hill Book Company, New York, 1965. (A pocket-sized book for checking spelling and word division.)

Oxford English Dictionary, Oxford University Press, New York, 1933.

The Random House Dictionary of the English Language, Random House, Inc., New York, 1966.

Roget's International Thesaurus, 3d ed., Thomas Y. Crowell Company, New York, 1962. (A word book for finding a word to fit an idea.)

Webster's New World Dictionary of the American Language, College Edition, The World Publishing Company, Cleveland, 1968.

Webster's Seventh New Collegiate Dictionary, G. & C. Merriam Company, Springfield, Mass., 1969. (Desk-sized.)

Webster's Third New International Dictionary, G. & C. Merriam Company, Springfield, Mass., 1966. (Unabridged.)

Encyclopedias

Columbia Encyclopedia, 3d ed., Columbia University Press, New York, 1963.

Encyclopaedia Britannica, Encyclopaedia Britannica, Inc., Chicago, 1969.

Encyclopedia Americana, Americana Corporation, New York, 1969.

Etiquette and Personal Development

Amy Vanderbilt's New Complete Book of Etiquette, Doubleday & Company, Inc., Garden City, N.Y., 1967.

Post, Elizabeth L., *Emily Post's Etiquette,* 12th rev. ed., Funk & Wagnalls Company, New York, 1969.

Whitcomb, Helen, and Laura Cochran, *Charm for Miss Teen,* Gregg Division, McGraw-Hill Book Company, New York, 1969.

———— and Rosalind Lang, *Charm: The Career Girl's Guide to Business and Personal Success,* Gregg Division, McGraw-Hill Book Company, New York, 1964.

Financial Information

Dun & Bradstreet Reference Book, Dun & Bradstreet, Inc., New York. (By subscription only; published bimonthly.)

Moody's manuals, Moody's Investors Service, Inc., New York. (There are five separate manuals: *Moody's Banks and Finance Manual, Moody's Industrial Manual, Moody's Municipal and Government Manual, Moody's Public Utilities Manual,* and *Moody's Transportation Manual;* published annually.)

Standard Corporation Records, Standard & Poor's Corporation, New York. (Published bimonthly.)

Geographical and Travel Information

Hotel & Motel Red Book, American Hotel Association Directory Corporation, New York. (Published annually.)

Rand McNally Commercial Atlas and Marketing Guide, Rand McNally & Company, Chicago. (Published annually.)

Webster's Geographical Dictionary, G. & C. Merriam Company, Springfield, Mass., 1967.

Travel information and road maps may be obtained from various automobile associations, oil companies, and map publishers. Local city maps are also available.

Grammar and Style Books

Fowler, H. W., *A Dictionary of Modern English Usage*, 2d ed., revised and edited by Sir Ernest Gowers, Oxford University Press, New York, 1965.

Hutchinson, Lois Irene, *Standard Handbook for Secretaries*, 8th ed., Gregg Division, McGraw-Hill Book Company, New York, 1969.

A Manual of Style, 12th ed., The University of Chicago Press, Chicago, 1969. (A standard reference for anyone who prepares typewritten copy for the printer.)

The New York Times Style Book for Writers and Editors, McGraw-Hill Book Company, New York, 1962.

Nicholson, Margaret, *A Dictionary of American-English Usage*, Oxford University Press, New York, 1957. (Based on Fowler's *Modern English Usage*.)

Perrin, Porter G., *Writer's Guide and Index to English*, 4th ed., Scott, Foresman and Company, Glenview, Ill., 1965. (Consists of two parts: a writer's guide, which discusses general English topics, and an index to English, which gives details of grammar arranged alphabetically.)

Skillin, Marjorie E., and Robert M. Gay, *Words Into Type*, rev. ed., Appleton-Century-Crofts, New York, 1964.

United States Government Printing Office Style Manual, rev. ed., U.S. Government Printing Office, Washington, 1967.

Postal and Shipping Information

Bullinger's Postal and Shippers Guide for the United States and Canada, Bullinger's Guides, Inc., Westwood, N.J. (Published annually.)

Directory of International Mail, U.S. Government Printing Office, Washington.

Directory of Post Offices, U.S. Government Printing Office, Washington.

Dun & Bradstreet Exporters' Encyclopaedia, Dun and Bradstreet Publications Corporation, New York. (Published annually.)

National ZIP Code Directory, U.S. Post Office Department Publication 65, Washington. (Revised periodically.)

Postal Manual, U.S. Government Printing Office, Washington.

Quotations

Bartlett's Familiar Quotations, 14th ed., Little, Brown and Company, Boston, 1968.

The Oxford Dictionary of Quotations, 2d ed., Oxford University Press, New York, 1953.

Secretarial Handbooks

Agnew, Peter L., et al., *Secretarial Office Practice*, 7th ed., South-Western Publishing Company, Cincinnati, 1966.

Anderson, Ruth I., et al., *The Administrative Secretary: Resource*, Gregg Division, McGraw-Hill Book Company, New York, 1970.

Bredow, Miriam, *Medical Secretarial Procedures*, 5th ed., Gregg Division, McGraw-Hill Book Company, New York, 1966.

Doris, Lillian, and Besse May Miller, *Complete Secretary's Handbook,* rev. ed., Prentice-Hall, Inc., Englewood Cliffs, N.J., 1960.

Gregg, John Robert, et al., *Applied Secretarial Practice,* 6th ed., Gregg Division, McGraw-Hill Book Company, New York, 1968.

Hanna, J Marshall, et al., *Secretarial Procedures and Administration,* 5th ed., South-Western Publishing Company, Cincinnati, 1968.

Hutchinson, Lois Irene, *Standard Handbook for Secretaries,* 8th ed., Gregg Division, McGraw-Hill Book Company, New York, 1969.

Leslie, Louis A., and Kenneth B. Coffin, *Handbook for the Legal Secretary, Diamond Jubilee Series,* Gregg Division, McGraw-Hill Book Company, New York, 1968.

Miller, Besse May, *Legal Secretary's Complete Handbook,* Prentice-Hall, Inc., Englewood Cliffs, N.J., 1953.

Place, Irene, and Charles B. Hicks, *College Secretarial Procedures,* 3d ed., Gregg Division, McGraw-Hill Book Company, New York, 1964.

Statistics

Statistical Abstract of the United States, U.S. Bureau of the Census, Washington. (Statistics on social, political, and economic organization; published annually.)

Index

This index contains many entries for individual words. If you are looking for a specific word that is not listed, refer to ¶ 715, which contains a 12-page guide to words that are frequently confused because they sound alike or look alike (for example, *affect-effect* or *stationary-stationery*).

NOTE: The boldface numbers in this index refer to *paragraph* numbers; the lightface numbers refer to *page* numbers.

268